Keys, Foreign Keys, and

Relational Theory

Definitions, Explanations, and

Critical Analysis

C. J. Date

Published by:

115 Linda Vista, Sedona, AZ 86336 USA
https://www.TechnicsPub.com

Cover design by Lorena Molinari

First Printing 2023

Copyright © 2023 C. J. Date. All rights reserved.

Printed in the United States of America.

ISBN, print ed.	9781634624053
ISBN, Kindle ed.	9781634624060
ISBN, ePub ed.	9781634624077
ISBN, PDF ed.	9781634624084

Library of Congress Control Number: 2023944225

Today, if you have a well designed database management system,
you have the keys to the kingdom
of data processing and decision support.

—E. F. Codd:
The Relational Model for Database Management Version 2 (1990)

... [Two] locked caskets,
each of which contains the key to the other.

—Isak Dinesen:
A Consolatory Tale (1942)

You will find it a very good practice always
to verify your references, sir.

—Martin Joseph Routh:
quoted in J. W. Burgon, *Memory of Dr Routh* (1878)

[There] is no scorn more profound, or on the whole more justifiable,
than that of the men who make for the men who explain.
Exposition, criticism, appreciation, is work for second-rate minds.

—G. H. Hardy:
A Mathematician's Apology (1940)

——— ♦ ♦ ♦ ♦ ♦ ———

To all those friends and family who have helped
in so many ways during the tribulations of the last few years

About the Author

C. J. Date is an independent author, lecturer, researcher, and consultant, specializing in relational database technology. He is best known for his book *An Introduction to Database Systems* (8th edition, Addison-Wesley, 2004), which has sold close to a million copies at the time of writing and is used by several hundred colleges and universities worldwide. He is also the author of numerous other books on database management, including most recently:

- From Morgan Kaufmann: *Time and Relational Theory: Temporal Databases in the Relational Model and SQL* (with Hugh Darwen and Nikos A. Lorentzos, 2014)

- From O'Reilly: *Relational Theory for Computer Professionals: What Relational Databases Are Really All About* (2013); *View Updating and Relational Theory: Solving the View Update Problem* (2013); *SQL and Relational Theory: How to Write Accurate SQL Code* (3rd edition, 2015); *The New Relational Database Dictionary* (2016); *Type Inheritance and Relational Theory: Subtypes, Supertypes, and Substitutability* (2016)

- From Apress: *Database Design and Relational Theory: Normal Forms and All That Jazz* (2nd edition, 2019)

- From Technics: *Logic and Relational Theory: Thoughts and Essays on Database Matters* (2020); *Fifty Years of Relational, and Other Database Writings: More Thoughts and Essays on Database Matters* (2020); *Stating the Obvious, and Other Database Writings: Still More Thoughts and Essays on Database Matters* (2020); *E. F. Codd and Relational Theory, Revised Edition: A Detailed Review and Analysis of Codd's Major Database Writings* (2021); *Database Dreaming, Volumes I and II: Relational Writings Revised and Revived* (2022); *On Cantor and the Transfinite* (2023)

Mr Date was inducted into the Computing Industry Hall of Fame in 2004. He enjoys a reputation that is second to none for his ability to explain complex technical subjects in a clear and understandable fashion.

Contents

Preface

People often skip prefaces. For that reason, I considered not writing a preface to this book at all; intead, I thought, I could cover the necessary prefatory material (the technical material, at any rate) in a chapter of its own, as a kind of prefix or preliminary to the existing Chapter 1. Certainly there's a lot I need to discuss before I can start getting into the real substance of the book, material that you really shouldn't skip. Rightly or wrongly, however, I decided to stick with tradition and present the material in question here. So here goes; I mean, here's an overview, or summary, of technical matters that I'm going to be assuming later on that you're familiar with and understand.

Sets

Sets—mathematical sets, I mean—are one of the principal foundations of the relational model (the other is logic). Here are some pertinent definitions:

> **Definition (set):** A collection of objects, called elements or members, with the property that given an arbitrary object x, it can be determined whether or not x appears in the collection. An example is the collection $\{a,b,c\}$, which can equivalently be written as, e.g., $\{b,a,c\}$, since sets have no ordering to their elements. Sets don't contain duplicate elements. Every subset or superset of a set is itself a set.

> **Definition (subset):** Set s_2 is a subset of set s_1 ("$s_2 \subseteq s_1$") if and only if every element of s_2 is also an element of s_1—in which case s_1 is said to include s_2 (equivalently, s_2 is included in s_1). Every set is a subset of itself. Note the logical difference between containment and inclusion—a set contains its elements but includes its subsets.

> **Definition (superset):** Set s_1 is a superset of set s_2 ("$s_1 \supseteq s_2$") if and only if s_2 is a subset of s_1. Every set is a superset of itself.

> **Definition (proper subset):** Set s_2 is a proper subset of set s_1 ("$s_2 \subset s_1$") if and only if it's a subset of s_1 and s_1 and s_2 are distinct.

Definition (proper superset): Set s_1 is a proper superset of set s_2 ("$s_1 \supset s_2$") if and only if s_2 is a proper subset of s_1.

Definition (set union): The union of sets s_1 and s_2 ("$s_1 \cup s_2$") is the set of all elements x such that x is contained in at least one of s_1 and s_2.

Definition (set intersection): The intersection of sets s_1 and s_2 ("$s_1 \cap s_2$") is the set of all elements x such that x is contained in both s_1 and s_2.

Definition (set difference): The difference between sets s_1 and s_2, in that order ("$s_1 - s_2$"), is the set of all elements x such that x is contained in s_1 and not in s_2.

Definition (cardinality): The number of elements in a set.

Definition (empty set): The unique set of cardinality zero.

Definition (singleton set): Any set of cardinality one.

Definition (doubleton set): Any set of cardinality two.

The Third Manifesto

The Third Manifesto ("the *Manifesto*" for short), by Hugh Darwen and myself, is an attempt to define precisely what a true relational DBMS would or should look like to the user. Like Codd's first few papers on the relational model, the *Manifesto* is quite abstract; at the same time, it's much more specific than those papers of Codd's, inasmuch as it lays out—as those papers did not (nor of course were they ever meant to do)—a specific, detailed set of requirements that Darwen and I claim a database language needs to adhere to in order to qualify as "truly relational." Here's the reference:

- C. J. Date and Hugh Darwen: *Databases, Types, and the Relational Model: The Third Manifesto*, 3rd edition (Addison-Wesley (2007).

See also the *Manifesto* website *www.thethirdmanifesto.com*.

Tutorial D

The Third Manifesto isn't a language definition; rather, it's a prescription for the functionality that Hugh Darwen and I claim a language must provide in order to be considered truly relational. But we did need a way of referring generically to any such language within our *Manifesto*, and we used the name **D** for that purpose. Note carefully, therefore, that **D** isn't a language as such, it's a family of languages; there could be any number of individual languages all qualifying as a valid member of that family, and **Tutorial D** is one such.[1]

Tutorial D is based on the relational algebra; it's defined more or less formally in the *Manifesto* book, and it's used throughout that book and elsewhere (the present book included) as a basis for examples. In fact, I and others have been using that language for such purposes in books and presentations for many years now, and I think our experience in that regard has shown that it's both well designed and fairly self-explanatory.[2]

That said, I need to make it clear too that **Tutorial D** is only a toy language, in a sense. To be specific, it includes no exception handling and no I/O. To repeat, however, I do believe the language is well designed as far as it goes, and it could well form the basis for a language—occasionally referred to by Darwen and myself as **Industrial D**—that does include that missing functionality.

Note that the names **D** and **Tutorial D** (and **Industrial D**) are always set in **bold**.

Foreign Keys

Despite their obvious practical significance, *The Third Manifesto* doesn't insist that foreign keys as such be explicitly supported; it insists only that the system support a language that allows constraints of arbitrary complexity to be defined, and foreign key constraints in particular can then be defined using that general purpose language. And one reason it doesn't insist on such explicit support is that foreign key constraints are self-evidently not fundamental—unlike, e.g., integrity constraints in general, or key constraints in particular.[3]

---

[1] By contrast, SQL isn't.

[2] It can be and has been used for real applications, too. If you're interested in trying it out for yourself, an implementation known as *Rel*, by Dave Voorhis of the University of Derby in the U.K., is available as a free download from the *Manifesto* website.

[3] Actually key constraints aren't fundamental either (or an argument could be made to that effect, at any rate), but in the case of keys the practical benefits of providing explicit support are overwhelming.

Given the foregoing, it won't surprise you to learn that **Tutorial D** doesn't include explicit foreign key support either. And yet ... In other writings and live presentations, I've almost always found it necessary to use a hypothetical dialect of **Tutorial D** that does include such support—partly because foreign keys are indeed part of the relational model as usually understood and therefore often need to be discussed, and partly because there's no question that foreign keys are of major practical importance. And in this book I'll do the same (assume such support is included, I mean).

Commalists

The term *commalist* is used heavily in syntax definitions in what follows (also, unsurprisingly, in the official **Tutorial D** grammar at the *Manifesto* website). It's short for "comma separated list." It can be defined as follows:

- Let *xyz* be some syntactic construct (for example, "attribute name"). Then the term *xyz commalist* denotes a sequence of zero or more *xyz*'s in which each pair of adjacent *xyz*'s is separated by a comma.

- Within any given commalist, spaces appearing immediately before the first item or any comma, or immediately after the last item or any comma, are ignored.

For example, let *A*, *B*, and *C* be attribute names. Then the following are all attribute name commalists:

```
A , B , C

C , A , B

B

A , C
```

So too is the empty sequence of attribute names.

Relvars

Note: This particular topic is discussed in much greater detail in Chapter 1.

"Relvar" is short for *relation variable*. What all too many people still call just "relations" (meaning by that term constructs in the database) are indeed really variables; after all, their value does change over time as INSERT, DELETE, and UPDATE operations are performed, and "changing over time" is exactly what makes them variables. In fact, *not* distinguishing clearly between relation values and relation variables—or table values and table variables, in SQL—has led to an immense amount of confusion in the past, and indeed continues to do so to this day. In our work on *The Third Manifesto*, therefore, Hugh Darwen and I decided to face up to this problem right from the outset. To be specific, in that *Manifesto* we framed all of our remarks in terms of relation values when it really was relation values that we meant, and in terms of relation variables when it really was relation variables that we meant, and we abided by this discipline rigorously (indeed, 100%). However, we also introduced two abbreviations: We allowed "relation value" to be abbreviated to just *relation* (exactly as we allow, e.g., "integer value" to be abbreviated to just *integer*), and we allowed "relation variable" to be abbreviated to a new term, *relvar*.

Suppliers and Parts

You won't be surprised to learn that many of the examples in this book make use of the familiar suppliers and parts database. That database contains three relvars (more specifically, three base relvars)—relvar S (suppliers); relvar P (parts); and relvar SP (shipments of parts by suppliers). Here are **Tutorial D** definitions for these relvars:

```
VAR S BASE RELATION    /* suppliers */
   { SNO    SNO ,
     SNAME  NAME ,
     STATUS INTEGER ,
     CITY   CHAR }
   KEY { SNO } ;

VAR P BASE RELATION    /* parts */
   { PNO    PNO ,
     PNAME  NAME ,
     COLOR  CHAR ,
     WEIGHT RATIONAL ,
     CITY   CHAR }
   KEY { PNO } ;
```

```
VAR SP BASE RELATION   /* shipments */
  { SNO SNO ,
    PNO PNO   ,
    QTY INTEGER }
  KEY { SNO , PNO }
  FOREIGN KEY { SNO } REFERENCES S
  FOREIGN KEY { PNO } REFERENCES P ;
```

And here's a picture showing the usual sample values:[4]

S

SNO	SNAME	STATUS	CITY
S1	Smith	20	London
S2	Jones	10	Paris
S3	Blake	30	Paris
S4	Clark	20	London
S5	Adams	30	Athens

P

PNO	PNAME	COLOR	WEIGHT	CITY
P1	Nut	Red	12.0	London
P2	Bolt	Green	17.0	Paris
P3	Screw	Blue	17.0	Oslo
P4	Screw	Red	14.0	London
P5	Cam	Blue	12.0	Paris
P6	Cog	Red	19.0	London

SP

SNO	PNO	QTY
S1	P1	300
S1	P2	200
S1	P3	400
S1	P4	200
S1	P5	100
S1	P6	100
S2	P1	300
S2	P2	400
S3	P2	200
S4	P2	200
S4	P4	300
S4	P5	400

As a matter of fact, those relvar definitions do vary a little bit from one book of mine to another, deliberately. For example, in some books it suits my purposes better to make attribute COLOR be of a user defined type instead of (as here) the system defined type CHAR. Here, however, the only attributes with user defined types are SNO (supplier number), which is of a user defined type of that same name SNO; PNO (part number), which is of a user defined type of that same name PNO; and SNAME and PNAME (supplier name and part name, respectively), both of which are of a user defined type called NAME. Since the specifics of user defined types in general aren't particularly relevant to the

---

[4] The significance of the double underlining in the picture is that the corresponding attribute participates in a key for the relvar concerned. In fact, of course, it so happens in the example that each relvar has just a single key, which you can therefore think of as the *primary* key if you like. See Chapter 1 for further discussion.

principal theme of this book, I omit the definitions of these types here for simplicity.

As for the system defined types in this example: Type INTEGER is self-explanatory; type CHAR is character strings of arbitrary length; and type RATIONAL is rational numbers.

SQL

SQL— the official pronunciation is *ess cue ell*, but the language was originally called SEQUEL, and many people pronounce it as if it still were—is both the de facto and de jure standard "relational" language. Please understand, however, that I set "relational" in quotes here because, as is well known, SQL departs in all too many ways from relational theory as such. Be that as it may, here for reference purposes is a definition in SQL, analogous (more or less) to the **Tutorial D** definition already shown, for the suppliers and parts database:

```
CREATE TABLE S
  ( SNO    SNO          NOT NULL ,
    SNAME  NAME         NOT NULL ,
    STATUS INTEGER      NOT NULL ,
    CITY   VARCHAR(25)  NOT NULL ,
    UNIQUE ( SNO ) ) ;

CREATE TABLE P
  ( PNO    PNO                   NOT NULL ,
    PNAME  NAME                  NOT NULL ,
    WEIGHT FIXED DECIMAL(5,2)    NOT NULL ,
    COLOR  VARCHAR(10)           NOT NULL ,
    CITY   VARCHAR(25)           NOT NULL ,
    UNIQUE ( PNO ) ) ;

CREATE TABLE SP
  ( SNO SNO       NOT NULL ,
    PNO PNO       NOT NULL ,
    QTY INTEGER NOT NULL ,
    UNIQUE ( SNO , PNO ) ,
    FOREIGN KEY ( SNO ) REFERENCES S ( SNO ) ,
    FOREIGN KEY ( PNO ) REFERENCES P ( PNO ) ;
```

Concluding Remarks

That brings us to the end of the technical preliminaries. But there a few more introductory remarks I need to make. The first is this. Keys and foreign keys are pretty simple concepts; yet, counting front matter and index pages, this book is almost 300 pages long! How could anyone write so much about so little?

Well, that's a good question (which is what people always say when they don't really have a good answer). But I suppose one part of the answer has to be that the concepts in question are in fact not quite as simple as they might seem on first acquaintance. And another is that, regardless of how simple those concepts might actually be, people are very good at making things more complicated—sometimes much more complicated—than they really are, or ought to be.[5] (To put the point another way: It's easy to make things difficult, and hard to make them simple.) So part of the complexity I'm going to have to address in these pages isn't complexity that's intrinsic to the matter at hand; rather, it's complexity that has been introduced, for one reason or another. As we'll see—or as I hope to show, at any rate.

By the way, I don't mean to exclude myself from the foregoing strictures. Over the years I've written a fair number of papers and books that are relevant, to a greater or lesser degree, to the matter at hand—and I have to say now, looking back at those publications, that they were often not as clear as they might have been. Sometimes they weren't too bad; but sometimes they were muddled, and sometimes, I'm afraid, they were flat out wrong. Let me take this opportunity, therefore, to apologize to anyone who might have been led astray by those earlier writings. *Mea culpa.*

So let me say a word about the structure of the book. There are six longish chapters, as follows:

- Chapter 1 lays the necessary theoretical groundwork; it goes over the pertinent aspects of relational theory in reasonably rigorous fashion but, I hope, without excessive formality.

- Chapter 2 then uses the groundwork from Chapter 1 to investigate in detail the concepts we're primarily interested in (iviz., keys and foreign keys), and to build up thereby a clear and precise understanding of those concepts.

- Chapter 3 offers a historical and somewhat critical survey of Codd's writings on these matters.

---

[5] SQL itself is prima facie evidence in support of this point.

■ With a view to redressing the balance a little, perhaps, Chapter 4 offers an extended critical analysis of an early (and rather lengthy) paper of my own on the subject.

■ By way of a detailed case study, Chapter 5 then examines the pertinent features of the SQL standard.

■ Finally, and by way of another case study, Chapter 6 discusses the pertinent features of the IBM products DB2 and SQL/DS.

There's also an appendix containing definitions of the most important concepts introduced in the foregoing chapters.

C. J. Date
Morristown, Vermont
2023

Chapter 1

Laying the Foundations

A building is only as strong as its foundations.
—Walter J. Clark (attrib.)

This first chapter consists essentially of a series of definitions, with examples and detailed explanation where necessary, of concepts that are relevant to the matter at hand. The definitions are based on ones in my book *The New Relational Database Dictionary* (O'Reilly, 2016), though I've made a few cosmetic changes here and there for contextual reasons. I've also divided the chapter up into sections in order to make the various individual topics a little easier to digest. Please understand, however, that those sections are definitely not independent of one another—rather, they're meant to be read in sequence as written, and I've done my best to keep forward references to a minimum. Unfortunately, though, such references sometimes seem to be unavoidable—and as a consequence I'm afraid you might find it necessary to read the chapter, or parts of it, twice over in order to understand and digest everything it says. Please accept my apologies for this state of affairs.

Now, when I first set out to write this chapter, it was my intention to cover not the whole of relational theory, but only those aspects that directly pertained to my chosen subject, keys and foreign keys. But I'd forgotten something! To paraphrase something I said in my book *SQL and Relational Theory: How to Write Accurate SQL Code* (3rd edition, O'Reilly, 2015):

> John Muir (famous naturalist, conservationist, and founder of the Sierra Club) once said: "When we try to pick out anything by itself, we find it hitched to everything else in the universe"—often quoted in the form "Everything is connected to everything else." Muir was talking about to the natural world, of course, but he might just as well have been talking about the relational model. The fact is, the various features of the model are highly interconnected: Remove just one of them, and the whole edifice crumbles.

In other words, what I'd planned to do—cover just those parts of the theory that are relevant to keys and foreign keys, I mean—turned out to be an almost impossible task. Everything really is connected to everything else! So this chapter wound up covering a lot more material (and, sadly, being quite a bit longer) than I originally anticipated. Though as a matter of fact it did also turn out that there were a few topics, certainly not very many, that I felt I could skip without causing myself too much trouble later on: details of some of the more obscure relational operators, for example. But even in those cases it was sometimes a difficult decision; I mean, I did have to wonder sometimes whether it might not be better to include them after all.

With that apology out of the way, let me now get on with the exposition.

DOMAINS vs. TYPES

> **Definition (domain):** A type.

I begin with domains because domains played such a crucial role in Codd's early writings on the relational model. The truth is, though, what Codd called a domain in those writings is nothing more nor less than what the programming languages world calls a type—possibly a system defined type, more generally one that's user defined.

Now, I'm sorry to have to say that, although the foregoing claim on my part is undoubtedly correct, it took me an embarrassingly long time to realize it (to realize that domains and types are the same thing, I mean). One of the reasons it took me so long was that Codd himself rejected that claim for many years. In fact, he made several attempts, in writing, to argue the opposite point of view, namely, that domains and types were different things.[1] Despite Codd's position, however—or opposition, I suppose I have to call it—I finally saw the light in the early 1990s or so, and I've adhered firmly to the true state of affairs ever since.

Note: With hindsight—which is always perfect, of course—it's my belief that the reason Codd took the position he did on this matter had more to do with his personal professional history in IBM than it did with impartial science. It would be inappropriate to elaborate on this point here, and I won't; suffice it to say that, eventually, Codd did come to agree that domains and types are the same thing after all. He made that admission on June 30th, 1994 (a red letter day!—I

---

[1] My own short paper "A Type Is a Type Is a Type" (Chapter 11 of my book *Database Dreaming Volume I*, Technics, 2022) provides my own detailed technical analysis of those arguments of Codd's.

noted it in my diary at the time). Though even then I'm not sure he ever documented that change in his opinions in anything he wrote subsequently.

Anyway, so a domain's a type—but what's a type? Here's a definition:

> **Definition (type):** A named—and in practice finite—set of values; not to be confused with the internal or physical representation of the values in question, which is an implementation issue. Every value, every variable, every attribute, every read-only operator, every parameter, and every expression is of some type.[2] Types can be either scalar or nonscalar (in particular, they can be tuple or relation types); as a consequence, attributes of relations in particular can also be either scalar or nonscalar. Types can also be either system defined or user defined. They can also be generated or "constructed" (see the next definition below).

Here's an example of a type definition (irrelevant details omitted):

```
TYPE POINT ... X RATIONAL , Y RATIONAL
               CONSTRAINT ( X^2 + Y^2 ) ≤ 10000 ) ;
```

POINT here is a user defined type, values of which denote geometric points in two-dimensional space. For a given point, the values X and Y, both of which are of the system defined type RATIONAL (rational numbers), denote the corresponding cartesian coordinates. Points in general (which is to say, values of type POINT) are subject to a type constraint—imposed somewhat arbitrarily, and purely for the sake of the example—that says, in effect, that the only points of interest are those that lie on or inside a circle with center the origin and radius of length 100. (The symbol "^" denotes exponentiation.)

> **Definition (type generator):** An operator that's invoked at compile time instead of run time and returns a type instead of a value; also known as a type constructor. For example, conventional programming languages typically support an array type generator, which lets users specify an unlimited number and variety of individual array types. In the relational model, the tuple and (especially) relation type generators are the important

---

[2] In fact, of exactly one type, except possibly if type inheritance is supported. But there's no need to deal with type inheritance in this book (at least, not in any detail), so no harm is done if we stay with that "exactly one type" limitation here. PS: Perhaps I should elaborate on a couple of the cases mentioned in the definition, since they might be a little less obvious than the rest. Basically, the type of a read-only operator is the type of the result an invocation of that operator returns. And the type of an expression is the type of the value that expression denotes.

ones; they allow users to specify an unlimited number and variety of individual tuple and relation types.

Consider this definition of relvar S from the suppliers and parts database:

```
VAR S BASE RELATION
   { SNO SNO , SNAME NAME , STATUS INTEGER , CITY CHAR }
     KEY { SNO } ;
```

I don't want to explain every aspect of this example just yet; all I want to do for the moment is note that it includes an invocation of the RELATION type generator (syntactically, everything from the keyword RELATION to the closing brace following the keyword CHAR, inclusive). That invocation returns a specific relation type—namely, the type whose name is, precisely,

```
RELATION
     { SNO SNO , SNAME NAME , STATUS INTEGER , CITY CHAR }
```

So this type is in fact a generated type—as indeed are all relation types, and all tuple types also.

Note that the attributes that go to make up this generated type are themselves typed. To be specific:

- Attribute SNO is of a user defined type also called SNO.

- Attribute SNAME is of a user defined type called NAME.

- Attributes STATUS and CITY are of the system defined types INTEGER and CHAR, respectively.

Observe, moreover, that nongenerated types such as SNO, NAME, INTEGER, and CHAR are always scalar (see the section after next for further explanation). By contrast, generated types—e.g., the particular relation type shown in the example above—are typically nonscalar; however, they don't have to be. For example, the SQL type CHAR(25) is a generated type, but it's scalar.

Aside: I should explain that CHAR in SQL is a type generator (not, as is commonly supposed, a type as such); the length specification 25 in the example is the argument to that specific invocation of that generator. Thus, e.g., CHAR(24) and CHAR(25) are different types—as should in fact be obvious, since the corresponding sets of values are certainly not the same. Analogous remarks apply to many other SQL so called types also—for example, VARCHAR, FLOAT, and NUMERIC are all type generators, and VARCHAR(4), FLOAT(32), and NUMERIC(5,2) are examples of corresponding (generated) types. *End of aside.*

One last remark on types: As I'm sure you're aware, the relational model prohibits pointers.[3] The reasons for that prohibition are too well known to need rehearsing here, but it might at least be helpful to state the rule a little more precisely, thus:

> *No attribute of any relation in the database is allowed to be of any pointer type.*

VALUES vs. VARIABLES

One of the great realizations I and my friend and colleague Hugh Darwen came to in the early 1990s—I might almost call it an epiphany—was that there's a logical difference between values and variables. Well, *obviously* there's a logical difference between values and variables—but it's so obvious, perhaps, that we don't usually bother to spell it out, with the result that much confusion can and does occur. For example, nowhere in Codd's writings is the difference even mentioned, and I believe those writings do display a certain amount of confusion as a consequence.[4] SQL too suffers from a considerable amount of muddle in this regard. So let me give some more definitions:

> **Definition (value):** An "individual constant" (for example, the individual constant three, denoted by the integer literal 3). Values can be of arbitrary complexity; in particular, they can be either scalar or nonscalar (for example, a value might be an array). Values have no location in time or

---

[3] SQL doesn't, incidentally!—a strong argument right there in support of the claim that SQL is a long way from being truly relational.

[4] For example, in his famous 1970 paper "A Relational Model of Data for Large Shared Data Banks" (*Communications of the ACM 13*, No. 6), he talks about what he calls "time varying" relations, and explains that term thus: "As time progresses, each *n*-ary relation may be subject to insertion of additional *n*-tuples, deletion of existing ones, and alteration of components of any of its existing *n*-tuples." Yet his own definition of the term "relation" earlier in that same paper makes it very clear that relations (tuples too, come to that) are *values* and simply aren't, and can't possibly be, "time varying."

space; however, they can be represented in memory by means of some encoding, and those representations (or encodings, or occurrences) do have location in time and space—indeed, distinct occurrences of the same value can appear at any number of distinct locations in time and space, meaning, loosely, that the very same value can occur as the value of any number of distinct variables, at the same time or at different times. Note that, by definition, a value can't be updated, because if it could, then after such an update it would no longer be that value. Note too that every value is of some type—in fact, of exactly one type (and types are thus disjoint).[5]

Definition (variable): A holder for a representation of a value. Unlike values, variables (a) do have location in time and space and (b) can be updated (that is, the current value of the variable can be replaced by another value). Indeed, to be a variable is to be updatable, and to be updatable is to be a variable; equivalently, to be a variable is to be assignable to, and to be assignable to is to be a variable. Every variable is declared to be of some type.

Let me get back to values for a moment. I said a value is "an individual constant"—that's a term logicians use—and I gave as an example the individual constant three, which I said could be denoted by the integer literal 3. Observe, therefore, that's there another logical difference here: namely, that between values as such, on the one hand, and literals, which are symbols that denote values, on the other.[6] In fact, let me give another definition:

Definition (literal): Loosely, a self-defining symbol; a symbol that denotes a value that can be determined at compile time. More precisely, a literal is a symbol that denotes a value that's fixed and determined by the symbol in question (and the type of that value is therefore also fixed and determined by the symbol in question). Every value of every type, tuple and relation types included, is—in fact, must be—denotable by means of some literal.

Here are some examples:

---

[5] Again, except possibly if type inheritance is supported (see footnote 2).

[6] Be aware, however, that some systems, including certain object oriented systems in particular, very unfortunately use the term *literal* to mean a value as such. *Caveat lector.*

```
4                  /* a literal of type INTEGER              */

'ABC'              /* a literal of type CHAR                  */

FALSE              /* a literal of type BOOLEAN               */

SNO('S1')          /* a literal of type SNO                   */

TUPLE { SNO SNO('S1') , PNO PNO('P1') , QTY 300) }
           /* a literal of type                              */
           /* TUPLE { SNO SNO , PNO PNO , QTY INTEGER }      */

RELATION
  { TUPLE { SNO SNO('S1') , PNO PNO('P1') , QTY 300 } ,
    { TUPLE { SNO SNO('S5') , PNO PNO('P6') , QTY 100 } }
           /* a literal of type                              */
           /* RELATION { SNO SNO , PNO PNO , QTY INTEGER } */
```

ASSIGNMENT

Here again is one particular sentence from the definition I gave above for the term *variable*:

> [To] be a variable is to be updatable, and to be updatable is to be a variable; equivalently, to be a variable is to be assignable to, and to be assignable to is to be a variable.

So now I need to define assignment!

> **Definition (assignment):** An operator, denoted ":=" in **Tutorial D**, that assigns a value (the source, denoted by an expression) to a variable (the target, denoted by a variable reference); also, the operation performed when that operator is invoked. The source and target must be of the same type, and the operation overall is required to abide by (a) *The Assignment Principle* (always), as well as (b) **The Golden Rule** (if applicable). Every update operator invocation is logically equivalent to some assignment (albeit possibly a multiple assignment—see later).

Points arising from this definition:

- Note the final sentence in particular! I'll have more to say about it in the next section, but basically what it means is that the familiar relational operators INSERT, DELETE, and UPDATE are all, in the final analysis, nothing but shorthand for certain relational assignments (see the next bullet item).

- Relational assignment in turn is simply an operation that assigns a relation value of type *T* to a relation variable of that same type *T*. *Note:* Relation values and relation variables are discussed in detail in the next section.

- *The Assignment Principle* states that after assignment of value *v* to variable *V*, the comparison *v* = *V* is required to evaluate to TRUE.
     Note: Of course, this requirement is obvious (it's really nothing more than a definition of what assignment means). At least, you'd be forgiven for thinking so. But it's like that business of values vs. variables already discussed: It's worth spelling out explicitly precisely because it's violated so ubiquitously (in SQL in particular). See Chapter 2, "Assignment," of my book *Stating the Obvious, and Other Database Writings* (Technics, 2020) for an exhaustive treatment of the issue.

- **The Golden Rule**—the name is set in **bold** because of the rule's fundamental importance—is the rule that no database is ever allowed to violate any integrity constraint. I'll be discussing constraints in great detail later in the chapter.

In closing this section, let me draw your attention to that remark, in the bullet item above on *The Assignment Principle*, concerning "the comparison *v* = *V*." As you now know (if you didn't before), the source and target in an assignment are required to be of the same type; and you'd probably expect the same to be true of the comparands in an equality comparison like *v* = *V*. Well, if you did expect that, then you'd be absolutely right; but once again we're talking about a requirement that's worth spelling out explicitly, because it's violated so ubiquitously (in SQL in particular). See Chapter 1, "Equality," of my book *Stating the Obvious, and Other Database Writings* (Technics, 2020) for an exhaustive treatment of the issue.

RELATION VALUES vs. RELVARS

As soon as we realized the importance of the logical difference between values and variables in general, Hugh Darwen and I also realized that it applied—of course!—to relation values and variables in particular. Moreover, we also realized that it was a lack of clarity over that particular logical difference that accounted for so much of the confusion I've already alluded to, both in Codd's writings and in SQL. Let me elaborate.[7]

Forget about databases for a moment; consider instead the following simple programming language example. Suppose I say in some programming language:

```
DECLARE N INTEGER ... ;
```

Observe now that N here *isn't an integer*. Rather, it's a *variable*, whose *values* are integers as such—different integers at different times. We all understand that. Well, in exactly the same way, if I say in SQL—

```
CREATE TABLE T ... ;
```

—then T *isn't a table*: Rather, it's a variable, a table variable or (as I'd prefer to say, ignoring various SQL quirks such as duplicate rows and left to right column ordering) a relation variable, whose values are relations as such—different relations at different times.

Take another look at the picture of the suppliers and parts database in the preface to this book. That picture shows three relation *values*: namely, the relation values that happen to exist in the database at some particular time. But if we were to look again at some different time, we'd probably see three different relation values appearing in their place. In other words, S, P, and SP in that database are really variables: relation variables, to be precise. For example, suppose the suppliers relation variable S currently has the value—the relation value, that is—shown in the preface, and suppose we delete the set of tuples for suppliers in Paris:

```
DELETE S WHERE CITY = 'Paris' ;
```

Here's the result:

---

[7] The discussion that follows is based on one in my book *SQL and Relational Theory: How to Write Accurate SQL Code* (3rd edition, O'Reilly, 2015).

SNO	SNAME	STATUS	CITY
S1	Smith	20	London
S4	Clark	20	London
S5	Adams	30	Athens

Conceptually, what's happened here is that the old value of S has been replaced in its entirety by a new value. Of course, the old value (with five tuples) and the new one (with three) are rather similar, in a sense, but they certainly are different values. In fact, the DELETE just shown is logically equivalent to, and indeed shorthand for, the following relational assignment:

```
S := S MINUS ( S WHERE CITY = 'Paris' ) ;
```

As with all assignments, the effect here is that (a) the *source expression* on the right side is evaluated and then (b) the result of that evaluation—a relation value in the case at hand, since the source expression is a relational expression—is then assigned to the *target variable* (a relation variable in the case at hand) on the left side, with the overall result already explained.

So, to repeat, DELETE is just shorthand for a certain relational assignment—and, of course, an analogous remark applies to INSERT and UPDATE also: They too are basically just shorthand for certain relational assignments. Thus, relational assignment is the fundamental update operator in the relational model. Indeed, it's the only update operator we need, logically speaking.

So there's a logical difference between relation values and relation variables. The trouble is, the database literature has historically used the same term, *relation*, to stand for both, and that practice has certainly led to confusion.[8] Throughout this book, therefore, I'll take care to distinguish very carefully between the two—I'll talk in terms of relation values when I mean relation values and relation variables when I mean relation variables. However, I'll also abbreviate *relation value*, most of the time, to just *relation* (exactly as we abbreviate *integer value* most of the time to just *integer*). And I'll abbreviate *relation variable* most of the time to **relvar**; for example, I'll say the suppliers and parts database contains three *relvars* (three base relvars, to be precise).

---

[8] SQL makes essentially the same mistake, of course, because it too has just one term, *table*, that has to be understood as meaning sometimes a table value and sometimes a table variable.

With the foregoing discussion by way of motivation, let me now proceed to give the necessary definitions. There are quite a lot of them, but I'll present them in a sequence that builds up as gradually as possible.

> **Definition (scalar):** (*Of a type, attribute, value, or variable*) Having no user visible component parts. The term is also often used as a noun, in which case it refers to a scalar value specifically. (*Of an operator*) Returning a scalar result.

> **Definition (nonscalar):** Not scalar; i.e., having user visible component parts. The most important nonscalar constructs in the relational model are tuples and (especially) relations themselves, where the "user visible component parts" are, of course, the pertinent attributes (and the pertinent tuples as well, in the case of a relation).

Before going any further, however, I must make it clear that the scalar and nonscalar concepts are only informal. To put it another way, there's no such thing as "absolute scalarness" (or "absolute atomicity," as it's sometimes called)—the concept is necessarily somewhat relative. For example, a phone number might be perceived equally well as either (a) an "atomic" (i.e., scalar) value or (b) a tuple value consisting of country code, area code, and local number. (I note in passing that a database design involving phone numbers ought to be capable of supporting both of these perceptions.)

I must make it clear too that, precisely because the terms are indeed only informal, the relational model nowhere depends on the scalar vs. nonscalar distinction in any formal sense.

Now let me move on to matters that are perhaps more obviously relevant to relations as such.

First of all, tables in SQL are made up of rows and columns, of course. But the relational model doesn't talk in terms of rows and columns (or tables, come to that)—it talks about *tuples* instead of rows, and *attributes* instead of columns. Please note immediately that the equivalences aren't exact!—for example, rows in SQL have a left to right ordering to their components, whereas tuples in the relational model don't. Precise definitions follow.

> **Definition (attribute):** Formally, a pair of names of the form <attribute name, type name>, where the first name of the pair (the attribute name) identifies the attribute in question, of course, and the second name of the

pair (the type name) identifies the corresponding type. But it's common to ignore the type name in informal contexts.

Note: Ignoring the type name in this way is acceptable when the heading (see below) of which the attribute in question is a component is known, because (a) attribute names within any given heading are required to be unique, and hence (b) if the heading is known, the attribute name effectively implies the corresponding type name.

Examples: In the suppliers and parts database, the pair <SNAME,NAME> is an attribute of relvar S, and the pair <SNO,SNO> is an attribute of both relvar S and relvar SP. We might also say, more simply but less formally, just that SNAME is an attribute of S and SNO is an attribute of both S and SP , and that these attributes are of types NAME and SNO, respectively.

Definition (heading): A set of attributes, in which by definition each attribute is a pair of the form <A,T>, where A is an attribute name and T is a type name (i.e., T is the name of the type of attribute A). Every subset of a heading is a heading. Within any given heading, (a) distinct attributes are allowed to have the same type name, but not the same attribute name; (b) the number of attributes is the degree (of the heading in question).

Note: Given that it's common to refer to an attribute, informally, by its attribute name alone, it's also common to regard a heading, informally, as a set of attribute names alone.

Here by way of example is the heading of the suppliers relvar S (**Tutorial D** syntax):

```
{ SNO SNO , SNAME NAME , STATUS INTEGER , CITY CHAR }
```

The following subset of the foregoing heading, corresponding to a certain projection of the suppliers relvar, is also a heading:

```
{ CITY CHAR , SNAME NAME }
```

These two headings might be represented less formally thus:

```
{ SNO , SNAME , STATUS , CITY }

{ CITY , SNAME }
```

Of course, headings are sets—sets of attributes—and sets have no ordering to their elements; thus, the order in which attributes are mentioned in examples, when those examples are expressed in written form as in the case at hand, is irrelevant.

Definition (tuple): [9] Let *H* be a heading, and let *t* be a set of pairs of the form *<<A,T>,v>*, called components, obtained from *H* by attaching to each attribute *<A,T>* in *H* some value *v* of type *T*, called the attribute value in *t* for attribute *A*. Then, and only then, *t* is a tuple value (or just a tuple for short) with heading *H* and the same degree and attributes as *H*. Every subset of a tuple is a tuple.

Here by way of example is a literal—a tuple literal, of course—representing the tuple for supplier S1 from the suppliers relation shown in the preface:

```
TUPLE { SNO SNO('S1') , SNAME NAME('Smith') ,
                    STATUS 20 , CITY 'London' }
```

The type names are omitted from the concrete syntax here because, by definition, the type of each attribute mentioned must be the same as the type of the corresponding specified attribute value, and each such attribute value implies the corresponding type. To be specific:

- The implied type of attribute SNO is SNO, because SNO is the type of the specified attribute value SNO('S1'): more precisely, of the literal SNO('S1'), since it's by means of that literal that the pertinent attribute value is specified.

- The implied type of attribute SNAME is NAME, because NAME is the type of the specified attribute value NAME('Smith'): more precisely, of the literal NAME('Smith').

- The implied type of attribute STATUS is INTEGER, because NAME is the type of the specified attribute value 20: more precisely, of the literal 20.

---

[9] The term *tuple* is an abbreviation of *n-tuple*, where *n* is the degree. It's pronounced to rhyme with "couple."

■ The implied type of attribute CITY is CHAR, because CHAR is the type of the specified attribute value 'London': more precisely, of the literal 'London'.

Note: It's sloppy, of course, but in informal contexts we sometimes drop the attribute names, as in this example:

```
TUPLE { SNO('S1') , NAME('Smith') , 20 , 'London' }
```

And in *very* informal contexts we might even simplify this example still further, to something like the following:

```
{ S1 , Smith , 20 , London }
```

But let me stress the fact that you should indulge in such simplifications only if both you and your audience really understand the true state of affairs—for otherwise they (the simplifications, that is) can be dangerously misleading. *Exercise:* In what ways, exactly?

Definition (tuple type): Let H be a heading; then, and only then, TUPLE H denotes a tuple type—in fact, the sole tuple type—with the same degree and attributes as H.

Definition (tuple variable): A variable whose type is some tuple type; referred to as a tuplevar for short. Let tuple variable V be of type T; then V has the same heading (and therefore attributes and degree) as type T does.
　　Note: Tuple variables aren't required by the relational model as such, but they're likely to be needed in the external environment. For example, such a variable will probably be needed to serve as the target for retrieval of some tuple from some relation.

Definition (relation type): Let H be a heading; then, and only then, RELATION H denotes a relation type—in fact, the sole relation type—with the same degree and attributes as H.

Definition (body): A set of tuples all of the same type. The number of tuples in that set is the cardinality (of the body in question). Every subset of a body is a body. In particular, the set of tuples appearing in some given relation—especially the relation that's the value of some given relvar at some given time—is a body, and so is any subset of such a set.

Definition (relation): Let H be a heading, let B be a body consisting of tuples with heading H, and let r be the pair $<H,B>$. Then, and only then, r is a relation value (or just a relation for short), with heading H and body B, and with the same degree and attributes as H and with the same cardinality as B.

Definition (relation variable): A variable whose type is some relation type; referred to as a relvar for short. Let relvar R be of type T; then R has the same heading (and therefore the same attributes and degree) as type T does. Let the value of R at some given time be r; then R has the same body and cardinality at that time as r does.

Let me briefly illustrate some of these latter definitions. First of all, here again is the suppliers relation from the preface:

SNO	SNAME	STATUS	CITY
S1	Smith	20	London
S2	Jones	10	Paris
S3	Blake	30	Paris
S4	Clark	20	London
S5	Adams	30	Athens

Now, I've just said this is a relation, but of course it isn't—it's a *picture* of a relation. Certainly there's a logical difference between a thing and a picture of a thing! Here's a list of some of the many differences that exist between this "tabular picture" (as I'll refer to it, just for the time being) and the relation it's supposed to depict:[10]

■ Each attribute in the heading of a relation involves a type name, but those type names are usually omitted from such tabular pictures.

---

[10] This list is based on one in my book *SQL and Relational Theory: How to Write Accurate SQL Code* (3rd edition, O'Reilly, 2015).

- Each component of each tuple in the body of a relation involves a type name and an attribute name, but those type and attribute names are usually omitted from tabular pictures.

- Each attribute value in each tuple in the body of a relation is a value of the applicable type, but those values (or literals denoting those values, rather) are usually shown in some abbreviated form—for example, S1 instead of SNO('S1'), London instead of 'London'—in tabular pictures.

- The columns in such tabular pictures have a left to right ordering, but the attributes of a relation don't.[11]

- The rows in such tabular pictures have a top to bottom ordering, but the tuples of a relation don't.

- A table in such a picture might contain duplicate rows, but a relation never contains duplicate tuples.

There are other differences, too, but they're beyond the scope of the present discussion.

All of that being said, let me now ignore these logical differences—as much as I can, at any rate!—and use the example as promised to illustrate the definitions.

- *Heading:* The heading of the relation depicted is:

```
{ SNO SNO , SNAME NAME , STATUS INTEGER , CITY CHAR }
```

This heading has four attributes and is thus of degree four. Each attribute has an attribute name and a type name.

- *Body:* The body of that relation is:

---

[11] Columns in SQL tables do have a left to right ordering, though. One implication of this fact is that (unlike attributes in the relational model) columns in SQL can have duplicate names, or even no names at all—no user known names, at any rate. For example, consider the SQL expression SELECT DISTINCT S.CITY, 2 * S.STATUS, P.CITY FROM S, P. What are the column names in the result of this expression?

S1	Smith	20	London
S2	Jones	10	Paris
S3	Blake	30	Paris
S4	Clark	20	London
S5	Adams	30	Athens

This body has five tuples and is thus of cardinality five.

■ *Relation type, tuple type:* The type of the foregoing relation is:

```
RELATION { SNO SNO , SNAME NAME ,
                STATUS INTEGER , CITY CHAR }
```

The type of each tuple in that relation (or in the body of that relation, to be more precise) is:

```
TUPLE { SNO SNO , SNAME NAME ,
             STATUS INTEGER , CITY CHAR }
```

■ *Relation variable (relvar):* The relation depicted could be, and indeed is meant to be, a possible value of a relvar of the relation type just shown.

■ *Tuple variable (tuplevar):* The example under discussion doesn't involve any tuplevars. But we could define a tuplevar—call it TV—of the same tuple type as that of the tuples in the relation depicted, and then we could perform an operation to extract a tuple from that relation, say the tuple for supplier S1, and assign it to that tuplevar TV.

LOGICAL DIFFERENCE

I've already mentioned the term *logical difference* several times; now it's time to say a little more about it. What it means, of course, is a difference that's logical, not (e.g.) merely psychological, in nature. It derives from a maxim of Wittgenstein's:

All logical differences are big differences.

The relevance of this maxim for database systems in particular, and in fact for computing systems in general, can be explained as follows:

- The relational model is a formal system (just as a DBMS is, or an operating system, or indeed any computer program).

- Formal systems are what computers are—or can be made to be—good at.

- And since the basis of any formal system is logic, it follows that in such contexts differences that are logical in nature are very important ones, and we need to pay careful attention to them.

In those same contexts, by contrast, differences that aren't logical in nature are comparatively unimportant. Thus, in programming languages in particular, semantic differences are very significant, while mere syntactic differences are much less so. By way of illustration, consider **Tutorial D**. In that language, there's a clear syntactic difference, but no semantic or logical difference, between the expressions

```
S { SNO } MINUS SP { SNO }
```

and

```
S { SNO } NOT MATCHING SP
```

—both evaluate to a relation of just one attribute, SNO, that contains the supplier numbers of just those suppliers that are represented in the current value of relvar S and not in the current value of relvar SP. In other words, both expressions are formal representations of the query "Get supplier numbers of suppliers who currently supply no parts."

For further discussion of the notion of logical difference in general, I refer you to Chapter 4 ("All Logical Differences Are Big Differences") of my book *Database Dreaming Volume I* (Technics, 2022).

NULLS – JUST SAY NO

I haven't yet mentioned nulls in this chapter. And there's a good reason for that omission!—as far as I'm concerned, nulls, at least as that term is usually understood (e.g., in SQL), have no part to play in a carefully constructed formal system such as the relational model is supposed to be. In fact, nulls were for many years my biggest area of disagreement with Codd; he thought nulls were a good idea, and I don't.

Now, I've documented my reasons for rejecting nulls in many places—see, e.g., Chapter 18, "Why Three- and Four-Valued Logic Don't Work," in my book *Date on Database: Writings 2000-2006* (Apress, 2006)—and I don't want to repeat those arguments here.[12] I'll content myself with simply repeating the following extract from *The New Relational Database Dictionary* (very slightly paraphrased here):

> **Definition (null):** A construct, used in SQL in particular, for representing "missing information"—or, rather, for representing the fact that some piece of information is unavailable for some reason.
>
> *Note:* By definition, nulls aren't values (they're sometimes said to be *marks*). It follows that—check the definitions if you don't believe me—a "type" that contains a null isn't a type; a "tuple" that contains a null isn't a tuple; a "relation" that contains a null isn't a relation; and a "relvar" that contains a null isn't a relvar. It follows further that nulls do serious violence to the relational model, and in this chapter I therefore have very little to say regarding them, or matters related to them.

RELATIONAL OPERATORS

I'm sure you're broadly familiar with the usual relational operators, but I'll give definitions, slightly simplified for present purposes, of three such in this section, viz., restriction, projection, and join. *Note:* My main reason for giving such definitions at all is just to illustrate the relevant **Tutorial D** syntax, which I'll be making much use of in examples later (though I won't be limiting myself to just those three operators).

> **Definition (restriction):** Let r be a relation and let bx be a restriction condition (which is to say, bx is a boolean expression of a certain limited kind—see below). Then, and only then, the expression r WHERE bx denotes the restriction of r according to bx, and it returns the relation with heading the same as that of r (i.e., the result is of the same type as r) and

---

[12] Except to note that Codd invented the relational model in 1969 and didn't add nulls until 1979, and so the model managed perfectly well (in fact better) without them for some ten years.

with body consisting of just those tuples of *r* for which *bx* evaluates to
TRUE.

Example: The following **Tutorial D** expression denotes a restriction of the
relation that's the current value of relvar P:

```
P WHERE WEIGHT < 17.5
```

Points arising:

■ Restriction is often referred to as selection (especially in later writings by
   Codd), but this term is deprecated, slightly, because of the potential
   confusion with the SELECT operator of SQL. The SELECT operator of
   SQL—meaning, more precisely, just the SELECT portion of an SQL
   SELECT expression—can be loosely characterized as a combination[13] of
   the relational summarize, extend, rename, and "project" operators
   ("project" in quotes because SELECT in SQL doesn't eliminate duplicates
   unless explicitly requested to do so, via DISTINCT). Note, therefore, that
   "selection" in the sense of restriction is precisely *not* one of the operations
   performed by the SELECT portion of an SQL SELECT expression.

■ Let *r* be a relation; then a *restriction condition* on *r* is a boolean expression
   in which all attribute references are references to attributes of *r* and there
   are no relvar references.
   Note: WHERE clauses in real languages, including both SQL and
   Tutorial D, typically permit boolean expressions that are more general than
   simple restriction conditions on the pertinent relation. Here's a **Tutorial D**
   example:

```
S WHERE P { PNO }=
          ( ( SP RENAME { SNO AS ZNO } )
                            WHERE ZNO = SNO ) { PNO }
```

---

[13] I say "combination" here because I'm trying to be polite, but "muddle" might be more appropriate.
Certainly it's true that SELECT in SQL can be quite confusing and awkward to use—and this state of affairs
is, I believe, a direct consequence of the fact that the semantics are just not very clearcut. More specifically,
it's a consequence of the fact that the meaning of the SQL SELECT clause is highly context dependent.
Indeed, it's relevant to mention in this connection that the SQL standard document requires some eleven or
so pages to define just that one clause, and textually dense pages at that—and that's not counting all of the
numerous references within those eleven pages to concepts defined elsewhere in the document.

The boolean expression in the outer WHERE clause here isn't just a simple restriction condition on the relation that's the current value of relvar S, because (a) it contains attribute references that aren't references to attributes of that relation, and (b) it also contains two relvar references.

Exercises: Translate the overall expression in this example into natural language—in other words, answer the question: What natural language query does the expression represent? Also, give a formulation of that query in SQL.

■ Note that, technically, restriction is an operation on a *relation*, not a relvar. For example, the expression shown earlier—

```
P WHERE WEIGHT < 17.5
```

—denotes a restriction of the relation that's the current value of relvar P, not a restriction of relvar P as such. In other words, restriction certainly applies to those relations that happen to be the current values of relvars. But in some contexts (view processing, for example) it's convenient to use expressions like *a restriction of relvar R* with a slightly different meaning. To be specific, we might say, loosely but very conveniently, that some *relvar* (call it *R'*) is a restriction of that given relvar *R*—meaning, more precisely, that the value of *R'* at all times is equal to the specified restriction of the value of the specified relvar *R* at the time in question. In a sense, therefore, we can, and often do, talk in terms of restrictions of relvars per se, instead of just in terms of restrictions of relations (restrictions of relations that happen to be current values of relvars in particular).

Note: Remarks analogous to those of the foregoing paragraph apply to all of the other relational operators also, of course.

Definition (projection): Let relation r have attributes $<A_1,T_1>$, $<A_2,T_2>$, ..., $<A_n,T_n>$ (and possibly others). Then, and only then, the expression $r\{A_1,A_2,...,A_n\}$ denotes the projection of r on those attributes, and it returns the relation with heading $\{<A_1,T_1>, <A_2,T_2>, ..., <A_n,T_n>\}$ and body consisting of all tuples t such that there exists a tuple in r that has the same value for attributes $A_1, A_2, ..., A_n$ as t does.

Example: The **Tutorial D** expression

```
S { STATUS , CITY }
```

denotes a projection of the relation that's the current value of relvar S. That projection is a relation of type

```
RELATION { STATUS INTEGER , CITY CHAR }
```

The result contains all possible tuples of the form $<st,sc>$ (and no other tuples) such that there exists some supplier number *sno* and some name *sn* such that the tuple $<sno,sn,st,sc>$ appears in the current value of relvar S.[14] Note that, given our usual sample value for relvar S, the result has cardinality four, not five (in other words, "duplicates are eliminated").

A couple of points of syntax:

- Let *r* be a relation with heading *H*, and let {*X*} be a subset of the attribute names in *H*. Then **Tutorial D** allows the projection *r*{*X*} to be expressed in the alternative form *r*{ALL BUT *Y*}, where {*X*} and {*Y*} are disjoint and their set theory union is equal to the set of all attribute names in *H*. Thus, e.g., the projection shown above—S{STATUS,CITY}—could alternatively be formulated thus: S{ALL BUT SNO, SNAME}.

- Projection has the highest precedence in **Tutorial D** of all of the familiar relational operators. Thus, e.g., the expression S JOIN P{PNO} means S JOIN (P{PNO}), not (S JOIN P){PNO}.

  Definition (join): Let relations r_1 and r_2 be joinable (see below). Then, and only then, the expression r_1 JOIN r_2 denotes the join of r_1 and r_2, and it returns the relation with heading the set theory union of the headings of r_1 and r_2 and body the set of all tuples *t* such that *t* is the set theory union of a tuple from r_1 and a tuple from r_2.

  Example: The expression S JOIN SP denotes the join of the relations that are the current values of relvars S and SP. That join is a relation of type

```
RELATION { SNO SNO , SNAME NAME , STATUS INTEGER ,
           CITY CHAR , PNO PNO , QTY INTEGER }
```

---

[14] Please forgive the very sloppy notation I'm using for tuples in this sentence (and elsewhere too, occasionally). I adopt it for brevity. I hope it's clear.

As for the body of the result, it can be defined thus (albeit loosely): If the current values of relvars S and SP are *s* and *sp*, respectively, then the result consists of just those tuples of the form *<sno,sn,t,c,pno,q>* such that the tuple *<sno,sn,t,c>* appears in *s* and the tuple *<sno,pno,q>* appears in *sp*.

Points arising:

- What I'm here calling simply *join* is often referred to in the literature more specifically as *natural* join. Indeed, the literature refers to several different kinds of joins (natural join, inner join, theta join, and so on). But natural join is far and away the most important kind, which is why I use the unqualified term *join* to refer to the natural join specifically, and why **Tutorial D** does the same with its keyword JOIN.

- Join is defined above is a dyadic operator—it takes exactly two operands. But the operator is in fact both commutative and associative, and so it's possible, and desirable, to extend the definition to allow for any number *n* of relations to be joined ("*n*-adic join"). I omit the details here.

- Finally, joinability. Here's a definition of what it means for relations to be joinable:

  Definition (joinable): Relations r_1 and r_2 are joinable if and only if attributes with the same name are of the same type—equivalently, if and only if the set theory union of their headings is a legal heading.

For formal definitions of other relational operators—including UNION, MATCHING, EXTEND, SUMMARIZE, and many others—I refer you once again to my book *The New Relational Database Dictionary* (O'Reilly, 2016). *Note:* Slightly less formal definitions and explanations can also be found in various other books of mine, including in particular *SQL and Relational Theory: How to Write Accurate SQL Code* (3rd edition, O'Reilly, 2015).

BASE vs. DERIVED

Something else I haven't discussed in this chapter so far is the matter of base vs. derived relations, and base vs. derived relvars—though at least I've been careful to phrase all definitions (where appropriate, and where it makes any difference) in such a way as to apply to the derived case as well as the base one. Anyway, let me rectify the omission now.

It might help to begin with the following very rough equivalences, or parallels:

■ First, a *base relvar* corresponds to what SQL calls a base table (and the value of any given base relvar at any given time is a base relation).

■ Second, a *derived relvar*—at least, the particular kind of derived relvar we're interested in here, which is a *virtual* relvar—corresponds to what SQL calls a view (and I'll often use the term *view* in what follows, for clarity). And the value of any given view at any given time is a derived relation, though I must immediately make it clear that it's not the only kind; in fact, the value of any given relational expression at any given time is a derived relation.

With these brief characterizations out of the way, let's get on with the definitions.

Definition (base relvar): A relvar not defined in terms of others.

Examples: Relvars S, P, and SP in the suppliers and parts database are base relvars (at least, that's what I said in the preface, and let's continue to assume as much until further notice, just to be definite).

By the way, it's a popular misconception—one that's unfortunately reinforced by all mainstream SQL products—that base relvars are physically stored,[15] in the sense that they correspond directly to physically stored files, and their tuples and attributes correspond directly to records and fields within those files. But the relational model has nothing to say about physical storage! In particular, it categorically *doesn't* say that base relvars, as such, are physically stored: not in the foregoing sense, and not in any other sense, either. The only requirement is that there must be some defined mapping between whatever is physically stored and what's perceived by the user (viz., base relvars or derived relvars or a mixture of both).

---

[15] And that views aren't.

Definition (derived relvar): A relvar defined in terms of others by means of some relational expression—for example, a virtual relvar or view.

As I've said, virtual relvars or views are in fact the only derived relvars that are relevant to the present discussion.[16] For present purposes, therefore, we can take the terms *derived relvar* and *virtual relvar* (or *view*) as synonymous.

Definition (virtual relvar): A view.

Definition (view): A relvar whose value at any given time is the result of evaluating a certain relational expression (the view defining expression, specified when the view itself is defined) at the time in question.

Example: The following is a possible definition for a view called LS ("London suppliers"):

```
VAR LS VIRTUAL ( S WHERE CITY = 'London' ) ;
```

The relation that's the value of view LS at any given time is equal to the value of the view defining expression

```
S WHERE CITY = 'London'
```

at the time in question.

Definition (base relation): The value of a given base relvar at a given time.

Examples: The relations that are the values of relvars S, P, and SP at some given time.

Definition (derived relation): A relation that results from evaluation of some relational expression; loosely, a relation defined in terms of others. Note carefully that the term isn't limited to meaning just the current value of some derived relvar. It's true that the current value of a derived relvar is indeed a derived relation as just defined; but so is the current value of any

---

[16] The others are snapshots, which I propose to ignore for most of this book.

relational expression *rx* (regardless in particular of whether *rx* happens to be the view defining expression for some view).[17]

Example: Consider the expression S JOIN SP. If the current values of relvars S and SP are *s* and *sp*, respectively, then this expression currently evaluates to the derived relation that's the join of *s* and *sp*.

There's one more issue I want to mention in connection with views (or virtual relvars), even though it takes us somewhat beyond where we really need to go for present purposes. Consider the suppliers relvar S. I've said I'm assuming that S is a base relvar, and I've defined relvar LS ("London suppliers") as a view of that relvar. Of course, I could if I wanted define another view NLS ("non London suppliers") too, like this:

```
VAR NLS VIRTUAL ( S WHERE CITY ≠ 'London' ) ;
```

So far, then, so good—relvar S is a base relvar and relvars LS and NLS are virtual relvars or views. *But observe now that it could have been the other way around.* That is, I could have defined LS and NLS as base relvars and S as a view (the view defining expression would be LS UNION NLS).[18]

As I hope you can see, then, what this example shows is the following: In a given database design, *which relvars are base ones and which ones are views is, in general, somewhat arbitrary* (at least from a formal point of view).[19] And one very significant logical consequence of this very significant realization is *The Principle of Interchangeability*:

> **Definition (*Principle of Interchangeability*):**   There must be no arbitrary and unnecessary distinctions between base and virtual relvars; i.e., virtual relvars should "look and feel" just like base ones so far as users are concerned.

---

[17] It's even true in the special case of a relational expression of the form simply *R*, where *R* is a base relvar name. In other words, base relations too are "derived relations"! But "most" derived relations aren't base ones.

[18] In order to guarantee that LS and NLS are together truly equivalent to the original S, there are certain constraints that would need to be enforced (including in particular constraints to the effect that every CITY value in LS is London and no CITY value in NLS is), but I choose to overlook such details here.

[19] Another thing it shows, or at least implies, is this: Which relvars—if any!—are physically stored and which ones aren't is arbitrary too. For example, even if S is a base relvar and LS and NLS are views, it could be the case that LS and NLS are physically stored and S isn't.

Here are some important implications of this principle:

- Views are subject to integrity constraints, just as base relvars are. (It's usual to think of constraints as applying to base relvars specifically, but *The Principle of Interchangeability* shows this position isn't really tenable.)

- In particular, views have keys.

- They might also have foreign keys, and foreign keys might refer to them.

- Perhaps most important of all, *views must be updatable*—because if they aren't, then that fact in itself would constitute the clearest possible violation of *The Principle of Interchangeability*.

    To put the point another way: Views are *relvars*, which means they're variables, which means they must be updatable. (To repeat something I said earlier: To be a variable is to be updatable, to be updatable is to be a variable.)

There's a huge amount more that could and needs to be said about these matters, as I'm sure you can imagine, but this isn't the appropriate place. For further details, I refer you to my book *View Updating and Relational Theory* (O'Reilly, 2013).

CONSTRAINTS

Now we come to integrity constraints, or just constraints for short: at last, you might be excused for thinking, since constraints—or certain kinds of constraints, at any rate—are what this book is supposed to be all about. But there's a lot of groundwork that needed to be covered first (a foundation for the foundation, you might say), and that's what I've been doing in this chapter up to this point. Foundations are important! After all, if we don't get the foundations right, then how can we guarantee that whatever we build on them is sound?

Definition (integrity constraint):[20] A named boolean expression, or something equivalent to such an expression, that's required to be

---

[20] This definition is slightly simplified. I'll have more to say about it in Chapter 2.

satisfied—i.e., to evaluate to TRUE—at all times, where "at all times" effectively means at statement boundaries (loosely, "at semicolons"), not merely at transaction boundaries. There are two basic kinds, type constraints and database constraints. The DBMS must reject any attempt to perform any update that would otherwise cause some integrity constraint to be violated (i.e., to evaluate to FALSE).

Well, there's a lot to unpack here. First of all, note that (as the definition says) there are two kinds of constraints:

■   The *type* constraint for a given type *T* is simply a definition of the set of values that go to make up type *T*. (See the user defined type POINT example near the beginning of this chapter for an illustration.) However, type constraints aren't particularly relevant to the main theme of this book, so I don't propose to discuss them any further here; from this point forward, you can take the unqualified term *constraint* to mean a database constraint specifically, unless the context demands otherwise.

Aside: I've said I'm not going to discuss type constraints further, but actually there's one point I'd like to note in passing, viz.:

> In SQL, the only type constraints supported for user defined types are ones that are a logical consequence of the underlying physical representation.

> This is a serious defect! For example, suppose the user defined type SHOE_SIZE, with the obvious interpretation, is defined to have an INTEGER physical representation. Then the only constraint on shoe sizes is that they must be representable as an integer. Thus, e.g., –5000 is apparently a valid shoe size, in SQL (!).

> PS: The reasons for this (on the surface, very strange, and obvious) defect are complex, and have to do with another major defect: namely, SQL's flawed approach to type inheritance. For a detailed discussion of the issue, I refer you to my book *Type Inheritance and Relational Theory* (O'Reilly, 2016). *End of aside.*

■ So a *database* constraint is any constraint that's not a type constraint. Here are some self-explanatory examples for suppliers and parts (they all make use of the boolean operator IS_EMPTY, which returns TRUE if its argument, a relation, is empty and FALSE if it isn't):

```
CONSTRAINT CX1
    IS_EMPTY ( S WHERE STATUS < 1 OR STATUS > 100 ) ;
    /* status values must be in the range 1-100 */

CONSTRAINT CX2
    IS_EMPTY ( P WHERE CITY = 'London'
                       AND COLOR ≠ 'Red' ) ;
    /* parts in London must be red */

CONSTRAINT CX3
    IS_EMPTY ( ( S JOIN SP )
               WHERE STATUS < 20 AND PNO = PNO('P6') ) ;
    /* no supplier with status less than 20 */
    /* can supply part P6                    */
```

(Are these constraints satisfied by our usual sample values?)

Key and foreign key constraints—to be discussed in more detail later—are also examples of database constraints, of course.

My next point is a very simple one, but it has far-reaching consequences. I'll introduce it by means of a kind of Socratic dialog.

Question: What is it that might cause a constraint to be violated?

Answer: Doing a database update (i.e., executing an update statement).

Question: What is it that gets updated when an update statement is executed?

Answer: A variable—in the present context, a relation variable, or relvar, specifically.

Question: So what is it that database constraints constrain?

Answer: Relvars in the database!

So database constraints in general (including key and foreign key constraints in particular, but in fact all database constraints) *apply to relvars, not to relations.* In particular, key and foreign key constraints apply to relvars, not to relations.

To put the point another way (and concentrating for the moment just on keys and the associated key constraints, for simplicity): It's relvars, not relations, that have keys. So when we define a key, we do so for a relvar, not for a relation.

Next: When we define a key K for a relvar R, we implicitly define a key constraint KC for R, and we say that R is *subject to KC*, or that *KC holds* in R, meaning that every relation r that can validly be assigned to R is required to *satisfy KC.* Note, therefore, that we draw a distinction—another logical difference, in fact—between a constraint's *holding* and its being *satisfied*: Constraints hold (or don't hold) for variables but are satisfied (or aren't satisfied, or in other words are violated) by values:

> **Definition (hold / subject to):** Constraint C holds for relvar R— equivalently, relvar R is subject to constraint C—if and only if every relation r that can ever be assigned to R satisfies C.

> **Definition (satisfy / violate):** Let C be a constraint that refers to relvars R_1, R_2, ..., R_n ($n \geqslant 0$) and no others. Then:

> - Relations r_1, r_2, ..., r_n (in that order) satisfy C if and only if evaluating C with R_1 equal to r_1, R_2 equal to r_2, ..., and R_n equal to r_n yields TRUE.

> - Relations r_1, r_2, ..., r_n (in that order) violate C if and only if evaluating C with R_1 equal to r_1, R_2 equal to r_2, ..., and R_n equal to r_n yields FALSE.

I note as an aside that the foregoing definitions are formulated in terms of *relation* variables and values specifically—but that's because we're specifically interested in this book in relation variables and values as such. In general, though, those definitions should, and can, be formulated in terms of variables and values of any kind whatsoever.

Keys

Now I want to focus on keys and key constraints specifically (once again there's quite a lot of ground to cover):

Definition (key): A candidate key (unless the context demands otherwise).

Definition (candidate key): Let K be a subset of the heading of relvar R; then K is a candidate key (or just a key for short) for, or of, R if and only if both of the following are true:

   a. *Uniqueness:* No possible value for R contains two distinct tuples with the same value for K.

   b. *Irreducibility:* No proper subset of K has the uniqueness property.

Examples: In the suppliers and parts database, {SNO}, {PNO}, and {SNO,PNO} are the sole "candidate keys"—or just keys, unqualified—for relvars S, P, and SP, respectively. Points arising from this example:

■ Note that {SNAME} isn't a key for S, because SNAME values aren't necessarily unique—though they do happen to be unique given our usual sample value for relvar S.

■ Note too that, e.g., {SNO,CITY} isn't a key for S either, because although its values are unique (necessarily so, in fact), it isn't irreducible—we could remove the CITY attribute, and what would be left would still have the uniqueness property.

■ Key irreducibility is desirable for several reasons, of which the most important is this: Without it, the system would be enforcing the wrong integrity constraint. For example, if the system knew only that {SNO,CITY} was a "key" for S, it couldn't enforce the constraint that supplier numbers are "globally" unique, but only the weaker constraint that they're unique within city.

■ Every relvar, base or derived, certainly does have at least one key. That's because the body of a relvar at any given time is a set, and sets don't contain duplicate elements; at the very least, therefore, the combination of all of the attributes (i.e., the heading) necessarily satisfies the uniqueness requirement.

■ A relvar can have more than one key. Such would be the case for the suppliers relvar S, for example, if suppliers were required to have both a unique supplier number and a unique supplier name.

■ Note clearly that keys are *sets* of attributes (and key values are therefore tuples). That's why I say that, e.g., {SNO} (with those set braces "{" and "}"), and not just SNO, is a key for S. However, if as in this example the set of attributes constituting some key contains just one attribute, then it's usual, though strictly incorrect, to speak informally of that attribute as such as being that key. I will *not* follow that practice in this book.

■ It's worth pointing out explicitly that if K is a key for relvar R, then the functional dependency

$$K \longrightarrow X$$

holds in R for all subsets X of the heading of R. (Functional dependencies are discussed in more detail in Chapter 2.)

■ Let me remind you (because it's important) that it's not just base relvars that have keys—all relvars do, including views in particular.

■ Finally, please understand that the term *candidate key* is basically just a hangover from earlier times, when more of a distinction was made between primary and alternate keys (see below) and a generic term was required to cover both. It could be dropped without serious loss, and usually is (and so it will be in this book, most of the time, from this point forward).

Definition (primary key): A key (or "candidate" key) that has been singled out for special treatment for some reason (special syntactic treatment, that is). While a given relvar can have any number n of candidate keys ($n > 0$), it can have at most one primary key. For a given relvar, however, whether some candidate key is chosen as primary, and if so which one, are essentially psychological issues, beyond the purview of the relational model as such.

Note: The relational model as originally formulated did insist that base relvars, at least, should always have a primary key. It also insisted that foreign keys reference primary keys specifically (partly because it further insisted that foreign key constraints were always between base relvars specifically—see the next subsection for further discussion). However, there were never good logical reasons for any of these rules, and in any case rules that apply to base relvars but not to other kinds are more than a little suspect anyway (because they violate *The Principle of Interchangeability*); thus, the primary key notion could be dropped without serious loss. I mention it here mainly because "everyone knows" there's such a thing as a primary key, and so I need to explain it.

> **Definition (alternate key):** Loosely, a key that isn't the primary key. More precisely, let relvar R have keys $K_1, K_2, ..., K_n$ (and no others), and let some K_i ($1 \leq i \leq n$) be chosen as the primary key for, or of, R; then each K_j ($1 \leq j \leq n, j \neq i$) is an alternate key for, or of, R. The term isn't much used.

> *Aside:* If you're already broadly familiar with relational ideas in general—which of course I'm assuming you are—then the suggestion that we should reject, or at any rate downplay, primary keys might come as a bit of a shock. So let me take a few moments to elaborate on my reasons for taking the position I do on this issue.
>
> It goes without saying that I do believe in keys in general. But I don't believe any longer in primary keys in particular—at least, not in any formal sense. In fact I think primary keys were another of Codd's mistakes (though not nearly as big a one as nulls!). I once wrote a paper to explain my position on this matter, "Why Primary Keys Are Nice but Not Essential," included as Appendix C of my book *Database Design and Relational Theory*, 2nd edition (Apress, 2019), and I'd like to quote from that appendix here:
>
> > Out of the ... set of keys possessed by a given relvar, the relational model as originally defined ascribes a primal role to an arbitrarily chosen member of that set called the *primary* key ... [But this state of affairs] has always been the source of some slight embarrassment to relational advocates, myself included. One of the strongest arguments in favor of the relational model is and always has been its claim to a solid logical foundation. However, whereas this claim is clearly justified for the most part, [the idea

of singling out one key and calling it primary]—i.e., the idea of having to choose one member from a set of equals and make it somehow "more equal than the others"—has always seemed to rest on grounds that don't enjoy the same degree of theoretical respectability. Certainly there doesn't seem to be any *formal* justification for the distinction; it seems to smack more of dogma than logic, which is why as I said I find the situation embarrassing. This appendix grew out of my own increasing dissatisfaction with the seeming lack of solid justification for the orthodox relational position on these matters. (As a friend of mine once said to me, these are the areas where in live presentations "You talk very quickly and hope no one will notice.")

What's more, not only does there seem to be no formal justification for [choosing one key as primary], there doesn't seem to be any formal way of making the choice, either. Indeed, Codd himself is on record as saying "The normal basis [for making the choice] is simplicity, *but this aspect is outside the scope of the relational model*" (my italics). But why should it be necessary to make the choice in the first place?—i.e., why, in those cases where a genuine choice does exist, should it be necessary, or desirable, to introduce such an element of arbitrariness?

End of aside.

So much for keys as such; I turn now to key constraints. The basic idea is straightforward, of course, but there are a few aspects and consequences of that idea that are worth calling out explicitly. Here first is the definition:

Definition (key constraint): A constraint to the effect that a given subset of the heading of a given relvar is a key for that relvar.

In **Tutorial D**, key constraints are defined by means of a KEY specification (typically part of the pertinent relvar definition).[21] For example, here again is the definition of base relvar S (suppliers):

---

[21] Recall, however, that a constraint in general is "a named boolean expression, or something equivalent to such an expression." A KEY specification is indeed equivalent to a certain boolean expression, though I omit the details here. But there's supposed to be a name, too—and so there is, in general, though again I omit the details. *Note:* Analogous remarks apply to FOREIGN KEY specifications also, mutatis mutandis (see the next subsection).

```
VAR S BASE RELATION
  { SNO SNO , SNAME NAME , STATUS INTEGER , CITY CHAR }
    KEY { SNO } ;
```

Note, however, that while the system certainly can and will enforce the uniqueness requirement implied by such a KEY specification, it can't in general enforce the corresponding irreducibility requirement as well. For example, suppose we were to specify KEY{SNO,CITY}, instead of KEY{SNO}, for the suppliers relvar S. As noted earlier, then, the system obviously wouldn't be able to enforce the constraint that supplier numbers as such, as opposed to supplier-number / city-name combinations, are unique. (On the other hand, if we were to specify *both* KEY{SNO,CITY} and KEY{SNO}, the system should at least be able to recognize that the second of these specifications logically implies the first, and so overlook or ignore, or even reject, that first one.)

> *Aside:* It follows from the foregoing that, technically speaking, specifying KEY {*K*} for relvar *R* means that {*K*} is certainly a *superkey* (i.e., a superset of a key), but not necessarily a key as such, for relvar *R*. But superkeys in general are beyond the scope of this chapter—though let me at least remind you that, in mathematics, every set is a superset of itself, and so every key is necessarily also a superkey. Let me remind you too that a superset of a given set *X* that's not identical to *X* is said to be a *proper* superset of *X*. In the relational world, analogously, a superkey of a given key *K* that's not identical to *K* is said to be a *proper* superkey. Finally, analogous remarks apply to subsets (and "subkeys") also, of course. *End of aside.*

To say it again, keys and key constraints apply to all relvars, not just to base ones. For example, here once again is the **Tutorial D** definition for the virtual relvar, or view, LS ("London suppliers"), but now with an explicit KEY specification:

```
VAR LS VIRTUAL ( S WHERE CITY = 'London' ) KEY { SNO } ;
```

Now, in many cases the DBMS should be able to perform some degree of *key inference*; in other words, it should be able to determine for itself at least some of the key constraints that apply to a given view. For example, if *K* is a key for relvar *R*, then values of *K* in any restriction of *R*—and in the case at hand, view LS is certainly a restriction of base relvar S—will clearly have the uniqueness property. (But what about the irreducibility property?) However, key inference in general is another topic I don't want to get sidetracked into discussing in detail at this point.

As a matter of fact, **Tutorial D** allows key constraints to be defined not just for relvars as such, but more generally for arbitrary relational expressions. Here's an example:

```
CONSTRAINT KX ( S JOIN SP ) KEY { PNO , CITY } ;
```

What this statement means is that if a view were to be defined with S JOIN SP as its defining expression, then that view would have {PNO,CITY} as a key. In other words, the statement effectively asserts the following:

> *If two suppliers are distinct but supply the same part, then they must be in different cities.*

(Is this constraint satisfied by our usual sample data?)

Let me close this subsection with an important point of clarification. When we say that *K* is a key, we mean that *K* has been specified as such *by means of explicit KEY syntax*. By contrast, if values of *K* are guaranteed to be unique only by virtue of some general integrity constraint and not by means of explicit KEY syntax, then the system might not be able to recognize that *K* is in fact a key, and will therefore not regard *K* as a key as such. Analogous remarks apply to foreign keys also (see the subsection immediately following).

Foreign Keys

I turn now to foreign keys. Yet again there's a lot to be said! First a definition:

> **Definition (foreign key):** Let R_1 and R_2 be relvars, not necessarily distinct, and let *K* be a key for R_1. Let *FK* be a subset of the heading of R_2 such that there exists a possibly empty set of attribute renamings on R_1 that maps *K* into *K'*, say, where *K'* and *FK* each contain exactly the same attributes (in other words, *K'* and *FK* are in fact one and the same).[22] Further, let R_1 and R_2 be subject to the constraint that, at all times, every tuple t_2 in R_2 has an

---

[22] Attribute renaming is yet another topic that I don't want to get sidetracked into discussing in detail in this chapter. For present purposes I'm just going to assume it makes obvious intuitive sense. At least I'll be giving an example in a few moments.

FK value that's the K' value for some necessarily unique tuple t_1 in R_1 at the time in question. Then *FK* is a foreign key; the associated constraint is a foreign key constraint (also known as a referential constraint); and R_2 and R_1 are the referencing relvar and the corresponding referenced relvar (or target relvar), respectively, for that constraint. Also, *K*—not *K'*—is the referenced key or target key.

Note: The referencing, referenced, and target terminology carries over to tuples in the obvious way; that is, tuples t_2 and t_1 in the foregoing paragraph are a referencing tuple and the corresponding referenced or target tuple, respectively.

And just for completeness:

Definition (foreign key constraint): See above.

Definition (referential constraint): See above.

Definition (referencing relvar): See above.

Definition (referenced relvar): See above.

Definition (target relvar): See above.

Definition (referenced key): See above.

Definition (target key): See above.

Definition (referencing tuple): See above.

Definition (referenced tuple): See above.

Definition (target tuple): See above.

Examples: In the suppliers and parts database, {SNO} and {PNO} in relvar SP are foreign keys corresponding to the keys {SNO} and {PNO} in relvars S and P, respectively. Note that, like keys, foreign keys are *sets* of attributes, and foreign key values are therefore tuples. That's why I say that, e.g., {SNO}— with those set braces—and not just SNO is a foreign key in SP. However, if as in this example the set of attributes constituting some foreign key contains just one attribute, then it's usual, though strictly incorrect, to speak informally of that attribute as such as being that foreign key. I will *not* follow that practice in this book.

Sometimes it's helpful to show foreign key or referential constraints diagrammatically, thus:

```
referencing relvar ──▶ referenced relvar
```

(The arrow means the relvar from which the arrow emerges has a foreign key that refers to some key of the relvar to which the arrow points.) Here's such a "referential diagram" for suppliers and parts:

```
S ◀── SP ──▶ P
```

Moreover, it can sometimes be helpful to label the arrow with the name of the corresponding constraint, but I generally won't bother to show such labels in my examples.

I note in passing that the arrows in a referential diagram can be seen as an extended form of the familiar functional dependency arrows. Certainly they represent many to one relationships, just as functional dependency arrows do.[23]

Here now is another example, one in which some attribute renaming is required (and note in this case how "the K' value" isn't actually part of, but rather is derived from, the pertinent target tuple):

```
VAR EMP BASE RELATION
    { ENO ENO , ... , MNO ENO , ... }
      KEY { ENO }
      FOREIGN KEY { MNO }
          REFERENCES ( EMP { ENO } RENAME { ENO AS MNO } ) ;
```

Attribute MNO in a given tuple of relvar EMP contains the employee number of the manager of the employee identified by the value of attribute ENO in that same tuple. (For example, the tuple for employee E3 might contain an MNO value of E2, which constitutes a reference to the tuple for employee E2.) Thus, {MNO} is a foreign key, and relvar EMP is thus *self-referencing*. Here's the referential diagram:

---

[23] Again, functional dependencies are discussed in more detail in Chapter 2.

EMP

Note: The parentheses in the REFERENCES specification in the foregoing example are logically unnecessary—they're included purely for clarity.
Points arising:

- As noted in the previous subsection, foreign keys don't have to reference primary keys. That is, given some specific foreign key, there's no requirement that the corresponding key in the referenced relvar be a primary key specifically.

- There's also no requirement that the referencing relvar and the referenced relvar be base relvars specifically; for example, there might be a foreign key constraint from a base relvar to a view, or from a view to a base relvar, or from one view to another.

- In fact, following on from the previous point, **Tutorial D** allows foreign key constraints to be specified between arbitrary relational expressions. Here's an example:

```
CONSTRAINT FKX ( S JOIN P )
             FOREIGN KEY { SNO , PNO } REFERENCES SP ;
```

What this statement means is that if a view were to be defined with defining expression S JOIN P—note that the join here is based on matching cities—then that hypothetical view would have {SNO,PNO} as a foreign key, referencing relvar SP. In other words, the statement effectively asserts the following:

If supplier sno and part pno are in the same city, then supplier sno must supply part pno.

(Again, is this constraint satisfied by our usual sample data?)
Here's another example: If it were part of the definition of relvar SP, the following specification—

```
FOREIGN KEY { SNO , PNO } REFERENCES ( S JOIN P )
```

—would mean that if a view were to be defined with defining expression S JOIN P, then the attribute combination {SNO,PNO} would be a key for that hypothetical view, and the attribute combination {SNO,PNO} in relvar SP would be a foreign key referencing that key. In other words, the statement effectively asserts the following:

> *If supplier sno supplies part pno, then supplier sno and part pno must be in the same city.*

(Once again, is this constraint satisfied by our usual sample data?)

To close out this subsection, here's a definition of referential integrity:

Definition (referential integrity): Loosely, the rule that no referencing tuple is allowed to exist if the corresponding referenced tuple doesn't exist. More precisely, let *FK* be some foreign key in some referencing relvar R_2; let *K* be the corresponding key in the corresponding referenced relvar R_1; and let *K'* be derived from *K* in the manner explained under the definition of "foreign key" above. Then the referential integrity rule states that there must never be a time at which there exists an *FK* value in R_2 that isn't the *K'* value for some (necessarily unique) tuple in R_1.

    Note: R_1 here might in fact be a "hypothetical view," in the sense of that term explained (or at least illustrated) above, and so might R_2.

Foreign Key Rules

Definition (foreign key rule): A rule specifying the action—the referential action—to be taken by the system to ensure that updates affecting the foreign key in question don't violate the associated foreign key constraint. Typical examples are CASCADE and NO ACTION.[24]

Example: Consider the foreign key constraint from relvar SP to relvar S, and consider also the "delete rule" specified in connection with that constraint for DELETE operations on relvar S.

---

[24] When they were first defined CASCADE and NO ACTION were spelled CASCADES and RESTRICTED, respectively (see Chapter 4).

■ Suppose that rule is NO ACTION; then an attempt to delete a supplier with existing shipments will fail.[25]

■ By contrast, suppose that rule is CASCADE; then an attempt to delete a supplier with existing shipments will "cascade" to delete those shipments as well.

Moreover, suppose relvar SP happens to be referenced by a foreign key in some other relvar (call it XYZ):

$$XYZ \longrightarrow SP \longrightarrow S$$

(I omit the arrow from SP to P because it's not relevant to the present discussion.) Then the effect of the "cascaded" DELETE on SP is exactly the same as if an attempt had been made to perform such a DELETE directly; i.e., it depends on the delete rule specified for the referential constraint from XYZ to SP. And if that cascaded DELETE fails because of the delete rule from XYZ to SP (or for any other reason), then the entire operation fails and the database remains unchanged. And so on, recursively, to any number of levels.

Exactly which referential actions should be supported the relational model doesn't currently say, but I think it's safe to say they should include the two mentioned above , viz., CASCADE and NO ACTION.

Further Definitions

I include these definitions here mainly for completeness. I'll have more to say about the concepts involved in later chapters.

Definition (referential path): Let relvars R_n, R_{n-1}, ..., R_2, R_1 be such that R_n has a foreign key referencing R_{n-1}, R_{n-1} has a foreign key referencing R_{n-2}, ..., and finally R_2 has a foreign key referencing R_1:

$$R_n \longrightarrow R_{n-1} \longrightarrow R_{n-2} \longrightarrow \ \ldots \ \longrightarrow R_2 \longrightarrow R_1$$

---

[25] Unless a *multiple assignment* is used to delete those shipments as well (see the final subsection within the present section).

Then the chain of such references from R_n to R_1 represents a referential path from R_n to R_1 (and that path is of length $n-1$). More precisely: There's a referential path, of length $n-1$, from R_n to R_1 if and only if (a) R_n references R_1 directly, or (b) R_n references some R_{n-1} directly and there's a referential path from R_{n-1} to R_1.

   Note: Any or all of R_n, R_{n-1}, ..., R_2, R_1 here might in fact be "hypothetical views," in the sense of that term explained earlier.

Definition (referential cycle): A referential path (of length n) from some relvar R_n to itself:

$$R_n \longrightarrow R_{n-1} \longrightarrow R_{n-2} \longrightarrow \ldots \longrightarrow R_2 \longrightarrow R_1 \longrightarrow R_n$$

Definition (self-referencing relvar): A relvar R with a foreign key that references some key of R itself (thereby giving rise to a referential cycle of length one).

Constraint Checking

Here's an abbreviated version of the definition I gave earlier for integrity constraints in general (but note that now I'm talking about database constraints specifically, not type constraints):

> **Definition (database constraint):** A named boolean expression, or something equivalent to such an expression, that's required to evaluate to TRUE at all times, where "at all times" effectively means at statement boundaries (or, loosely, "at semicolons"), not merely at transaction boundaries. The DBMS must reject any attempt to perform an update that would otherwise cause some integrity constraint to evaluate to FALSE.

The point I want to stress now is that business of "at all times" meaning at statement boundaries ("at semicolons"). If all constraints are to be satisfied at statement boundaries, then, to use conventional terminology, all integrity checking must be *immediate*, not *deferred*.

   Now, I'm sure you realize that this assertion on my part—this position statement, if you like—is *not* widely accepted in the database world at large. Instead, conventional wisdom is that:

a. There'll always be some situations where constraints simply can't be checked immediately (referential cycles provide an obvious case in point, though they're not the only one), and hence that

b. Checking in such cases has to be deferred to some later time, typically end of transaction (COMMIT time).

However, the fact that the foregoing is conventional wisdom doesn't mean it's correct, and it isn't. I don't want to repeat in detail here all of the reasons why it isn't; you can find those detailed arguments if you're interested in my book *SQL and Relational Theory: How to Write Accurate SQL Code* (3rd edition, O'Reilly, 2015). The overriding point, however, is simply this:

■ If a database is *ever* allowed to contain any inconsistencies (consistencies that persist from one statement to another, I mean), then that database is effectively a logical system that contains a contradiction.

■ And in a logical system that contains a contradiction, you can prove anything; for example, you can prove that $1 = 2$.

■ Translating this state of affairs into database terms, it means that you can get absolutely any answer whatsoever from a query against an inconsistent database.

In other words, all bets are off—you simply can't trust any answer you get from such a database.

Let's take a closer look at an example of a constraint where deferred checking seems on the face of it to be required. Consider suppliers and parts once again. In order to avoid irrelevant distractions, though, let's assume for once that attributes SNO and PNO are both of the system defined type CHAR, not (as elsewhere) of user defined types SNO and PNO, respectively. Now suppose the database is subject to the following constraint:

```
CONSTRAINT ...
    COUNT ( ( S WHERE SNO = 'S1' ) { CITY }
            UNION
          ( P WHERE PNO = 'P1' ) { CITY } ) < 2 ;
```

This constraint says that supplier S1 and part P1 must never be in different cities. To elaborate: If relvars S and P contain tuples for supplier S1 and part P1, respectively, then those tuples must contain the same CITY value (if they didn't, then the COUNT invocation would return the value two); however, it's legal for relvar S to contain no tuple for S1, or relvar P to contain no tuple for P1, or both (in which case the COUNT invocation will return either one or zero).

Given this constraint, then, together with our usual sample values, each of the following individual UPDATEs will fail under immediate checking:

```
UPDATE S SET CITY = 'Paris' WHERE SNO = 'S1' ;

UPDATE P SET CITY = 'Paris' WHERE PNO = 'P1' ;
```

Note that I show these UPDATEs in SQL, not **Tutorial D**, precisely because integrity checking *is* immediate in **Tutorial D** and the conventional solution to the problem therefore doesn't work in **Tutorial D** (nor is it needed, of course). What is that conventional solution? *Answer:* We defer the checking of the constraint to commit time, and we make sure the two UPDATEs are part of the same transaction, as in this SQL code:

```
START TRANSACTION ;
    UPDATE S SET CITY = 'Paris' WHERE SNO = 'S1' ;
    UPDATE P SET CITY = 'Paris' WHERE PNO = 'P1' ;
COMMIT ;
```

In this conventional solution, the constraint is checked at the end of the transaction (i.e., at the COMMIT), and the database is inconsistent between the two UPDATEs. Note in particular that if the transaction were to ask the question "Are supplier S1 and part P1 in different cities?" between the two UPDATEs (and assuming rows for S1 and P1 do exist), it would get the answer *yes*—in other words, it would see the database in an inconsistent state.

Aside: In case you were wondering, here's what deferred checking looks like in SQL:

- First of all, every SQL constraint is declared to be (a) either DEFERRABLE or NOT DEFERRABLE, and if DEFERRABLE then (b) either INITIALLY DEFERRED or INITIALLY IMMEDIATE. *Note:* Actually there are some exceptions to the foregoing, but those exceptions don't need to concern us here (especially since the standard itself—the version of the standard available to me, at any rate—isn't very clear on them anyway).

- Then at run time the statement SET CONSTRAINTS *<constraint name commalist> <option>*, where *<option>* is either DEFERRED or IMMEDIATE, sets the "mode" of the specified constraint(s) accordingly. (Of course, the constraint(s) in question must all have been defined to be DEFERRABLE for SET CONSTRAINTS to apply.)

- COMMIT forces all DEFERRABLE constraints into immediate mode. If some integrity check then fails, the COMMIT fails, and the transaction is rolled back.

End of aside.

Multiple Assignment

A much better solution to the foregoing problem—I mean, a solution that's logically correct, as well as being easier to deal with—is to support a *multiple* form of assignment: i.e., to allow any number of individual assignments to be performed "simultaneously," as it were. For example (switching back now to **Tutorial D**):

```
UPDATE S WHERE SNO = 'S1' : { CITY := 'Paris' } ,
UPDATE P WHERE PNO = 'P1' : { CITY := 'Paris' } ;
```

Explanation: First, note the comma separator, which means the two UPDATEs are part of the same overall statement. Second, UPDATE is really assignment, as we know, so the foregoing "double UPDATE" is really just shorthand for a double assignment of the following form:

```
S := ... , P := ... ;
```

This double assignment assigns one value to relvar S and another to relvar P, all as part of the same overall operation. In general, the semantics of multiple assignment are as follows:

- First, all of the source expressions on the right sides of the individual assignments are evaluated.

- Second, those individual assignments to the variables on the left sides are executed.

- Third, all pertinent constraints are checked.

(Actually this explanation requires a slight refinement in the case where two or more of the individual assignments specify the same target variable, but that refinement doesn't need to concern us here.)

Observe that, precisely because all of the source expressions are evaluated before any of the individual assignments are executed, none of those individual assignments can depend on the result of any other (and so the sequence in which they're executed is irrelevant; in fact, you can think of them as being executed in parallel, or "simultaneously"). Moreover, since multiple assignment is defined to be a semantically atomic operation, no integrity checking is performed "in the middle of" any such assignment—indeed, this fact is the major rationale for supporting the operation in the first place. In the example, therefore, the double assignment succeeds where the two separate single assignments failed. Observe in particular that there's now no way for the transaction to see an inconsistent state of the database between the two UPDATEs, because the notion of "between the two UPDATEs" now has no meaning. Note further that there's now no need for deferred checking at all.

Finally, let me point out in closing this subsection that multiple assignment actually isn't such a novel idea: It exists in some shape or form in many languages already (including SQL, as a matter of fact).[26] In the database context in particular, multiple assignment is involved implicitly in a variety of other operations already—for example, updating some join or union view, or cascading a delete.

DATABASE VALUES vs. DBVARS

Here again is the definition I gave earlier in the chapter for the term *variable*:

---

[26] What typically, but unfortunately, doesn't exist in those languages at the time of writing is an explicit multiple assignment in which the individual assignments are relvar assignments as such—and that, of course, is exactly what we need here.

Definition (variable): A holder for a representation of a value. Unlike values, variables (a) do have location in time and space and (b) can be updated (that is, the current value of the variable can be replaced by another value). Indeed, to be a variable is to be updatable, and to be updatable is to be a variable; equivalently, to be a variable is to be assignable to, and to be assignable to is to be a variable. Every variable is declared to be of some type.

Once again I'd like to draw your attention to the following text in particular (set now in **bold**, for emphasis):

[To] be a variable is to be updatable, and to be updatable is to be a variable.

It follows that the entire database itself is in fact a variable! After all, databases are surely updatable—indeed, they wouldn't be much use if they weren't[27]—and that makes them variables by definition.

Now, up to this point I've been talking as if the database were just a container for relvars, and indeed that's the way we usually think of them. And thinking of them that way doesn't do too much harm, most of the time. But in this section I want to take a brief look at a more accurate picture; that is, I want to explain the true state of affairs.

What I'm saying here, in essence, is that we can and should draw a distinction between database values and database variables, one that's precisely analogous to the one we already draw between relation values and relation variables. As a matter of fact, we—that is, Hugh Darwen and myself—did draw exactly such a distinction in the first (1998) version of *The Third Manifesto*. But in the next version we backed off from that position. Here's a quote, somewhat edited here, from the second (2000) edition of the *Manifesto* book:

> The first version of this *Manifesto* drew a distinction between databases per se (i.e., database values) and database variables ... It went on to suggest that, following the pattern already established in connection with relations, the unqualified term *database* be used to mean a database value

---

[27] Even so called "read only" databases have to be initialized, and that initialization is an update operation. I suppose we might say a database that's given an initial value when it's created and is never updated again is a database *constant*. But databases in general are variables.

specifically, and the term *dbvar* be used as shorthand for "database variable." While we still believe this distinction to be a valid one, we found it had little direct relevance to other aspects of the *Manifesto*. We therefore decided, in the interest of familiarity, to revert to more traditional terminology. [*In other words, we went on to use the term "database" to mean a database variable rather than a database value, and we didn't use the terms "database variable" or "dbvar" at all.*]

And of course I've done the same thing—I mean, I've used the term *database* in the traditional way, and I haven't used the terms *database variable* or *dbvar* at all—throughout the present book, prior to this section. However, the most recent (i.e., third, 2007) edition of the *Manifesto* book, after quoting the foregoing text, goes on to say:

> Now this bad decision has come home to roost! With hindsight, it would have been much better to "bite the bullet" and adopt the more logically correct terms *database value* and *database variable* (or dbvar), despite their lack of familiarity.

That same book gives arguments in support of this change of heart, of course, but I don't need to repeat those arguments here; the simple fact is, a database simply *is* a variable (its value changes over time), regardless of whether we call it a "dbvar" or just a database.

Now, it follows from the foregoing that when we "update some relvar" within some database, what we're really doing is updating the pertinent dbvar. (For clarity, I'll adopt the term *dbvar* for the remainder of the present section.) For example, the **Tutorial D** statement

```
DELETE SP WHERE QTY < 150 ;
```

"updates the shipments relvar SP" and thus really updates the entire suppliers and parts dbvar (the "new" database value for that dbvar being the same as the "old" one except that certain shipment tuples have been removed). In other words, while we might say a database "contains variables" (viz., the applicable relvars), such a manner of speaking is only approximate, and in fact quite informal. A more formal and more accurate way of characterizing the situation is this:

A database variable is a tuple variable.

Or more catchily:

A dbvar is a tuplevar.

(Refer to the section "Relation Values vs. Variables," earlier in this chapter, if you need to refresh your memory regarding tuple variables or *tuplevars*.)

The tuple variable in question has one attribute for each relvar in the dbvar (and no other attributes), and each of those attributes is relation valued.[28] In the case of suppliers and parts, for example, we can think of the entire dbvar as a tuple variable of the following tuple type:

```
TUPLE { S   RELATION { SNO SNO , SNAME NAME ,
                       STATUS INTEGER, CITY CHAR } ,
         P   RELATION { PNO PNO , PNAME NAME , COLOR CHAR ,
                       WEIGHT RATIONAL , CITY CHAR } ,
         SP RELATION { SNO SNO , PNO PNO , QTY INTEGER } }
```

Suppose we call the suppliers and parts dbvar (or tuple variable, rather) SPDB. Then the DELETE statement shown above might be regarded as shorthand for the following *tuple assignment*:

```
SPDB := TUPLE { S    ( S FROM SPDB ) ,
                P    ( P FROM SPDB ) ,
                SP ( ( SP FROM SPDB )
                       WHERE NOT ( QTY < 150 ) ) } ;
```

Explanation: The expression on the right side of this assignment is a tuple expression—technically, it's a *tuple selector invocation*—and it denotes a tuple with three attributes called S, P, and SP, each of which is relation valued. Within that tuple, (a) the value of attribute S is the current value of relvar S; (b) the value of attribute P is the current value of relvar P; and (c) the value of attribute SP is the current value of relvar SP, excluding those tuples for which the quantity is less than 150.

In sum, therefore: A dbvar is a tuple variable, and a database (i.e., the value of some given dbvar at some given time) is a tuple. What's more, given a relational assignment of the form

---

[28] In case you were wondering, yes, it's legal for an attribute of a relation, or of a relvar, to be "relation valued"—i.e., to have as its type some specific relation type. (If you go back and check, you'll find that none of the defintions I've given earlier in this chapter rule out such a possibility.) See my book *SQL and Relational Theory: How to Write Accurate SQL Code* (3rd edition, O'Reilly, 2015) for a more detailed discussion.

```
R := rx
```

(where *R* is a relvar reference—i.e., a relvar name—denoting a relvar in the database and *rx* is a relational expression of the same type as *R*), that relvar reference is essentially behaving as a *pseudovariable* reference (see the paragraph immediately following). In other words, that relational assignment is shorthand for a tuple assignment that "zaps" one component of the corresponding dbvar (which is, to repeat, really a tuple variable). It follows that "relation variables" (at least, relation variables in the database) aren't really variables at all; rather, they're a convenient fiction that gives the illusion that the database—or the dbvar, rather—can be updated in a piecemeal fashion, individual relvar by individual relvar.

A note on pseudovariables: Essentially, a pseudovariable reference consists of an operational expression appearing in the target position within an assignment operation. For example, let X be a variable of type CHAR, and let 'Middle' be the current value of X. Then the assignment SUBSTR(X,2,1) := 'u' has the effect of "zapping" the second character position within X, replacing the *i* by a *u*. The expression on the left side of that assignment is a pseudovariable reference. *Note:* The term *pseudovariable* is taken from the language PL/I. For a detailed discussion of pseudovariables in general, I refer you to Chapters 5 and 6 ("Types, Values, and Variables") of my book *Database Dreaming Volume II* (Technics, 2022).

CONCLUDING REMARKS

This brings us to the end of this overview of the relational model—or of those aspects of the model that are most relevant to the topic that's our principal concern in this book, viz., referential integrity and foreign keys—but I must stress that there are aspects of the model that I haven't touched on at all in this chapter, aspects that aren't directly relevant to our major theme. Be that as it may, here for review purposes is a list by section name of the topics I *have* covered:

- Domains vs. types

- Values vs. variables

- Assignment

- Relation values vs. relvars

- Logical difference

- Nulls – just say no

- Relational operators

- Base vs. derived

- Constraints

- Database values vs. dbvars

And the section "Constraints" in particular was divided into the following subsections:

- Keys

- Foreign keys

- Foreign key rules

- Further definitions

- Constraint checking

- Multiple assignment

So we've covered quite a lot of territory, and I'd like you to be sure you truly understand it all before you move on to the next chapter. Let me add that I really don't think the material is all that difficult—but there's a lot of it, and the overall impact can be a little overwhelming at first.

Well, perhaps I need to say too that if you're familiar with SQL, which I'm sure you are, then there are a few matters we've talked about in connection with which you might have to do some *un*learning—and unlearning can be hard, as we all know. I refer, of course, to points where SQL departs from the prescriptions of the relatonal model. For example, SQL tables allow duplicate rows, but relations don't allow duplicate tuples; likewise, SQL tables have a left to right ordering to their columns, but relations don't have any such ordering to their attributes. And then of course there's nulls. (There's *always* nulls.)

Chapter 2

Building on the Foundations

*This article may contain URLs that were valid when originally published,
but now link to sites or pages that no longer exist.
To maintain the flow of the article, we've left these URLs in the text,
but deleted the links.*
—from "Why We Need XML Server Technology"
(*www.software.ag*, August 1999)

This chapter uses the ideas introduced in Chapter 1 to home in and elaborate on the topic of integrity in particular: most particularly, on various matters related to keys and foreign keys. It consists primarily of a major expansion and rewrite of a paper—"Inclusion Dependencies and Foreign Keys"—that I originally wrote for the book *Database Explorations: Essays on The Third Manifesto and Related Topics*, by Hugh Darwen and myself (Trafford, 2010).

FUNCTIONAL DEPENDENCIES

First of all, I have a little unfinished business to attend to. I'll begin by repeating, albeit in abbreviated form, the following definition from the previous chapter:

> **Definition (integrity constraint):** A named boolean expression, or something equivalent to such an expression, that's required to be satisfied—i.e., to evaluate to TRUE—at all times, where "at all times" effectively means at statement boundaries (or, loosely, "at semicolons"), not merely at transaction boundaries.

You'll recall, however, that this definition was accompanied by a footnote saying it was "slightly simplified." Now I need to explain what I meant by that footnote. Well, you'll recall too that I referred several times in that previous chapter to the notion of logical difference, laying stress on the idea that *all logical differences are big differences.* But there was one such difference in particular that, though I didn't ignore it entirely, I deliberately blurred just a little at the time: namely, the difference between (a) an integrity constraint as such, on the one hand, and (b) whether the constraint in question actually holds, on the other. Let me elaborate; more specifically, let me take functional dependencies (FDs) as a familiar example to illustrate the point at issue.[1]

I'll start with a definition of what it means for a given FD to hold (you might think I should define FDs as such first—before worrying about whether or not they hold, I mean—but I have my reasons for wanting to do it this way around):

> **Definition (functional dependency holding):** Let X and Y be subsets of the heading of relvar R; then the functional dependency (FD)
>
> $$X \longrightarrow Y$$
>
> holds in R if and only if, whenever two tuples of R agree on X, they also agree on Y. ("Agree on," in contexts like the one at hand, is standard shorthand for "have the same value for.") X and Y here are the determinant and the dependant, respectively, and the FD overall can be read as "X functionally determines Y," or as "Y is functionally dependent on X," or more simply just as "X arrow Y."
>
> *Example:* Given the usual suppliers and parts database, the FD
>
> $$\{ \text{SNO} \} \longrightarrow \{ \text{CITY} \}$$

holds in relvar S, because whenever two supplier tuples have the same supplier number, they certainly have the same city. (Of course, if at any given time two tuples in relvar S have the same supplier number, they must in fact be the very same tuple; so they must certainly have the same city, and the FD in question must therefore certainly hold.)

More generally (but as I'm sure you know—in fact, I mentioned the point in passing in the previous chapter), FDs represent *many to one relationships*, or in other words "For one of these, there's one of those (but for any number of these, there can be the same one of those)." The sample FD just shown can thus

---

[1] The discussion that follows is based on one in my book *Database Design and Relational Theory*, 2nd edition (Apress, 2019).

be read, informally, as follows: "For one supplier number, there's one corresponding city (but any number of supplier numbers can have the same corresponding city)."

By the way, note the braces in the example—{SNO} and {CITY}, not just SNO and CITY. To repeat, X and Y in the definition are subsets of the heading of R, and are therefore sets (sets of attributes), even when, as in the example, they happen to be singleton sets. Note too, therefore, that X and Y values are *tuples*, even when, as in the example, they happen to be tuples of degree one. That said, let me quickly add that:

■ Informally, we often speak of Y as being functionally dependent on the attribute(s) in X, rather than on X as such. This practice is especially common if, as here, X happens to be of degree one. However, the practice is strictly incorrect, and can be misleading, and I won't adopt it in what follows.[2]

■ Likewise, we often speak of the attribute(s) in Y, rather than Y as such, as being functionally dependent on X. This practice is especially common if, as here, Y happens to be of degree one. Again, however, the practice is strictly incorrect, and can be misleading, and I won't adopt it in what follows.

So much for an FD holding; now let me turn now to the question of what an FD actually *is*.

Definition (functional dependency): Let H be a heading; then a functional dependency (FD) with respect to H is an expression of the form $X \longrightarrow Y$, where the determinant X and the dependant Y are both subsets of H. The phrase *with respect to H* can be omitted if H is understood.

Here are a couple of examples:

```
{ SNO }  ──▶ { CITY }
{ CITY } ──▶ { SNO }
```

Points arising:

---

[2] In fact, what we're dealing with here (and in the next bullet item also) is yet another logical difference— viz., the logical difference beween an element e and the set $\{e\}$ that contains just that element.

■ Note carefully that, contrary to popular opinion, FDs are defined with respect to some heading, not with respect to some relation or some relvar. Thus, for example, the two FDs just shown are defined with respect to any heading that contains attributes called CITY and SNO (as well as others, possibly).

■ Note too that from a formal point of view, an FD is just an expression: an expression that, when interpreted with respect to some specific relation, becomes a *proposition* that—by definition—evaluates to either TRUE or FALSE.[3] For example, if the two FDs shown above are interpreted with respect to the relation that's our usual sample value for relvar S, then the first evaluates to TRUE and the second to FALSE.

Of course, it's common informally to define such an expression to be an FD, in some specific context, only if it evaluates to TRUE in that context. But I must emphasize that such a definition is indeed informal, and in fact strictly incorrect. Why? Because that "definition" leaves us with no way of saying that a given relation fails to satisfy, or in other words violates, some given FD. Again, why? Because, by that "definition," an FD that isn't satisfied wouldn't be an FD in the first place! For example, we wouldn't be able to say that the relation that's our usual sample value for relvar S violates the second of the FDs shown above.

I really can't stress this point strongly enough. For most people, it represents a shift in thinking; however, it's a shift that has to be made if you really want to understand the subject at hand fully and properly.

That said, I should say too that in fact most writings on FDs— including in particular the early research papers by Codd that first introduced the concept, as well as early writings by myself—fall into this trap. That is, they don't actually define the *concept* of an FD, as such, at all! Instead, they say something along the lines of "*Y* is functionally dependent on *X* in relvar *R* if and only if, whenever two tuples of *R* agree on *X*, they also agree on *Y*." Which is perfectly true, of course—but it's not a definition of an FD as such; rather, it's a definition of what it means for an FD to hold. But if we want to develop a theory of FDs as such, then we

---

[3] A proposition in logic is a statement that's categorically either true or false. For example, "London is the capital of France" is a valid proposition: a false one, as it happens. By contrast, "Beethoven wrote exactly *N* symphonies" isn't a valid proposition—we can't say whether it's true or false until that variable *N* is replaced by some specific value *n* (at which point it becomes a different statement anyway).

clearly need to be able to talk about FDs as objects in their own right, divorced from the context of some particular relation or some particular relvar. More specifically, we need to divorce the idea of an FD as such from the idea that a given FD might have some interpretation, or meaning, in some given context.

So now we've finally reached a position where the formal definition of what it means for an FD to be satisfied or not should make sense:

Definition (satisfying or violating an FD): Let relation r have heading H and let $X \longrightarrow Y$ be an FD, F say, with respect to H. If all pairs of tuples t_1 and t_2 of r are such that whenever $t_1\{X\} = t_2\{X\}$, then $t_1\{Y\} = t_2\{Y\}$, then r satisfies F; otherwise r violates F.[4]

Observe that it's relations, not relvars, that satisfy or violate some given FD. For example, the relation that's the current value of relvar S satisfies both of these FDs—

```
{ SNO   }  ⟶  { CITY }
{ SNAME }  ⟶  { CITY }
```

—and violates this one:

```
{ CITY }  ⟶  { SNO }
```

And now I can give a revised (and simpler) definition of what it means for an FD to hold:

Definition (FD holding): The FD F holds in relvar R—equivalently, relvar R is subject to the FD F—if and only if every relation that can be assigned to relvar R satisfies F.

At the risk of boring you with undue repetition, let me stress once again the terminological distinction I'm drawing here: FDs are *satisfied* (or violated) by

---

[4] As you can see, this definition appeals to the fact—the obvious fact, I hope—that the concept of projection can be and is extended to apply to tuples as well as to relations (and the same goes for the corresponding syntax, of course). It follows that "whenever $t_1\{X\} = t_2\{X\}$, then $t_1\{Y\} = t_2\{Y\}$" is just a more elegant and precise way of saying "whenever t_1 and t_2 agree on X, they also agree on Y."

relations, but *hold* (or don't hold) in relvars. By way of example, the following FD holds in relvar S—

```
{ SNO }  ─▶  { CITY }
```

—and these two don't:

```
{ SNAME }  ─▶  { CITY }
{ CITY }   ─▶  { SNO }
```

(Contrast the examples following the previous definition.) So now, at last, we know precisely what it means for a given relvar to be subject to a given FD.

To close out the discussion, let me remind you that I've been using FDs in this section primarily as an illustration of points that actually apply to integrity constraints in general. To sum up, the points in question are as follows (and now I'm going to get a little formal for a moment):

■ Let C be a constraint. Fundamentally, then, C is nothing but a (named) boolean expression—though the name is often elided in concrete syntax, especially in the case of the constraints that are of the most immediate interest to us in this book (i.e., key and foreign key constraints). Moreover, again in the case of key and foreign key constraints in particular, the concrete syntax will typically be such that the fact that the constraint really is a boolean expression might not be very obvious.

■ Let C mention variables V_1, V_2, ..., V_n, and no others. (In the cases we're interested in, V_1, V_2, ..., V_n will all be relvars, of course, but in general they don't have to be.)

■ Let C_v be obtained from C by substituting the value v_1 for the variable V_1, the value v_2 for the variable V_2, ..., and the value v_n for the variable V_n. If C_v evaluates to TRUE, then the values v_1, v_2, ..., v_n satisfy C. If C_v evaluates to FALSE, then the values v_1, v_2, ..., v_n violate C.

■ If C is such that it can never be violated, then C holds for variables V_1, V_2, ..., V_n; equivalently, V_1, V_2, ..., V_n are subject to C. If C is such that it can be violated, then C does not hold for variables V_1, V_2, ..., V_n; equivalently, V_1, V_2, ..., V_n aren't subject to C.

INCLUSION DEPENDENCIES

The main topic I want to discuss in this chapter is foreign keys, of course. But foreign key constraints are actually just a special case—in practice, probably the most important special case—of a more general construct known as *inclusion dependencies* (INDs for short). Here's a definition:

> **Definition (inclusion dependency):** A named expression of the form *rx* ⊆ *ry*, where *rx* and *ry* are relational expressions of the same type.
>   *Note:* Recall from the preface that the symbol "⊆"denotes *set inclusion*; thus, the expression *rx* ⊆ *ry* can be read as "The relation denoted by *rx* is included in the relation denoted by *ry*"—or rather, and more precisely, "The set that's the body of the relation denoted by *rx* is included in the set that's the body of the relation denoted by *ry*."

And here's an example:

```
CONSTRAINT INDX P { CITY } ⊆ S { CITY } ;
```

In (stilted!) natural language, this expression says:

> If *pc* is all of the cities where a part is currently stored, and *sc* is all of the cities where a supplier is currently located, then *pc* is included in *sc*.

In other words, no part can be stored in a city unless there's at least one supplier in that city. (Usual question: Is this constraint satisfied by our usual sample data?)
    Points arising:

- I've said the symbol "⊆" denotes set inclusion. For obvious reasons, however, we often refer to it in the database context more specifically as *relational* inclusion.

- Also for obvious reasons, inclusion dependencies are sometimes known as subset constraints: "The set that's the body of the relation denoted by *rx* is a subset of the set that's the body of the relation denoted by *ry*."

■   The definition requires the expressions *rx* and *ry* in the IND *rx* ⊆ *ry* to be of the same type—which is to say, of course, it requires the relations denoted by those expressions to be of the same type, or in other words to have the same heading. For that reason, some attribute renaming is sometimes required. We'll see an example of such renaming in Example 4 later in this chapter.

■   In general, the expressions *rx* and *ry* in the IND *rx* ⊆ *ry* can be arbitrarily complex. In practice, however, they'll often be just simple projections of certain relvars, like this:

$$R_2 \ \{ \ \ldots \ \} \ \subseteq \ R_1 \ \{ \ \ldots \ \}$$

(Indeed, such is the case in the example above.) In such a case, relvars R_2 and R_1 are sometimes referred to as the source relvar and the target relvar, respectively, or just the source and the target for short.

Aside: SQL has no direct support for the "⊆" operator, and hence no direct support for inclusion dependencies. As a consequence, workarounds are needed. Here again is the boolean expression I used in the INDX example above:

```
P { CITY } ⊆ S { CITY }
```

And here's one possible SQL workaround for this expression (note the need for a double negative):

```
NOT EXISTS
  ( SELECT CITY
    FROM    P
    WHERE   NOT EXISTS
            ( SELECT CITY
              FROM    S
              WHERE   S.CITY = P.CITY ) )
```

Loosely: There's no city in P that's not in S. *End of aside.*

EQUALITY DEPENDENCIES

There's still one more topic I need to discuss before I can get to foreign keys as such: viz., equality dependencies (EQDs for short).[5] EQDs are an important special case of INDs; loosely speaking, they're INDs that "go both ways," as it were. Here's a definition:

> **Definition (equality dependency):** A named expression of the form *rx* = *ry*, where *rx* and *ry* are relational expressions of the same type.

And here's an example:

```
CONSTRAINT EQDX P { CITY } = S { CITY } ;
```

In (stilted!) natural language, this expression says:

> If *pc* is all of the cities where a part is currently stored, and *sc* is all of the cities where a supplier is currently located, then *pc* and *sc* are equal.

In other words: Every part city is also a supplier city and vice versa. (Once again, is this constraint satisfied by our usual sample data?)
Points arising:

■ This first point is obvious, but let me spell it out anyway: The EQD *rx* = *ry* is logically equivalent to, and can be regarded as shorthand for, the expression *rx* ⊆ *ry* AND *ry* ⊆ *rx*. That's what I meant when I said, loosely, that an EQD is an IND that "goes both ways."

■ EQDs occur surprisingly frequently in practice, as we'll see (which is why they're important, of course).

> *Aside:* I noted in the previous section that SQL has no direct support for the "⊆" operator (and hence no direct support for INDs), and that's true. In fact, it has no support for relational (or table) equality either, and hence no direct support for EQDs. So here again is the boolean expression from the EQD example above:

---

[5] Equality dependencies were first introduced in my book *Database Design and Relational Theory* (2nd edition, Apress, 2019).

```
P { CITY } = S { CITY }
```

And here's one possible SQL workaround for this expression:

```
NOT EXISTS
   ( SELECT CITY
     FROM   P
     WHERE  NOT EXISTS
            ( SELECT CITY
              FROM   S
              WHERE  S.CITY = P.CITY ) )
AND
NOT EXISTS
   ( SELECT CITY
     FROM   S
     WHERE  NOT EXISTS
            ( SELECT CITY
              FROM   P
              WHERE  P.CITY = S.CITY ) )
```

Loosely: There's no city in P that's not in S, and there's no city in S that's not in P.

Well ... I said that SQL has no direct support for equality comparisons on relations (or tables, rather, in SQL), and that's basically true. As a consequence, the following is *not* a legitimate way to test in SQL whether the set of cities in P is equal to the set of cities in S—

```
( SELECT DISTINCT CITY FROM P ) =
( SELECT DISTINCT CITY FROM S )
```

—not even if we do at least remember to specify those two DISTINCTs! But the odd thing is, SQL does have direct support for equality comparisons on *bags*,[6] including bags of rows in particular (which is what the bodies of tables are, in SQL). Let's take a closer look.

- First of all, a bag is like a set, except that it's allowed to contain duplicates. Thus, tables in SQL contain, in general, not sets but bags of rows.

---

[6] Bags are also known in mathematics as *multisets*, and SQL in fact uses this latter term—but I prefer *bags*, for brevity if nothing else.

- Regarding bag equality, here's the way the SQL standard defines it:

  > Two [bags] *A* and *B* are distinct if there exists a value *V* in the element type of *A* and *B*, including the null value [*sic!*], such that the number of elements in *A* that are not distinct from *V* does not equal the number of elements in *B* that are not distinct from *V*.

  I hope that's perfectly clear! Note that the extract quoted does indeed define what it means for two bags to be equal, because—simplifying considerably—if two values *A* and *B* aren't "distinct" in SQL terminology, then they must be equal. (Believe it or not, you really do have to worry, in SQL, about such matters—i.e., "do *not distinct* and *equal* mean the same thing?" It's a wonderful language.)[7]

- Moreover, SQL also has an operator for converting a table to a bag of rows. Note that such a conversion is necessary—in the context at hand, that is—because, although SQL tables do *contain* bags of rows, SQL tables *aren't* bags of rows as such. I mean, a table and a bag of rows aren't the same thing, because the operators that apply to tables aren't the same as the operators that apply to bags of rows. It's a wonderful language.

- So we can do the desired equality comparison in the example by converting the tables to bags of rows and then comparing those bags.

- Believe ir not, the operator for converting a table to a bag of rows in SQL is called *TABLE*. (I can't imagine what the SQL language designers were thinking here. The whole point of that operator is that the result is a bag of rows and not a table. It's a wonderful language.)

---

[7] In case you were wondering, they *don't* mean the same thing, thanks to nulls (were you surprised?). To be more specific: Are two nulls equal? *Answer:* Don't know (UNKNOWN). So are they distinct? *Answer:* No (FALSE). So we don't know if they're equal but we do know they're not the same. Got that?

■ Thus, the desired comparison can legitimately be formulated in SQL as follows:

```
TABLE ( SELECT DISTINCT CITY FROM P ) =
TABLE ( SELECT DISTINCT CITY FROM S )
```

But the foregoing trick only works for equality comparisons—SQL has no direct support for "⊆", nor any other comparison operators (certainly not for tables, and not for bags of rows either).[8] *End of aside.*

FOREIGN KEYS

So at last we come to foreign keys. A foreign key constraint is an inclusion dependency, of course, but it's a special case—the special case where the target relvar is "all key." In the suppliers and parts database, for example, there's a foreign key constraint from shipments to suppliers:

```
FOREIGN KEY { SNO } REFERENCES S
```

And this constraint is clearly equivalent to the combination of (a) the following IND—

```
SP { SNO } ⊆ S { SNO }
```

—and (b) the fact that {SNO} is a key for relvar S (i.e., S{SNO} is "all key").

Now, the foreign key concept was invented before INDs in general were defined—indeed, I daresay it's more familiar to you than INDs in general are—and a great deal of special terminology has grown up around it. For the record, therefore, I give below a definition that includes most if not all of the terms commonly encountered in practice. *Note:* The definition is basically just a repeat of material from the previous chapter—though there's one big, albeit subtle, difference!—but I give it here anyway, for convenience. I've broken it

---

[8] What's more, the standard doesn't guarantee that the single column, in those bags of rows resulting from the two TABLE invocations in the example, has any prescribed column name; in particular, it explicitly *doesn't* guarantee that the column name in question is CITY. Of course, this fact is probably insignificant in the present context, but it could easily be very significant indeed in other contexts. Stop me if I've said this before, but it's a wonderful language.

out into bullet items for clarity.

Definition (foreign key):

- Let R_1 and R_2 be relvars, not necessarily distinct, and let K be a key for R_1.

- Let FK be a subset of the heading of R_2 such that there exists a possibly empty set of attribute renamings on R_1 that maps K into K', say, where K' and FK each contain exactly the same attributes (in other words, K' and FK are in fact one and the same).

- Let FKC be a constraint to the effect that, at all times, every tuple t_2 in R_2 has an FK value that's the K' value for some necessarily unique tuple t_1 in R_1 at the time in question.

- Then FK is a foreign key; the associated constraint FKC is a foreign key constraint (also known as a referential constraint); and R_2 and R_1 are the referencing relvar and the corresponding referenced relvar (or target relvar), respectively, for that constraint. Also, K—not K'—is the referenced key or target key.

- The referencing, referenced, and target terminology carries over to tuples in the obvious way; that is, tuples t_2 and t_1 in the third bullet item above are a referencing tuple and the corresponding referenced or target tuple, respectively.

- Finally, note that R_1 here might in fact be a "hypothetical view" in the sense of that term explained in the previous chapter, and so might R_2.

So what's the "big, subtle difference" between the foregoing and the definition I gave for the foreign key concept in Chapter 1? *Answer:* I haven't said, here, that constraint *FKC* has to hold! If we want to insist that it does hold, we could add one more bullet item to the definition:

- Let R_1 and R_2 be subject to constraint FKC.

But if we did that (if we made that requirement part of the definition, I mean),

then we'd have no way to talk about a foreign key constraint being violated—
because, by such a definition, a foreign key constraint that's violated wouldn't be
a foreign key constraint in the first place.

Note: If you're having difficulty with this point, then I suggest you go back
and reread the section "Functional Dependencies" earlier in this chapter.

> *Aside:* Before I continue wth the main theme of this section, let me say a
> few words about SQL once again. The definition I just gave is of course a
> *relational* definition; thus, it might not accord with the way things are
> done in SQL, and in fact it doesn't. Note in particular that in the relational
> context an attribute of a given foreign key and the corresponding attribute
> of the corresponding target key are matched up by virtue of being one and
> the same attribute. In SQL, by contrast, such matching is performed on
> the basis of ordinal position—the "first" attribute (or column, rather) of
> the foreign key matches the "first" attribute (or column) of the target key,
> the "second" matches the "second," and so on—where "first," "second,"
> etc., refer not to the order in which the columns appear in their respective
> tables, but rather to the order in which they're listed in the applicable
> FOREIGN KEY specification. In other words, a FOREIGN KEY specification in
> SQL looks like this—
>
> ```
> FOREIGN KEY ( B₁ , B₂ , ... , Bₙ )
>          REFERENCES T ( A₁ , A₂ , ... , Aₙ )
> ```
>
> —where column B_1 is matched up with column A_1, column B_2 is matched
> up with column A_2, and so on. For all i $(1 \leq i \leq n)$, columns A_i and B_i are
> required to be of the same type, but they're not required to have the
> same name. Also, of course, the definition of the target table T must
> contain either a UNIQUE or a PRIMARY KEY specification in which the
> columns A_1, A_2, ..., A_n (and no others) are all mentioned—though they
> don't have to appear in that specification in the same sequence as they do
> in the FOREIGN KEY specification. (Optionally, they and the parentheses
> surrounding them can be omitted entirely from that FOREIGN KEY
> specification—but if so, then (a) they must appear in a PRIMARY KEY
> specification, not a UNIQUE specification, for table T, and (b) of course,
> they must also appear in that specification in the appropriate sequence.)
> *End of aside.*

Now let me get back to the main theme of the section. First, here are a few more definitions, just for completeness:

Definition (source relvar): For the general meaning, see the section "Inclusion Dependencies," earlier. In the foreign key context in particular, the term is a synonym for referencing relvar.

Definition (target relvar): For the general meaning, see the section "Inclusion Dependencies," earlier. In the foreign key context in particular, the term is a synonym for referenced relvar.

Definition (source tuple): Synonym for referencing tuple.

Definition (target tuple): Synonym for referenced tuple.

Syntax

The purpose of this subsection is simply to explain the syntax of foreign key definitions in **Tutorial D**—in particular, to inroduce the names I'll be using later in the chapter for various syntactic categories. Here by way of illustration is the **Tutorial D** definition (repeated from the preface) for the shipments relvar SP from the suppliers and parts database:

```
VAR SP BASE RELATION
  { SNO SNO , PNO PNO , QTY INTEGER }
    KEY { SNO , PNO }
    FOREIGN KEY { SNO } REFERENCES S
    FOREIGN KEY { PNO } REFERENCES P ;
```

Until further notice, let me concentrate on just this clause—

```
FOREIGN KEY { SNO } REFERENCES S
```

—which is an example of what I'm going to be calling from this point forward a *<foreign key def>*. The semantics of that clause are intuitively obvious, but let me spell them out here for the record:

■ The source or referencing relvar with respect to this particular *<foreign key def>* is relvar SP, because the *<foreign key def>* is contained within the definition of that relvar.

■ The set of attributes {SNO} of that referencing relvar constitutes a foreign key for that relvar, because that set of attributes is the one specified following the keywords FOREIGN KEY in the *<foreign key def>*.

■ The target or referenced relvar with respect to that *<foreign key def>* is relvar S, because that relvar is the one specified following the keyword REFERENCES in that *<foreign key def>*.

■ The referenced relvar S is required to have an attribute called SNO such that {SNO} is defined, via an appropriate KEY specification, to be a key for that relvar.

■ Attribute SNO of S is required to be of the same type as attribute SNO of SP (formally, in fact, they're required to be the very same attribute, since the names are required to be the same as well).

■ Specifying this *<foreign key def>* as part of the relvar definition for relvar SP means we want the corresponding foreign key constraint to hold. In other words, we want relvars SP and S to be subject to the following IND:

```
SP { SNO } ⊆ S { SNO }
```

So far, then, we can say that the syntactic category *<foreign key def>* is defined like this in **Tutorial D**:

```
<foreign key def>
    ::=    FOREIGN KEY { <attribute ref commalist>
                  REFERENCES <relation var ref>
```

The syntax has to permit a commalist of *<attribute ref>*s, of course, in order to cater for foreign keys consisting of two or more attributes. Every *<attribute ref>* in that *<attribute ref commalist>* must identify an attribute of the relvar in whose definition the *<foreign key def>* appears; moreover, the same set of *<attribute ref>*s must together identify a key of the relvar identified by the specified *<relation var ref>*.

For convenience, **Tutorial D** supports an ALL BUT form too, and so the syntax becomes:

```
<foreign key def>
    ::=   FOREIGN KEY { [ ALL BUT ] <attribute ref commalist>
                       REFERENCES <relation var ref>
```

For example, the foreign key constraint from shipments to suppliers could alternatively be specified as follows:

```
FOREIGN KEY { ALL BUT PNO , QTY } REFERENCES S
```

(ALL BUT isn't very useful in this example, of course, but it could be useful in other cases.)

We also allow the *<foreign key def>* to be named, so that error messages arising from attempts to violate the constraint can be specific as to just which constraint it is that's been violated. For simplicity, however, I'll ignore this detail for the rest of this chapter.

Advantages of Special Syntax

Foreign key specifications—*<foreign key def>*s, in **Tutorial D**—are actually redundant, in a sense. That's because the user language, be it **Tutorial D** or SQL or something else entirely, must certainly provide a means for specifying general integrity constraints (constraints of arbitrary complexity, that is); and given such a language, of course, foreign key constraints can obviously at least be formulated, though perhaps only in some roundabout way.

Assuming we do have such a general language, then—i.e., one that allows us to formulate those arbitrarily complex constraints—it clearly becomes a judgment call as to which constraints (if any) merit special syntactic treatment. But if I were allowed to be the judge, then I would argue, in the case of foreign key constraints in particular, that the arguments in favor of special casing are overwhelming. Here are some of them:

- ■ Special syntax effectively raises the level of abstraction (and hence the level of discourse) by giving an explicit name to, and thereby allowing us to talk explicitly in terms of, certain "bundles" of concepts that fit naturally together and often need to be discussed in the same breath as it were.
  Note: To me, this first advantage is the most important one. It accords well with what I've referred to elsewhere as *The Naming Principle*, which simply says that *everything we need to talk about should have a*

name (including that principle itself, of course!—and so it does; it's called *The Naming Principle*).[9]

■ Special syntax can be more user friendly; in particular, it can act as shorthand for what might otherwise require a comparatively longwinded formulation. As one reviewer of an early version of this chapter remarked (in connection with integrity constraints specifically), the shorthand can mean among other things that users don't have to devote time and effort to checking whether the constraint they've laboriously typed out in detail is really the one they meant. More particularly, they don't have to check that it doesn't have a subtle typo in it that converts it into something completely different.

Aside: The foregoing point, regarding user friendliness and "longwindedness," might sometimes be a little debatable in the case of foreign keys in particular. For example, the specification

```
FOREIGN KEY { SNO } REFERENCES S
```

can hardly be said to be "shorthand" for the specification

```
SP { SNO } ⊆ S { SNO }
```

—except inasmuch as the former implies that {SNO} must have been defined as a key for relvar S while the latter doesn't. On the other hand, the explicit IND syntax does require the pertinent attribute names to be written out twice, a consideration that could have the effect of sometimes making the FOREIGN KEY version truly a shorthand after all. *End of aside.*

■ Special syntax can make it easier for the system to recognize the special case and give it special treatment (by which I mean it can implement it more efficiently). Let me immediately add that I regard this particular advantage merely as a kind of bonus; I'm very much opposed to the idea of

---

[9] SQL manages to violate this principle in several places, though. (Were you surprised?) For example, it supports a construct it calls an exception handler, but such handlers have no name. Even columns are sometimes anonymous, in SQL! For example, the sole column in the the table that results from evaluating the SQL expression SELECT 10 * WEIGHT FROM P has no name—certainly no name that's known to the user, at any rate. (Actually the SQL standard says it does have a name, but that the name in question is "implementation dependent"—which effectively just means it's undefined.)

adding features to the user language (or indeed to the underlying model) if the sole, or even just the primary, motivation for them is simply performance.

EXAMPLE 1: A ONE TO ONE RELATIONSHIP

I now embark on a series of detailed examples, each of which is intended, broadly speaking, to introduce one new point. The first is taken from an early paper of my own;[10] it concerns two entity types, invoices and shipments, with a one to one relationship between them (by which I mean that each shipment has exactly one invoice and each invoice has exactly one shipment).

> *Aside:* I apologize for my use of the term *entity type* here, which, because it's so vague, is a term I usually try to avoid. Att least I'm not relying on it in any formal sense. By contrast, I *am* relying on the term *one to one relationship* in a formal sense. Here's the definition:
>
> > **Definition (one to one relationship):** A correspondence between two sets *s1* and *s2* (not necessarily distinct) such that each element of *s1* corresponds to exactly one element of *s2* and each element of *s2* corresponds to exactly one element of *s1*.
>
> *End of aside.*

The obvious first attempt at a design looks like this (INVNO is invoice number, SHIPNO is shipment number):

```
VAR INVOICE BASE RELATION
  { INVNO ... , SHIPNO ... , INV_DETAILS ... }
    KEY { INVNO }
    KEY { SHIPNO }
    FOREIGN KEY { SHIPNO } REFERENCES SHIPMENT ;
```

---

[10] "A Note on One to One Relationships," in my book *Relational Database Writings 1985-1989* (Addison-Wesley, 1990).

```
VAR SHIPMENT BASE RELATION
  { SHIPNO ... , INVNO ... , SHIP_DETAILS ... }
    KEY { SHIPNO }
    KEY { INVNO }
    FOREIGN KEY { INVNO } REFERENCES INVOICE ;
```

Well, maybe the design isn't so obvious, after all—clearly this "first attempt" involves a certain amount of redundancy, a point I'll come back to in the next section.

What's more, it's not at all obvious why we should have to deal with both invoice numbers and shipment numbers when the two are clearly in lock step, as it were. Let me state for the record, therefore, that the example is based on a real application, and the company in question really did use both invoice numbers to identify invoices and shipment numbers to identify shipments, and there really was a one to one relationship between the two, and the database really was designed in essentially the manner shown.

Observe, then, that in that "first attempt" design:

a. Each relvar has two keys.

b. Each relvar has a foreign key referencing the other.

c. Each foreign key is in fact also a key for the relvar that contains it.

Note too that, thanks to point b. here, the example involves a referential cycle (of length two):

I remark in passing that precisely because the two relvars are in lock step, INSERTs at least are going to require an explicit multiple assignment operation (see the previous chapter if you need to refresh your memory regarding multiple assignment). Why? Because whenever we insert a tuple into one relvar, we must simultaneously insert a tuple into the other one as well. (DELETEs are going to require multiple assignment too, of course, but in the DELETE case the necessary multiple assignments might be done "under the covers," as a consequence of a cascade delete rule. See Example 10, later.)

But wait a moment ... I've shown {SHIPNO} in relvar INVOICE as a foreign key referencing relvar SHIPMENT, but isn't {INVNO} in relvar INVOICE such a foreign key too? And similarly for {SHIPNO} in relvar SHIPMENT? In other words, don't we need to extend our design as follows?—

```
VAR INVOICE BASE RELATION
   { INVNO ... , SHIPNO ... , INV_DETAILS ... }
     KEY { INVNO }
     KEY { SHIPNO }
     FOREIGN KEY { SHIPNO } REFERENCES SHIPMENT
     FOREIGN KEY { INVNO }  REFERENCES SHIPMENT ;

VAR SHIPMENT BASE RELATION
   { SHIPNO ... , INVNO ... , SHIP_DETAILS ... }
     KEY { SHIPNO }
     KEY { INVNO }
     FOREIGN KEY { INVNO }  REFERENCES INVOICE
     FOREIGN KEY { SHIPNO } REFERENCES INVOICE ;
```

No, I don't think so! Let's reconsider. The point about the example is precisely its one to one, lock step nature. In other words, while the foreign key constraints specified by all those *<foreign key def>*s do indeed hold, what's really going on here is that the relvars are subject to a pair of equality dependencies (EQDs):

```
INVOICE { SHIPNO } = SHIPMENT { SHIPNO }
SHIPMENT { INVNO } = INVOICE { INVNO }
```

Now, we might consider extending the syntax of a *<foreign key def>* to make it explicit when the dependency implied by that definition is in fact an EQD instead of just an IND—perhaps by means of an AND VICE VERSA option, like this:

```
<foreign key def>
   ::=  FOREIGN KEY { [ ALL BUT ] <attribute ref commalist>
               REFERENCES <relation var ref>
               AND VICE VERSA
```

But the trouble with such a clause is that symmetry would seem to dictate that it be specified for all of the foreign keys involved:

```
VAR INVOICE BASE RELATION ...
    FOREIGN KEY { SHIPNO } REFERENCES SHIPMENT
            AND VICE VERSA
    FOREIGN KEY { INVNO }  REFERENCES SHIPMENT
            AND VICE VERSA ;

VAR SHIPMENT BASE RELATION ...
    FOREIGN KEY { INVNO }  REFERENCES INVOICE
            AND VICE VERSA
    FOREIGN KEY { SHIPNO } REFERENCES INVOICE
            AND VICE VERSA ;
```

Matters are getting worse, not better! The fact is, the syntax of *<foreign key def>*s as so far discussed works precisely because the implied dependency is usually an IND as such, not an EQD. I mean, it's the asymmetry inherent in INDs in general—their intrinsic many to one nature—that makes it intuitively reasonable to attach the *<foreign key def>* to just one of the relvars involved: namely, the source or referencing relvar, or in other words the relvar on the "many" side of the relationship. But when that implied dependency is an EQD instead of an IND, the asymmetry goes away, and there's no longer any good reason to attach the *<foreign key def>* to one of the relvars and not the other. (And attaching it to both is obviously redundant.)

For such reasons, I don't offer AND VICE VERSA as a serious syntax proposal. Indeed, I see no reasonable alternative to simply stating the EQDs explicitly—in which case, of course, the *<foreign key def>*s become 100% redundant (since they're implied by those EQDs) and can be dropped, and the database definition becomes:

```
VAR INVOICE BASE RELATION
    { INVNO ... , SHIPNO ... , INV_DETAILS ... }
    KEY { INVNO }
    KEY { SHIPNO } ;

VAR SHIPMENT BASE RELATION
    { SHIPNO ... , INVNO ... , SHIP_DETAILS ... }
    KEY { SHIPNO }
    KEY { INVNO } ;

CONSTRAINT EQD1A INVOICE { SHIPNO } = SHIPMENT { SHIPNO } ;

CONSTRAINT EQD1B SHIPMENT { INVNO } = INVOICE { INVNO } ;
```

Note, incidentally, that the definitions of the two relvars here can't really be considered complete until the two EQDs have been defined as well. At least updates to those relvars will probably have to be prohibited until the constraints are in place. Thus, something akin to multiple assignment—probably the ability to bundle up several definitions into a single statement—will be needed in order to permit the relvars and constraints to be defined in the first place.[11]

I haven't finished with this example—I'll come back to it in the section immediately following.

EXAMPLE 2: MORE ON ONE TO ONE RELATIONSHIPS

Perhaps you've already realized that there's still a problem with the invoices and shipments design, even with those explicit EQDs instead of the original *<foreign key def>*s. To be specific, the database is clearly required to satisfy the following constraint:

> If relvar INVOICE shows invoice *i* as corresponding to shipment *s*, then relvar SHIPMENT must show shipment *s* as corresponding to invoice *i*, and vice versa.

The design of the previous section fails to capture this constraint. For example, the configuration of values shown here is permitted by that design and yet violates the constraint:

INVOICE

INVNO	SHIPNO	. . .
i1	*s1*	. . .
i2	*s2*	. . .

SHIPMENT

SHIPNO	INVNO	. . .
s1	*i2*	. . .
s2	*i1*	. . .

Clearly what we need is another constraint—in fact, another EQD:

```
CONSTRAINT EQD2A
   INVOICE { INVNO , SHIPNO } = SHIPMENT { INVNO , SHIPNO } ;
```

But oberve now that enforcing this constraint will have the effect of enforcing constraints EQD1A and EQD1B automatically!—which means there's

---

[11] In fact, of course, a similar observation will apply (a) whenever a constraint is defined by means of a separate CONSTRAINT statement instead of as part of a relvar definition, as well as (b) whenever a constraint that *is* specified as part of a relvar definition references some other relvar.

now no need to state those constraints explicitly, and they can be dropped.

> *Aside:* In practice, faced with a situation like the one just discussed, users sometimes "cheat" by (a) declaring the sole key for each of the relvars to be the combination {INVNO,SHIPNO} and then (b) declaring that same combination additionally to be a foreign key in each of the relvars that references the other. Now, it's true that this subterfuge will have the effect of enforcing constraint EQD2A. However, it'll also have the effect of *not* enforcing uniqueness for any of the true keys!
>
> Moreover, suppose the user attempts to overcome this latter objection by additionally defining {INVNO} and {SHIPNO} to be keys for both relvars. Then the system should reject the attempt to define the combination {INVNO,SHIPNO} as a key as well, since it manifestly violates the irreducibility requirement. As noted in Chapter 1, however, whether the system will indeed reject that attempt is another matter. As a matter of fact, in the case of SQL in particular, an implementation that did reject the attempt would actually be "nonconforming"!—that is, it would actually be in violation of the prescriptions of standard.[12] *End of aside.*

Let's get back to the main thread of the discussion. The next point is that if we do indeed include constraint EQD2A in our design (and if it's enforced, of course), then that design will clearly lead to redundancy in the database as such. To be specific, every {INVNO,SHIPNO} combination appearing in either of the two relvars will now necessarily appear in the other.[13]

Now, we could avoid that redundancy by combining the two relvars into one ("INV_SHIP"), thus:

---

[12] To be fair, the fact that it would be in violation was probably unintended—I think the SQL standardizers were probably just trying to prevent the possibility of declaring the same key twice, but they muddled the wording. (For the record, the actual wording is: "The set of columns in the <unique column list> shall be distinct from the unique columns of any other unique constraint descriptor that is included in the base table descriptor of T." I think the phrase "distinct from" here should probably be "not identical to.")

[13] Well, that's the whole point of constraint EQD2A, of course. In fact, you could argue that EQDs always imply data redundancy of some kind. I don't want to get sidetracked too much into that particular debate here; I'll just make the point that redundancy can certainly cause problems if it's not properly controlled, but it can be perfectly acceptable otherwise—even a good thing, sometimes. See my book *Database Design and Relational Theory*, 2nd edition (Apress, 2019) for further discussion.

```
VAR INV_SHIP BASE RELATION
  { INVNO ... , SHIPNO ... , INV_DETAILS ..., SHIP_DETAILS }
    KEY { INVNO }
    KEY { SHIPNO } ;
```

An immediate advantage of this combination design is that it eliminates not only the redundancy as such, but also the need to state and enforce constraint EQD2A. What's more, we could if we want go on to define invoices and shipments as views—specifically, projection views—of INV_SHIP, thus allowing a user who's mainly interested in invoices to ignore shipments and vice versa:

```
VAR INVOICE VIRTUAL ( INV_SHIP { INVNO , INV_DETAILS } )
    KEY { INVNO } ;

VAR SHIPMENT VIRTUAL ( INV_SHIP { SHIPNO , SHIP_DETAILS } )
    KEY { SHIPNO } ;
```

Note, however, that the updates on these views will almost certainly be limited to updates to INV_DETAILS and SHIP_DETAILS (no INSERTs, no DELETEs, no key updates).

EXAMPLE 3: A SIXTH NORMAL FORM DESIGN

For my next example, I return to suppliers and parts. Suppose we decide to represent suppliers, not by a single relvar S as before, but rather by a set of relvars in *sixth normal form,* 6NF. Here's a definition of 6NF:

> **Definition (sixth normal form):** Relvar R is in sixth normal form, 6NF, if and only if it can't be nonloss decomposed at all, other than trivially (i.e., into the corresponding identity projection).[14] Equivalently, relvar R is in 6NF if and only if it's in 5NF, is of degree n, and has no key of degree less than $n-1$.[15] *Note:* A relvar in 6NF is sometimes said to be irreducible.

---

[14] The identity projection of a relation r is the projection of r on all of its attributes, which is of course identically equal to r. And the identity projection of a relvar R has as its value at any given time the identity projection of the relation r that's the value of relvar R at the time in question.

[15] For a detailed explanation of normal forms in general, including 6NF and 5NF in particular, again I refer you to my book *Database Design and Relational Theory* (2nd edition, Apress, 2019).

Examples: Relvar SP is in 6NF, since it can't be nonloss decomposed at all other than trivially; in other words, it's irreducible. (Observe that it's certainly in 5NF; it's of degree three; and it has no key of degree less than two.) By contrast, relvars S and P aren't in 6NF, because they can each be nonloss decomposed, nontrivially, into two or more projections (in several different ways, in fact).

6NF is the ultimate normal form with respect to normalization as conventionally understood, and there are strong arguments for making sure as far as possible that base relvars, at least, are always in 6NF. By way of example, if we were to apply that recommended discipline in the case of suppliers, we would replace the original relvar S by three projections, like this:

```
VAR SN BASE RELATION { SNO SNO , SNAME NAME }
    KEY { SNO } ;

VAR ST BASE RELATION { SNO SNO , STATUS INTEGER }
    KEY { SNO } ;

VAR SC BASE RELATION { SNO SNO , CITY CHAR }
    KEY { SNO } ;
```

In fact, there are also strong arguments for including another relvar in our design whose purpose is simply to record the supplier numbers for all suppliers currently represented in the database. Let's reuse the original name S to refer to that "suppliers master list" relvar:

```
VAR S BASE RELATION { SNO SNO }
    KEY { SNO } ;
```

Also, let's assume for the moment that if supplier *sno* is represented in any of these relvars, then that supplier *sno* must in fact be represented in all of them. Then the following EQDs clearly hold:

```
CONSTRAINT EQD3A SN { SNO } = S { SNO } ;
CONSTRAINT EQD3B ST { SNO } = S { SNO } ;
CONSTRAINT EQD3C SC { SNO } = S { SNO } ;
```

Of course, the following EQDs hold as well:

```
CONSTRAINT EQD3D SN { SNO } = ST { SNO } ;
CONSTRAINT EQD3E ST { SNO } = SC { SNO } ;
CONSTRAINT EQD3F SC { SNO } = SN { SNO } ;
```

But there's no need to declare these last three, because they're logical consequences of the first three. In other words, if EQD3A, -B, and -C are enforced, then EQD3D, -E, and -F will be enforced automatically.

Incidentally, another strong argument in favor of including that "master list" relvar S has to do with the shipments relvar SP (which is already in 6NF, as we know). The point is, given that master relvar, we can retain the conventional *<foreign key def>* from SP to S:

```
FOREIGN KEY { SNO } REFERENCES S
```

Without it, the situation is much messier (see Example 9).

Suppose now that it's not the case after all that if supplier *sno* is represented in any of relvars S, SN, ST, and SC, then that supplier *sno* is represented in all of them. To be more specific, suppose it's the case—a not unreasonable situation in practice—that:

a. If supplier *sno* is represented in any of SN, ST, and SC, then supplier *sno* must be represented in S.

b. If supplier *sno* is represented in S, then supplier *sno* can also be represented in any or all of SN, ST, and SC (possibly in none of them at all).

Then none of the foregoing EQDs will hold any more; instead, we'll be back to a situation involving nothing more than conventional foreign keys (or INDs), and conventional foreign key syntax—i.e., *<foreign key def>*s as so far defined—will suffice. The design will now look like this:

```
VAR S BASE RELATION { SNO SNO }
    KEY { SNO } ;

VAR SN BASE RELATION { SNO SNO , SNAME NAME }
    KEY { SNO }
    FOREIGN KEY { SNO } REFERENCES S ;

VAR ST BASE RELATION { SNO SNO , STATUS INTEGER }
    KEY { SNO }
    FOREIGN KEY { SNO } REFERENCES S ;

VAR SC BASE RELATION { SNO SNO , CITY CHAR }
    KEY { SNO }
    FOREIGN KEY { SNO } REFERENCES S ;
```

To spell the point out explicitly: This design allows us to represent a supplier with no known name, and/or no known status, and/or no known city, without having to resort to nulls, three-valued logic, or other such suspect method of dealing with "missing information." Indeed, this fact in itself is a strong argument in favor of such a design.

> *Aside:* At this point, I can hear some obvious objections being raised. First, you might be thinking (especially if you're steeped in the kinds of implementations to be found on the market today, where each base relvar maps to its own stored file, pretty much), that the kind of design I'm talking about here is bound to perform horribly. All those joins, right? But things don't have to be that way: The fact is, there's a radically different approach to implementation, the so called TransRelational™ approach (TR for short).[16] And 6NF and TR are actually a perfect marriage—not least because, in TR, *join costs are linear.* That is, using M for million and T for trillion, joining two million-tuple relations takes $O(2M)$ time in TR, whereas in classical implementations it takes $O(1T)$ time—i.e., it's 500,000 times slower, in those classical implementations.
>
> Second, you might be thinking that even if we use 6NF to eliminate all nulls from the database as such, we're still going to need nulls in generated results. In fact, you're probably thinking the joins I was talking about in the previous paragraph are going to have to be *outer* joins, and they're going to generate nulls all over the place. Well, again, things don't have to be that way. I've shown elsewhere[17] how we can get "don't know" answers—when "don't know" is the right answer, of course!—out of a database without nulls, without having to generate nulls and without ever having to depart from good old two-valued logic. *End of aside.*

EXAMPLE 4: SIMPLE RENAMING

As promised earlier, I now take up the issue of attribute renaming. Let's go back to the original version of suppliers and parts, where relvars S and P are in fifth normal form (5NF) but not in sixth. For the sake of the example, though, let the

---

[16] See my book *Go Faster! The TransRelational™ Approach to DBMS Implementation* (2002, 2011), available from *http://bookboon.com/en/go-faster-ebook* as a free download.

[17] In Chapter 5, "*The Closed World Assumption,*" of my book *Logic and Relational Theory* (Technics, 2020).

supplier number attribute in relvar S be named SNUM instead of SNO. Now, an expression of the form

```
SP { SNO } ⊆ S { SNUM }     /* warning: illegal! */
```

is illegal—it fails on a type error, because (as we know from the previous chapter) relations with different headings are of different types. In the example, therefore, some attribute renaming is required in order to make the comparison legal.

Now, in principle we could do that renaming either on the referencing side or on the referenced side of the constraint. Renaming on the referencing side would look like this:

```
( SP RENAME { SNO AS SNUM } ) { SNO } ⊆ S { SNUM }
```

And renaming on the referenced side would look like this:

```
SP { SNO } ⊆ ( S RENAME { SNUM AS SNO } ) { SNO }
```

Both of these expressions are syntactically legal. Corresponding *<foreign key def>*s might look like this:

```
FOREIGN KEY { RENAME { SNO AS SNUM } } REFERENCES S

FOREIGN KEY { SNO } REFERENCES S RENAME { SNUM AS SNO }
```

Syntactically speaking, therefore, it might seem as if we could go either way; i.e., we could do the renaming on either side. However, there are reasons—possibly not overwhelming ones, but reasons nonetheless—to prefer the referenced side:[18]

- Renaming on the referencing side effectively requires us to introduce a new syntactic category: specifically, a new kind of *<attribute ref>*, of the form RENAME {*<attribute ref>* AS *<introduced name>*}. The question then arises as to whether such *<attribute ref>*s should be allowed in all contexts where *<attribute ref>*s are currently allowed—and if so, what they might mean in those contexts.

---

[18] And I therefore now explicitly disavow the syntax tentatively proposed in various earlier writings of mine, which effectively involved renaming on the referencing side instead.

■ Renaming on the referencing side also means that what we surely think of intuitively as the foreign key as such—viz., {SNO} in SP, in the example—isn't what actually appears following the keywords FOREIGN KEY in the *<foreign key def>*.

By contrast, renaming on the referenced side avoids these problems. So let's try that. If we do, we'll have reached a point where a *<foreign key def>* looks like this—

```
<foreign key def>
    ::=   FOREIGN KEY { [ ALL BUT ] <attribute ref commalist>
              REFERENCES <relation var ref>
                [ RENAME { <renaming commalist> } ]
```

—where a *<renaming>* in turn looks like this:

```
<attribute ref> AS <introduced name>
```

So just to be clear, the SP relvar definition becomes:

```
VAR SP BASE RELATION
  { SNO SNO , PNO PNO  , QTY INTEGER }
  KEY { SNO , PNO }
  FOREIGN KEY { SNO } REFERENCES S RENAME { SNUM AS SNO }
  FOREIGN KEY { PNO } REFERENCES P ;
```

Now, you might be thinking that renaming on the referenced side as I'm suggesting here just means we have to introduce a new syntactic construct on the referenced side instead of on the referencing side. But it doesn't—the construct

```
<relation var ref> RENAME { <renaming commalist> }
```

is just a special case of a syntactic category that already exists in **Tutorial D**. To be specific, it's a special case of a *<rename>*, whose more general form is:

```
<relation exp> RENAME { <renaming commalist> }
```

And a *<rename>* in turn is itself just a special case of a *<relation exp>*. So now we've reached the point where the target in a *<foreign key def>* might be specified by means of one particular special case, at least, of a general *<relation exp>*.

Observe now that if we agree that, when it's used to specify the target in a *<foreign key def>*, the syntactic construct

```
<relation var ref> RENAME { <renaming commalist> }
```

can be interpreted as a *<relation exp>*, then we've tacitly also agreed that the target of a foreign key reference in general doesn't necessarily have to be a base relvar! After all—reverting now to our original example from the beginning of this section—we could certainly make

```
S RENAME { SNUM AS SNO }
```

the defining expression for a virtual relvar (or view), like this:

```
VAR SV VIRTUAL ( S RENAME { SNUM AS SNO } )
    KEY { SNO } ;
```

And now we could define {SNO} in the shipments relvar SP as a foreign key from SP to that virtual relvar SV:

```
VAR SP BASE RELATION
  { SNO SNO , PNO PNO , QTY INTEGER }
    KEY { SNO , PNO }
    FOREIGN KEY { SNO } REFERENCES SV ;
```

So now we have the idea that the target for a given foreign key might be a view—or, more generally, something that could be a view if we chose to define it as such.[19] I'll explore this possibility in more detail later (see Example 6).

EXAMPLE 5: MORE ON RENAMING

Recall this example from Chapter 1.

```
VAR EMP BASE RELATION
  { ENO ENO , ... , MNO ENO , ... }
    KEY { ENO }
    FOREIGN KEY { MNO }
        REFERENCES EMP { ENO } RENAME { ENO AS MNO } ;
```

---

[19] Of course, a more fundamental implication is that the target for an arbitrary IND might be a view, or something that could be a view if we were to define it as such.

As I explained when I discussed this example in Chapter 1, attribute MNO in a given tuple of relvar EMP contains the employee number of the manager of the employee identified by the value of attribute ENO in that same tuple (for example, the tuple for employee E3 might contain an MNO value of E2, which constitutes a reference to the tuple for employee E2). Thus, {MNO} is a foreign key, and relvar EMP is thus self-referencing:

```
EMP
```

Observe now that the *<foreign key def>* in this example involves renaming on the target or referenced side again. More specifically, the target is specified by means of an expression that is, again, more complicated than just a simple *<relation var ref>*:

```
EMP { ENO } RENAME { ENO AS MNO }
```

But this target expression doesn't involve just a RENAME as in Example 4—it involves a projection (of EMP on {ENO}) as well. And in fact it must. For suppose we tried to write the target expression as follows, without that projection:

```
EMP RENAME { ENO AS MNO }
```

Then the RENAME would fail, because EMP already has an attribute called MNO. (By contrast, the projection of EMP on {ENO} doesn't.) Here for the record is the relational comparison (to be more specific, the IND) that's implied by the *<foreign key def>* in the example—

```
EMP { MNO } ⊆ ( EMP { ENO } RENAME { ENO AS MNO } ) { MNO }
```

—which incidentally could be simplified (because the expression in parentheses on the right side denotes a result with just one attribute, viz., MNO) to just:

```
EMP { MNO } ⊆ ( EMP { ENO } RENAME { ENO AS MNO } )
```

Again, therefore, the example illustrates the point that a foreign key target doesn't necessarily have to be a base relvar. In particular, we could define a view like this:

```
VAR EMPV VIRTUAL
  ( EMP { ENO } RENAME { ENO AS MNO } )
    KEY { MNO } ;
```

And now we could define {MNO} to be a foreign key from the base relvar
EMP to the virtual relvar EMPV:

```
VAR EMP BASE RELATION
  { ENO ENO , MNO ENO , ... }
    KEY { ENO }
    FOREIGN KEY { MNO } REFERENCES EMPV ;
```

But this example raises another point. (Actually, Example 4 raised the
same point, but I deliberately ducked the issue in the previous section.) Consider
the generic *<foreign key def>*

```
FOREIGN KEY K REFERENCES R
```

In this *<foreign key def>*, the target *R* is required to have a key of the same
type—involving, therefore, the same attribute name(s)—as *K*; thus, in the
example under discussion, the target is required to have {MNO} as a key.
    Now, in the version of the example that specified the target relvar as view
EMPV, I explicitly defined {MNO} to be a key for that view, and the *<foreign
key def>*

```
FOREIGN KEY { MNO } REFERENCES EMPV
```

thus clearly satisfied the foregoing requirement.[20] But what about the original
version of the example (i.e., the one without the explicit view definition) from
the beginning of the section? Here again is the *<foreign key def>* from that
version:

```
FOREIGN KEY { MNO } REFERENCES
            EMP { ENO } RENAME { ENO AS MNO }
```

---

[20] When I defined view EMPV a short while back, I explicitly defined {MNO} to be a key, precisely in
order to avoid having to have the present discussion at that point. Please note, however, that **Tutorial D**
doesn't actually require explicit KEY specifications on views; if they're omitted, then the system is
supposed to work out for itself what keys the view in question might possess (see the discussion of *key
inference* in the next section). As for SQL, explicit KEY specifications—or their analog, rather—on views
aren't even permitted.

So the question is: Does the system know that the result of evaluating the expression

```
EMP { ENO } RENAME { ENO AS MNO }
```

satisfies the constraint that {MNO} is a key?—i.e., that {MNO} values are unique in that result? Equivalently, does the system know that if that expression were used as the defining expression for a view, then a specification of the form KEY {MNO} would apply to the view?

Well, first let me remind you that specifying KEY *K* as part of the definition of relvar *R* means only that *K* is a superkey, and not necessarily a key as such, for that relvar. In the case at hand, then, the system does at least know that {ENO} is a superkey for EMP, thanks to the specification KEY {ENO} in the definition of that relvar. From this fact, it follows that {ENO} is certainly a superkey for the projection of EMP on {ENO}. And from *this* fact, it follows that {MNO} is at least a superkey for the result of the renaming. Thus, the system should certainly be able to infer that {MNO} is a superkey for the target of the foreign key in this particular example—and so the situation is logically equivalent to that in which the foreign key target is specified as view EMPV and the definition of that view includes the explicit specification KEY {MNO}. In other words, in this example at least, the requirement under discussion is again clearly satisfied. (And I hope it's obvious that it was satisfied in Example 4 also.)

EXAMPLE 6: GENERALIZING THE TARGET

Consider the supplier and parts database once again, with its relvars S, P, and SP. Suppose the following business rule is currently in effect:

> *At this time there's an embargo on suppliers in Athens, and no such supplier is allowed to supply any parts.*

Formally:

```
SP { SNO } ⊆ ( S WHERE CITY ≠ 'Athens' ) { SNO }
```

This expression is clearly another example of an inclusion dependency (by which I mean the generalized form of such a dependency, in which the target doesn't necessarily have to be a base relvar as such). However, it's not a foreign key constraint—at least, not as foreign key constraints are conventionally understood. But it does look awfully like one! Now, we've already seen cases in the last two sections where the target for a *<foreign key def>* has to be specified by means of a *<relation exp>* that's a little more general than just a simple *<relation var ref>*. So why not go the whole hog, as it were, and extend the syntax of *<foreign key def>*s to allow the target to be specified by a *<relation exp>* of arbitrary complexity, like this?—

```
<foreign key def>
    ::=  FOREIGN KEY { [ ALL BUT ] <attribute ref commalist>
             REFERENCES <relation exp>
```

The example at hand could then be expressed as follows:

```
VAR SP BASE RELATION
  { SNO SNO , PNO PNO , QTY INTEGER }
    KEY { SNO , PNO }
    FOREIGN KEY { SNO }
            REFERENCES ( S WHERE CITY ≠ 'Athens' ) ;
```

(The parentheses surrounding the expression S WHERE CITY ≠ 'Athens' here are unnecessary but legal, because one form of *<relation exp>* in **Tutorial D** consists of a *<relation exp>* enclosed in parentheses. I include them for clarity.)

If this solution isn't available to us, then instead we'll have to write something like this:

```
VAR SP BASE RELATION
  { SNO SNO , PNO PNO , QTY INTEGER }
    KEY { SNO , PNO }
    FOREIGN KEY { SNO } REFERENCES S ;

CONSTRAINT ...
    IS_EMPTY ( ( SP JOIN ( S WHERE CITY = 'Athens' ) ) ) ;
```

But if we have to write out that separate constraint definition anyway, why not just write one that takes care of the foreign key constraint as well, like this?—

```
CONSTRAINT ...
    SP { SNO } ⊆ ( S WHERE CITY ≠ 'Athens' ) { SNO } ;
```

If we did that, then the *<foreign key def>* as such—i.e., the specification

```
FOREIGN KEY { SNO } REFERENCES S
```

—wouldn't be needed at all! So what exactly does the conventional FOREIGN KEY syntax buy us, in this particular example?

On the other hand ... Suppose we did in fact extend the syntax of *<foreign key def>*s to allow specifications like the one under discussion:

```
FOREIGN KEY { SNO } REFERENCES ( S WHERE CITY ≠ 'Athens' )
```

Then we'd be faced with a key inference problem once again: to be specific, the problem of ensuring, in the particular case at hand, that if the expression S WHERE CITY ≠ 'Athens' were used to define a view, then that view would be subject to the constraint KEY {SNO}. But once again the inference is straightforward, because the system certainly knows that {SNO} is a superkey for S, and from this fact it follows immediately that {SNO} is also a superkey for any restriction of S (which is what S WHERE CITY ≠ 'Athens' is, of course).

More generally, if we want to permit *<relation exp>*s of arbitrary complexity to be used to specify foreign key targets, then we need to be sure that the key inference problem can be solved for any such *<relation exp>*. But that problem *has* been solved, at least to a large extent. To be specific, Hugh Darwen has given solutions for *<relation exp>*s involving any of the following relational operations: rename, project, restrict, join, product, intersect, union, difference, extend, and summarize. For more specifics, I refer you to Hugh's paper "The Role of Functional Dependence in Query Decomposition," in our book *Relational Database Writings 1989-1991* (Addison-Wesley, 1992).

EXAMPLE 7: MORE ON GENERALIZING THE TARGET

Note: This section takes a slightly closer look at an example previously discussed in Chapter 1.

Here's another example to illustrate the usefulness of being able to specify the target of a foreign key constraint by means of an arbitrarily complex *<relation exp>*. Again consider the supplier and parts database, with its relvars S, P, and SP. Suppose the following business rule is currently in effect:

If supplier sno supplies part pno, then supplier sno and part pno must be in the same city.

Formally:

```
VAR SP BASE RELATION
  { SNO SNO , PNO PNO , QTY INTEGER }
    KEY { SNO , PNO }
    FOREIGN KEY { SNO , PNO } REFERENCES ( S JOIN P ) ;
```

Observe that (a) the expression S JOIN P denotes the join of suppliers and parts on {CITY} (since CITY is the sole attribute common to relvars S and P), and (b) the combination {SNO,PNO} is clearly a key for that join.

EXAMPLE 8: GENERALIZING THE SOURCE

Again consider the supplier and parts database, with its relvars S, P, and SP. Suppose the following business rule is currently in effect:

Only suppliers in London can supply parts in a quantity greater than 200.

Formally:

```
( SP WHERE QTY > 200 ) { SNO } ⊆
                    ( S WHERE CITY = 'London' ) { SNO }
```

Now, we've already agreed that we can allow the target of a *<foreign key def>* (or, more generally, an IND) to be specified by means of an arbitrarily complex *<relation exp>*—so the obvious question is: Can't we do the same with the source?

Well, note first that, as the formal statement of the constraint under discussion suggests, we've effectively already done this in connection with inclusion dependencies in general; that is, we've already allowed the source in an IND to be specified by means of an arbitrarily complex relational expression. Turning to *<foreign key def>*s in particular, here's a formulation that looks as if it might work:

```
VAR SP BASE RELATION
   { SNO SNO , PNO PNO , QTY INTEGER }
     KEY { SNO , PNO }
     WHEN QTY > 200 THEN FOREIGN KEY { SNO } REFERENCES
                                 ( S WHERE CITY = 'London' ) ;
```

Of course, we'd still need to say that every supplier number in relvar SP also appears in relvar S, even if the quantity is 200 or less. A conventional *<foreign key def>* of the form

```
FOREIGN KEY { SNO } REFERENCES S
```

would suffice. But we might want to be a little more sophisticated:

```
VAR SP BASE RELATION
   { SNO SNO , PNO PNO , QTY INTEGER }
     KEY { SNO , PNO }
     WHEN QTY > 200 THEN FOREIGN KEY { SNO } REFERENCES
                             ( S WHERE CITY = 'London' )
     WHEN QTY ≤ 200 THEN FOREIGN KEY { SNO } REFERENCES S ;
```

Or even:

```
VAR SP BASE RELATION
   { SNO SNO , PNO PNO , QTY INTEGER }
     KEY { SNO , PNO }
     CASE
        WHEN QTY > 200 THEN FOREIGN KEY { SNO } REFERENCES
                                ( S WHERE CITY = 'London' )
        WHEN QTY ≤ 200 THEN FOREIGN KEY { SNO } REFERENCES S
     END CASE ;
```

Here's the same example formulated in terms of explicit views:

```
VAR SPV VIRTUAL ( SP WHERE QTY > 200 ) KEY { SNO , PNO }
    FOREIGN KEY { SNO }
           REFERENCES ( S WHERE CITY = 'London' ) ;

VAR SPW VIRTUAL ( SP WHERE QTY ≤ 200 ) KEY { SNO , PNO }
    FOREIGN KEY { SNO } REFERENCES S ;
```

In other words, it should certainly be possible to specify a view as the source, as well as the target, for a *<foreign key def>*; indeed, *The Principle of Interchangeability* (see Chapter 1) effectively demands as much. However, I don't think I want to offer the foregoing syntax, using WHEN, as a serious proposal (except possibly as a basis for a well defined shorthand), because it isn't sufficiently general. Consider the following business rule:

> *If supplier sno and part pno are in the same city, then supplier sno must supply part pno.*

(Like Example 7, this one was previously discussed, briefly, in Chapter 1. It's the inverse of that previous one, in a sense.) Formally:

```
( S JOIN P ) { SNO , PNO } ⊆ SP { SNO , PNO }
```

Now, we might consider representing this IND by means of a *<foreign key def>* for which an appropriate view serves as the source, like this:

```
VAR SPZ VIRTUAL ( S JOIN P ) KEY { SNO , PNO }
    FOREIGN KEY { SNO , PNO } REFERENCES SP ;
```

But we surely don't want to have to go through all of the effort and overhead of defining a view if the sole purpose of that view is just to serve as the source for some *<foreign key def>*. Instead, why not allow *<foreign key def>*s to be attached directly, within a constraint definition, to an arbitrary *<relation exp>*?[21] Then we could formulate the example at hand like this:

```
CONSTRAINT ...
    ( S JOIN P ) FOREIGN KEY { SNO , PNO } REFERENCES SP ;
```

Now, this particular example is slightly longer than its IND analog—which, to remind you, looks like this:

```
CONSTRAINT ...
    ( S JOIN P ) { SNO , PNO } ⊆ SP { SNO , PNO } ;
```

But (as I pointed out once before in this chapter) this latter kind of formulation requires the pertinent attribute names to be written out twice, which the FOREIGN KEY analog doesn't. Thus, the FOREIGN KEY equivalent might truly be a shorthand in more complicated cases. I conclude that (a) not only can

---

[21] After all, I've already said in Chapter 1 that we should be able to do the same for key definitions (as opposed to foreign key definitions, I mean). Here's the example I used in that chapter: CONSTRAINT ... (S JOIN SP) KEY {PNO,CITY}. (Meaning: *If two suppliers are distinct but supply the same part, then they must be in different cities.*) PS: Of course, another key constraint, KEY {SNO,PNO}, also applies to S JOIN SP—but that one's a logical consequence of the fact that {SNO} is a key for S and {PNO} is a key for P.

*<foreign key def>*s be a useful shorthand in connection with explicit relvar definitions (as of course everyone knows), but (b) they can also be useful, sometimes, in connection with arbitrary *<relation exp>*s.

EXAMPLE 9: MORE THAN ONE TARGET?

In 1981 I wrote a paper[22] in which I proposed an extension to the original foreign key concept. According to that proposal, a *<foreign key def>* would look like this (the principal difference is in the REFERENCES specification):

```
<foreign key def>
    ::=   FOREIGN KEY { [ ALL BUT ] <attribute ref commalist>
            REFERENCES
              [ <quantifier> ] { <relation exp commalist> }
```

The *<quantifier>* is EXACTLY ONE OF, AT LEAST ONE OF, or ALL OF, and I assume for present purposes that each of these possibilities has the intuitively obvious semantics. *Note:* The *<quantifier>* can be omitted entirely, along with the braces enclosing the *<relation exp commalist>*, if and only if that commalist contains exactly one *<relation exp>*.

So much for syntax. In a later paper,[23] however, I backed away from the foregoing proposals; in fact, I rejected them entirely (they turned out to be nothing but a blind alley). To be frank, I wish I'd thought about them a bit more carefully before committing them to paper in the first place! Fortunately, they had essentially no impact on anything important, so not too much harm was done by that original lack of forethought on my part. Nevertheless, I think it's worth taking a brief look at them here, if only because they might serve as an object lesson of some kind.

EXACTLY ONE OF

On the face of it, EXACTLY ONE OF might seem to be the most useful of the

---

[22] "Referential Integrity," Proc. 7th International Conference on Very Large Data Bases, Cannes, France (September 1981); republished in revised form in my book *Relational Database: Selected Writings* (Addison-Wesley, 1986). I'll refer to this paper in the rest of this chapter as *the 1981 paper*. PS: In the interest of accuracy, let me add that the 1981 paper didn't allow arbitrary *<relation exp>*s, but only *<base relvar name>*s, following that optional *<quantifier>*.

[23] "Referential Integrity and Foreign Keys Part I: Basic Concepts; Part II: Further Considerations," in my book *Relational Database Writings 1985-1989* (Addison-Wesley, 1990). See Chapter 4.

three cases. For example, suppose the database contains a relvar representing an audit trail for a certain bank, and suppose that relvar contains a tuple for every commercial transaction carried out by that bank over a certain period of time. Suppose further that each such transaction is exactly one of the following: a deposit, a withdrawal, or a request for balance information. Then we could certainly imagine a situation in which each tuple in the audit trail relvar has to reference exactly one of the following: a tuple in the deposits relvar, a tuple in the withdrawals relvar, or a tuple in the balance requests relvar.

For a more concrete example, I turn to suppliers and parts once again. Suppose the original suppliers relvar S is replaced by a set of relvars, one for each supplier city, thus:

```
VAR AS BASE RELATION        /* Athens suppliers */
   { SNO SNO , SNAME NAME , STATUS INTEGER }
     KEY { SNO } ;

VAR LS BASE RELATION        /* London suppliers */
   { SNO SNO , SNAME NAME , STATUS INTEGER }
     KEY { SNO } ;

VAR PS BASE RELATION        /* Paris suppliers */
   { SNO SNO , SNAME NAME , STATUS INTEGER }
     KEY { SNO } ;
```

(I assume for the sake of discussion that there are just three possible supplier cities. Note that attribute CITY can now be dropped from each of the three relvars, and indeed has been.)

In the shipments relvar SP, then, we could have a *<foreign key def>* involving EXACTLY ONE OF:

```
VAR SP BASE RELATION
   { SNO SNO , PNO PNO , QTY INTEGER }
     KEY { SNO , PNO }
     FOREIGN KEY { SNO }
             REFERENCES EXACTLY ONE OF { AS , LS , PS } ;
```

However, let me now point out that this EXACTLY ONE OF syntax is logically redundant. To see why, note first that (in terms of the example under discussion) we'll need a constraint to ensure that no supplier number appears at any given time in more than one of AS, LS, and PS:

```
CONSTRAINT SNO_GLOBALLY_UNIQUE IS_EMPTY
    ( UNION { AS { SNO } INTERSECT LS { SNO } ,
              LS { SNO } INTERSECT PS { SNO } ,
              PS { SNO } INTERSECT AS { SNO } } ) ;
```

Explanation: The union of these three intersections will be empty if and only if those intersections are all empty. And those intersections will be empty if and only if no supplier number is common to any two of AS, LS, and PS—in which case no supplier number will be common to all three, a fortiori.[24]

Clearly, then, if constraint SNO_GLOBALLY_UNIQUE is enforced, as it should be, then the *<foreign key def>* can be stated more simply as:

```
FOREIGN KEY { SNO } REFERENCES UNION { AS , LS , PS }
```

Or if we're not confident that the system will be able to recognize that {SNO} is a key for that union:

```
CONSTRAINT ...
    SP { SNO_} ⊆ ( UNION { AS , LS , PS } ) { SNO } ;
```

So EXACTLY ONE OF isn't logically necessary. Perhaps more to the point, though, I also think it's not very useful; it seems to me now that an apparent need for that quantifier is really an indication that the database isn't very well designed. Let me elaborate.

Observe first, with respect to the example discussed above, that London, Paris, and Athens suppliers can all be regarded as *subtypes* of the more general type, or *supertype*, "suppliers"—where the supertype has various common properties that apply to suppliers in general, while each subtype has certain special properties of its own that don't apply to the other subtypes (though no such special properties were shown in the example). Surely, therefore, there should be a single "master" or supertype relvar S, containing the common properties, and then relvars LS, PS, and AS should contain just the special properties that apply to London, Paris, and Athens suppliers, respectively. And the foreign key {SNO} in the shipments relvar SP would then reference that supertype relvar:

---

[24] I note in passing that support for an operator of the form DISJOINT {*<relation exp commalist>*}, defined to return TRUE if and only if no two of its argument relations have a tuple in common, might be a useful thing to have in practice. I proposed such an operator in my book *View Updating and Relational Theory* (O'Reilly, 2013).

```
FOREIGN KEY ( SNO ) REFERENCES S
```

(Of course, an exactly similar foreign key constraint would also apply to each of the relvars LS, PS, and AS.)

Overall, this seems to me to be a much cleaner design. Note in particular what would happen to the {SNO} foreign key constraint in relvar SP with this design, vs. what would have happened with the previous version, if new supplier cities—Rome, Oslo, Madrid, etc.—became legal.

> *Aside:* The mention of supertypes and subtypes in the foregoing discussion isn't exactly wrong, but it might be a little unfortunate—even misleading, in a way. The fact is, relvars in the relational model don't *represent* types; rather, they *have* types. (After all, relvars are variables, and variables aren't types. Note the logical difference here!)
>
> Similar remarks apply to relations also, of course. That is, relations too have types, but don't represent types. (Relations are values, and values aren't types.)
>
> By the way, SQL in particular does support a feature it calls "supertables and subtables," and that feature *might* be useful in connection with examples like the one discussed above. (I'm skeptical, though, because supertables and subtables in SQL behave in ways that are ... well, a little strange, to say the least.) But even so—even if they turn out to be useful for problems like the one at hand, I mean—the one thing supertables and subtables aren't is an example of type inheritance as such, because (to say it again, albeit now using SQL terms) tables aren't types.
>
> For a detailed look at these issues and numerous related matters, please see my book *Type Inheritance and Relational Theory* (O'Reilly, 2016). *End of aside.*

AT LEAST ONE OF

It's hard to come up with an intuitively reasonable example of the *<quantifier>* AT LEAST ONE OF—but in any case there's no need to, because (like EXACTLY ONE OF) it's clearly logically redundant. To be specific, the *<foreign key def>*

```
FOREIGN KEY FK
           REFERENCES AT LEAST ONE OF { R₁ , R₂ , ... , Rₙ }
```

is clearly equivalent to this one:

```
FOREIGN KEY FK REFERENCES UNION { R₁ , R₂ , ... , Rₙ }
```

(At least, it is so long as R_1, R_2, ..., R_n are all of the same type; otherwise some projections and/or renamings will be required, as in Examples 4 and 5). So I don't offer AT LEAST ONE OF as a serious proposal at this time, either.

ALL OF

Finally, consider the *<foreign key def>*

```
FOREIGN KEY FK REFERENCES ALL OF { R₁ , R₂ , ... , Rₙ }
```

I note in passing that such a *<foreign key def>* might conceivably appear as part of the definition of relvar SP if, as in Example 3, suppliers are represented by the three 6NF relvars SN, ST, and SC (assuming for the moment that the master relvar S is *not* included). Be that as it may, every pair of relvars in R_1, R_2, ..., R_n clearly has to satisfy a certain equality dependency (EQD), and we need a constraint to ensure that this is so:[25]

```
CONSTRAINT ...
    UNION     { R₁ { fk } , R₂ { fk } , ... , Rₙ { fk } } =
    INTERSECT { R₁ { fk } , R₂ { fk } , ... , Rₙ { fk } } ;
```

Explanation: The symbol *fk* here denotes a commalist of all of the attributes in *FK*. The union and the intersection of a collection of sets will be equal if and only if all of the sets in the collection are in fact the same set.

Assuming this constraint is enforced, then, the *<foreign key def>* can be stated more simply as just

```
FOREIGN KEY FK REFERENCES Rᵢ
```

---

[25] Again a shorthand might be useful—perhaps an operator of the form IDENTICAL {*<relation exp commalist>*}, defined to return TRUE if and only if its argument relations are all equal. Again, I proposed such an operator in my book *View Updating and Relational Theory* (O'Reilly, 2013).

for some arbitrary i $(1 \le i \le n)$.[26] So ALL OF too is logically redundant. But more to the point, though, I also don't think it's useful; it seems to me now that an apparent need for that quantifier is (like that for EXACTLY ONE OF) really an indication that the database isn't very well designed. Let me elaborate.

Again recall Example 3, where suppliers were represented by the three 6NF relvars SN, ST, and SC (and again assume for the moment that the master relvar S is *not* included). In that example, the following EQDs held:

```
CONSTRAINT ... SN { SNO } = ST { SNO } ;
CONSTRAINT ... ST { SNO } = SC { SNO } ;
CONSTRAINT ... SC { SNO } = SN { SNO } ;
```

Or equivalently:

```
CONSTRAINT ...
    UNION     { SN { SNO } , ST { SNO } , SC { SNO } } =
    INTERSECT { SN { SNO } , ST { SNO } , SC { SNO } } ;
```

Without going into details, surely it would again be better to introduce a "master" suppliers relvar S (even if that relvar contains nothing but supplier numbers). Then, as in the case of EXACTLY ONE OF above, the foreign key SNO in the shipments relvar SP would reference that master relvar—

```
FOREIGN KEY ( SNO ) REFERENCES S
```

—and ALL OF would then no longer be necessary. As for those EQDs, they would need to be revised thus:

```
CONSTRAINT ... SN { SNO } = S { SNO } ;
CONSTRAINT ... ST { SNO } = S { SNO } ;
CONSTRAINT ... SC { SNO } = S { SNO } ;
```

I remind you also that it's an advantage of this design that it can handle suppliers for whom at least one of the three properties name, status, and city is missing. If we assume for the sake of the example that name and city can be missing but status can't be, then the first and last of the EQDs just shown can be replaced by the following *<foreign key def>* on relvars SN and SC:

---

[26] Though I admit that the arbitrariness of the choice as to which of R_1, R_2, ..., R_n is to play the role of the target is a little bothersome. But I don't think it matters, given what follows.

```
FOREIGN KEY ( SNO ) REFERENCES S
```

The net of the discussions in these three subsections is this: I don't believe it's necessary at this time to extend the syntax of *<foreign key def>*s to allow for two or more targets, or to support any of the *<quantifier>*s, just so long as other recommendations in this chapter are implemented—in particular, the recommendation that it should be possible to specify the target by means of an arbitrarily complex *<relation exp>*.

EXAMPLE 10: COMPENSATORY ACTIONS

For the final example in this series I return once again to the original suppliers and parts database, and in particular to the *<foreign key def>* relating shipments to suppliers:

```
FOREIGN KEY { SNO } REFERENCES S
```

Here's a complete list of updates that could cause this constraint to be violated (the wording is pretty loose, of course, but it's good enough for present purposes):

- Inserting an SP tuple, if the SNO value doesn't currently appear in relvar

- Changing the SNO value in an SP tuple, if the new SNO value doesn't currently appear in relvar S

- Deleting an S tuple, if the SNO value currently appears in relvar SP

- Changing the SNO value in an S tuple, if the old SNO value currently appears in relvar SP

- Any relational assignment that's logically equivalent to one of the foregoing cases

Now, in this chapter so far I've assumed, tacitly, that any update that would otherwise cause some constraint to be violated will simply be rejected. For example, consider the following DELETE:

```
DELETE S WHERE SNO = SNO('S1') ;
```

If (a) this DELETE means *exactly* what it says—i.e., if it means "delete the tuple for supplier S1 from relvar S," no more and no less—and if (b) relvar SP currently contains at least one tuple for supplier S1, then (c) under the foregoing assumption, the DELETE will simply fail. But sometimes we can do better than that, and that's what foreign key rules are all about. The basic idea is that sometimes it might be possible for the system to perform an appropriate "compensatory action" that will guarantee that the overall result does still satisfy the foreign key constraint after all. In the example, the obvious compensatory action is for the system to "cascade" the DELETE to delete the SP tuples for supplier S1 as well. We can make sure this happens by extending the pertinent *<foreign key def>* as follows:

```
FOREIGN KEY { SNO } REFERENCES S
             ON DELETE CASCADE
```

The specification ON DELETE CASCADE defines a "delete rule" for this particular foreign key, and the specification CASCADE is the corresponding compensatory action.

Foreign key rules were first proposed by myself in the 1981 paper (see footnote 22). The discussion that follows is based on ideas from that paper, but it differs considerably at the detail level.[27] I'll begin with some definitions (the first of which is repeated from Chapter 1):

Definition (foreign key rule): A rule specifying the action to be taken by the system—the referential action—to ensure that updates affecting the foreign key in question don't violate the associated foreign key constraint.

Definition (delete rule): A foreign key rule that specifies the action to be taken by the system if some tuple t_2 exists that contains a foreign key value referencing some tuple t_1 and—speaking rather loosely—tuple t_1 is deleted.

---

[27] Mainly because I no longer believe in nulls, and therefore now reject the various nulls-related options proposed in the original paper.

Definition (update rule):[28]   A foreign key rule that specifies the action to be taken by the system if some tuple t_2 exists that contains a foreign key value referencing some tuple t_1 and—speaking very loosely—the corresponding target key in tuple t_1 is updated.

Definition (referential action):   The action specification portion of a foreign key rule (e.g., CASCADE); also used to mean the corresponding action itself.

Definition (compensatory action):   An action performed automatically by the system in addition to some requested update, with the aim of avoiding some integrity violation that might otherwise occur. Cascading a delete operation is a typical example.

Several points arise from the foregoing definitions. First of all, note that compensatory actions in general aren't actually prescribed by the relational model—but neither are they proscribed. In other words, while the relational model is certainly the foundation of the database field, it's *only* the foundation, and there's no reason why additional features shouldn't be built on top of that foundation—just so long as those additions don't violate the prescriptions of the model, of course (and are in the spirit of the model and can be shown to be useful, I suppose I should add).

Second, observe that I distinguish between compensatory and referential actions. A referential action is what the system has to do when an update is attempted that might violate some referential constraint. A compensatory action is what the system has to do when an update is attempted that might violate some constraint (not necessarily a referential constraint). Thus, all referential actions are compensatory actions but some compensatory actions aren't referential actions, and it's useful to have different terms for the two concepts.

Third, such actions should of course be specified declaratively, and users should be aware of them. That is, users certainly need to understand when their update requests are shorthand for some more extensive set of actions—for otherwise they might perceive an apparent violation of *The Assignment Principle* (see later).

---

[28] It's an unfortunate but well known fact that the term *update* is used in database contexts with two different meanings: Sometimes it's used to mean the INSERT, DELETE, and UPDATE (and assignment) operators considered collectively; sometimes it's used to mean just the UPDATE operator specifically. Well, I'll simply have to hope that my intended meaning is always clear from context. If you find this state of affairs confusing, then I sympathize, but please don't blame me.

Fourth, note that I propose a foreign key delete rule and a foreign key update rule but no foreign key insert rule. The rationale here, with reference to suppliers and shipments by way of illustration, is that shipments are in a sense subordinate to suppliers. (Certainly they're "existence dependent" on them—a given shipment can't exist if the corresponding supplier doesn't exist.) And an insert rule, if such a thing could be defined, would presumably mean that insertion of a shipment could cause some kind of compensatory action to be performed on suppliers—an intuitively unreasonable "tail wags the dog" kind of situation, it seems to me.

For analogous reasons, there's no update rule that applies to updates to the foreign key in relvar SP.

Last, the only referential actions that I believe—at the time of writing, at any rate— make sense are CASCADE and NO ACTION (which I referred to as CASCADES and RESTRICTED, respectively, in the 1981 paper):

- CASCADE: I've already explained this one, informally, in the context of a delete rule. In the context of an update rule, its effect is as follows (I'll explain it in terms of suppliers and shipments, again just by way of illustration): If the SNO value in an S tuple is changed, then that same change is cascaded to all corresponding SP tuples.

- NO ACTION: This one is the default, and it means what it says: Don't do any compensatory action. Thus, in terms of suppliers and shipments once again, ON DELETE NO ACTION means that an attempt to delete an S tuple will fail if there are any corresponding SP tuples; ON UPDATE NO ACTION means that an attempt to change the SNO value in an S tuple will fail if there are any corresponding SP tuples.

Aside: SQL actually supports five referential actions: SET NULL, SET DEFAULT, CASCADE, RESTRICT, and NO ACTION. I reject SET NULL for obvious reasons. I also reject SET DEFAULT, at least for now, because any such support would clearly have to be part of some kind of comprehensive scheme for default values and **Tutorial D** includes no such scheme at this time. CASCADE is OK. As for RESTRICT and NO ACTION, I believe they'd be equivalent if updates were treated as they should be—i.e., as proper set level operators, not row or tuple level operators. (This latter issue, set vs. tuple level operators, is discussed further in the section "Implementation Issues," later.) *End of aside.*

So I'm extending the syntax of *<foreign key def>*s once again:

```
<foreign key def>
    ::=   FOREIGN KEY { [ ALL BUT ] <attribute ref commalist>
                  REFERENCES <relation exp>
          [ ON DELETE [ NO ] CASCADE ]
          [ ON UPDATE [ NO ] CASCADE ]
```

Now, I said above that users need to be aware of compensatory actions, because otherwise they might perceive an apparent violation of *The Assignment Principle*. Here just to remind you is a definition of that principle:

> **Definition (*Assignment Principle*):** After assignment of value *v* to variable *V*, the comparison *v* = *V* is required to evaluate to TRUE.

Let me spell the point out in detail, because it's important. The easiest way to appreciate that point is to think of the entire database as just one big variable (which in fact it is, as we saw in Chapter 1). So consider the following scenario:

- There's a foreign key constraint relating S and SP, with an associated cascade delete rule.

- But suppose you're not aware of that constraint, and hence not aware of that delete rule.

- Suppose too, for simplicity, that the database currently contains just three tuples—one for S1 in relvar S, one for P1 in relvar P, and one for S1 and P1 in relvar SP.

- You delete the tuple for S1 from S, thus:

  ```
  DELETE S WHERE SNO = SNO('S1') ;
  ```

- Then what you thought was an operation to remove just one tuple from the database will in fact remove two. To you, that looks like an *Assignment Principle* violation.

In other words, if ON DELETE CASCADE is specified in connection with the foreign key from relvar SP to relvar S, then the user must be aware that the statement

```
DELETE S WHERE SNO = SNO('S1') ;
```

—which is usually understood to be just shorthand for the *single* assignment

```
S := S MINUS ( S WHERE SNO = SNO('S1') ) ;
```

—is in fact shorthand for the following *double* assignment:

```
S  := S  MINUS ( S  WHERE SNO = SNO('S1') ) ,
SP := SP MINUS ( SP WHERE SNO = SNO('S1') ) ;
```

Or if you prefer:

```
DELETE S  WHERE SNO = SNO('S1') ,
DELETE SP WHERE SNO = SNO('S1') ;
```

Note: For an extended discussion of this idea—the idea, that is, that compensatory actions need to be exposed to the user—please see my book *View Updating and Relational Theory* (O'Reilly, 2013).

———— ♦ ♦ ♦ ♦ ♦ ————

There are a few further points I need to make in connection with compensatory actions in general. First, as the foregoing example indicates, if some update does cause some compensatory action to be performed, then the original update and the compensatory action together must be treated as semantically atomic (all or nothing); in other words, they must definitely be treated as part of the same overall multiple assignment, which means among other things that no database constraint checking must be done until all of the individual assignments have been done.

Second, there's a lot more to multiple assignment in general than I want or need to discuss here, which is why I omit a formal definition. For an exhaustive discussion of the topic, please see my book *Database Dreaming Volume II* (Technics, 2022).

Next, I haven't lost sight of the fact that *<foreign key def>*s, and therefore compensatory actions, can be specified for views as well as base relvars. Thus, compensatory actions in general imply the need to support at least some kinds of view updating. Again I refer you to my book *View Updating and Relational*

Theory (O'Reilly, 2013) for further discussion.

Next, I observe that if foreign key constraints aren't specified by means of special case syntax—i.e., by *<foreign key def>*s, to use the terminology of the present chapter—but instead by means of expressions in some general purpose constraint language, then that language would presumably need to support the declarative specification of foreign key rules also. Further research is probably needed in connection with this point.

Finally, the question arises: If some specific update would require some compensatory action to be performed if it were expressed as an explicit DELETE or UPDATE, what should happen if that update is expressed by some means of some general relational assignment instead? Further research is probably needed in connection with this point also.

IMPLEMENTATION ISSUES

Although this book is deliberately not much concerned with matters of implementation, I do want to make a few remarks here in connection with the implementation of delete rules in particular. The first concerns certain implementation restrictions to be found in certain SQL products today. For example, IBM's DB2 product used to have—as far as I know, it still does have—a limitation in connection with self-referencing relvars to the effect that the delete rule must be CASCADE. Part of the justification for this state of affairs is as follows. Consider the following self-referencing relvar (repeated from Example 5):

```
VAR EMP BASE RELATION
    { ENO ENO , ... , MNO ENO , ... }
      KEY { ENO }
      FOREIGN KEY { MNO }
          REFERENCES EMP { ENO } RENAME { ENO AS MNO } ;
```

Here's the referential diagram:

And here's a sample value:

```
EMP   ┌──────┬──────┬──────┐
      │ ENO  │ MNO  │ ...  │
      ╞══════╪══════╪══════╡
      │  E1  │  E1  │ ...  │  (tuple 1)
      │  E2  │  E1  │ ...  │  (tuple 2)
      └──────┴──────┴──────┘
```

Observe now that (by default) the delete rule for the foreign key in this example is NO ACTION—meaning, loosely, that it's OK to delete a tuple only if no other tuple refers to it. So consider the following DELETE statement:

```
DELETE EMP ;
```

This DELETE is, of course, shorthand for the following:

```
DELETE EMP WHERE TRUE ;
```

In other words, the user is trying to delete all the tuples from EMP.

Suppose now that the system, in response to this DELETE, tries to delete tuple 2 first and then tuple 1, checking the foreign key constraint for each of those tuples as it does so. Then the update overall will succeed. But if it tries to delete tuple 1 first, then it'll see that tuple 2 refers to it, and so the update overall will fail. So the argument—the argument used by the DB2 designers, that is, or at least so I presume—goes like this:

> In order to guarantee a predictable result no matter which tuple is deleted first, the delete rule *must* specify CASCADE.

However, I regard this argument as logically flawed. The flaw consists in checking, or attempting to check, the foreign key constraint one tuple at a time. Operations in the relational model are set at a time, not tuple at a time—which means, in the case of update operations in particular, that they update entire relvars en bloc, not piecemeal. And one consequence of this fact is that (a) compensatory actions mustn't be done until all of the requested updating has been done, and (b) database constraint checking mustn't be done until all of the compensatory actions have been done. To say it again, a set level update mustn't be treated as a sequence of individual tuple level updates. Thus, the conceptual algorithm for implementing the general DELETE statement

```
DELETE EMP WHERE bx ;
```

(with a NO ACTION delete rule) has to look something like this:

```
unmark all tuples in EMP ;
do for each tuple t in EMP in some sequence ;
    if t satisfies bx
        then mark t for deletion ;
end do ;
do for each unmarked tuple t in EMP in some sequence ;
    if MNO FROM t = ENO FROM some marked tuple in EMP
        then quit /* DELETE fails */ ;
end do ;
do for each marked tuple t in EMP in some sequence ;
    remove t from EMP ;
end do /* DELETE succeeds */ ;
```

Observe that this algorithm amounts, in effect, to a tuple at a time implementation of a set level operation. Of course, it can and should be improved in numerous ways in practice, but such considerations are beyond the scope of the present discussion.

The other implementation issue I want to discuss briefly is as follows.[29] It's well known—or frequently claimed, at any rate—that certain combinations of

a. Referential structures (by which I mean sets of relvars that are interrelated via foreign key constraints),

b. Specific foreign key rules, and

c. Specific data values in the database,

can together lead to conflicts. Consider, for example, the following referential structure:

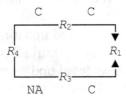

---

[29] Actually I think it's the same issue, though you might disagree.

As you can see, relvar R_4 here references both relvars R_2 and R_3, each of which in turn references relvar R_1, and so there are two referential paths from R_4 to R_1. I'll refer to the one via R_2 as the upper path and the one via R_3 as the lower path.

Now let's think about the delete rules. Suppose those rules are as indicated in the diagram (C = CASCADE, NA = NO ACTION). Assume for simplicity that each relvar has just one attribute, A, and further that $\{A\}$ is both the sole key for each of the four relvars and also the necessary foreign key in R_4, R_3, and R_2 (actually both foreign keys, in the case of R_4); assume also that each relvar contains just one tuple, containing the same value a in every case. Finally, suppose we try to delete the single tuple from relvar R_1. What happens?

- If the system applies the delete rules in the upper path first, the single tuple in R_2 and the single tuple in R_4 will both be deleted, because the rules on that path are both CASCADE. When the system then applies the delete rules in the lower path, an attempt will be made to delete the single tuple from R_3; this attempt will succeed, because there's now no matching tuple in R_4 that (thanks to the NO ACTION rule) will cause that attempt to fail. The net effect is that all four tuples will be deleted.

- If on the other hand the system applies the delete rules in the lower path first, the net effect is that the database will remain unchanged. For the tuple in R_4 will cause the attempt to delete the tuple from R_3 to fail (thanks to the NO ACTION delete rule), and hence the overall operation will fail also.

In other words, the result is unpredictable—and if so, then it's to be hoped that the implementation will detect and reject the conflicting definitions in the first place, so that such unpredictability can't occur.

Aside: I've said the result in this example is unpredictable—but is that really true? Wasn't I, in effect, appealing to tuple at a time thinking once again? It seems to me rather that the system should implement that DELETE on R_1 by going through essentially the same conceptual algorithm as before, like this:

- First, it should unmark all tuples.

- Next, it should mark tuples that the user has asked to be deleted.

(Note that the procedure for this step will be invoked recursively, because of the CASCADE rules.) Following the upper path causes the tuples in R_1, R_2, and R_4 to be marked; following the lower path causes the tuples in R_1 (again) and R_3 to be marked. No matter which path is followed first, therefore, the net effect is that all four tuples are marked.

■ Next, it should check to see that no unmarked tuple includes a reference to any marked tuple. In the example, this check succeeds.

■ Finally, it should actually delete all marked tuples. In the example, this step has the effect of deleting the tuples from all four of R_1, R_2, R_3, and R_4.

However, despite the foregoing argument, I'll continue to assume for the sake of the rest of this section that unpredictable results are indeed a possibility, in general. *End of aside.*

Now, some critics have used examples like the one above as a basis for arguing that the notion of foreign key rules as such (or compensatory actions, at any rate) is problematic, possibly logically flawed. Myself, I don't find such arguments totally convincing. The rules and compensatory actions specified in any given situation are surely supposed to reflect policies in operation in whatever the enterprise is that the database is meant to serve. Thus, it seems to me that if some combination of definitions leads to unpredictability, then those definitions must be logically incorrect—i.e., they can't properly reflect the situation existing in the real world. (Unless the "real world" is logically incorrect too, I suppose I should add; but then I would argue that having the policies stated declaratively instead of procedurally can only improve the chances of the enterprise detecting the error and coming up with a remedy.)

Let's take a closer look at these matters. It's clear in the foregoing example that if the four delete rules had all been the same—either all CASCADE or all NO ACTION—then the question of unpredictability wouldn't have arisen. So you might be thinking that situations involving a mixture of CASCADE and NO ACTION rules shouldn't be allowed. But sometimes such a mixture might be exactly what's wanted. Let's look at another example:

```
VAR P BASE RELATION { PNO PNO , ... } KEY { PNO } ;

VAR PP BASE RELATION { MAJOR_PNO PNO , MINOR_PNO PNO , ... }
    KEY { MAJOR_PNO , MINOR_PNO }
    FOREIGN KEY { MAJOR_PNO }
         REFERENCES P RENAME { PNO AS MAJOR_PNO }
         ON DELETE CASCADE
    FOREIGN KEY { MINOR_PNO }
         REFERENCES P RENAME { PNO AS MINOR_PNO }
         ON DELETE NO ACTION ;
```

This is the well known "bill of materials" example—relvar P contains a master list of parts, and relvar PP shows which parts (MAJOR_PNO) contain which other parts (MINOR_PNO) as components. Each part can contain any number of components and each part can be a component of any number of parts, so there's a many to many relationship between parts and parts; hence the need for a separate relvar (PP) to represent that relationship. So the referential structure looks like this:

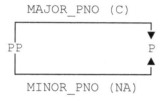

There are two (very short!) referential paths from PP to P, and I've labeled them with the pertinent attribute names to make it clear which is which. Using the same shorthand as before, I've also shown the delete rules for those two paths (C = CASCADE, NA = NO ACTION). As you can see, therefore, again we have a situation involving a mixture of CASCADE and NO ACTION rules, and so there seems to be just as much potential for conflict as there was in the previous example. But here that mixture seems a little more reasonable; I mean, it seems reasonable on the face of it to say that deleting a part:

a. Cascades to those PP tuples where the pertinent part number appears as a MAJOR_PNO value (meaning: "delete linkages from the part in question to component parts"), but

b. Doesn't cascade to those tuples where the same part number appears as a MINOR_PNO value (meaning: "don't delete linkages to the part in question from parts of which it's a component").

But wait a minute ... Point b. here implies that if, say, part P1 contains part P2 as a component, and if we delete the tuple from P for P2, then PP will now contain a tuple (for P1 and P2) that references a part that no longer exists! So maybe that CASCADE / NO ACTION mixture makes no sense after all.

What do you think?

CONCLUDING REMARKS

Note: As indicated earlier, this chapter, or the bulk of it at any rate, is heavily based on an earlier paper by myself, published as Chapter 13 ("Inclusion Dependencies and Foreign Keys") in the book Database Explorations: Essays on The Third Manifesto and Related Topics, by Hugh Darwen and myself (Trafford, 2010). The present section is repeated more or less verbatim from that earlier paper. The remarks concerning SQL are new, though.

This chapter grew in the writing. My original motivation for embarking on it was a nagging concern over the attribute renaming issue (see Examples 4 and 5); I'd been worrying about that issue off and on for quite a long time, and I wanted to get it pinned down once and for all. However, the more I thought about the subject in general, the more I found I wanted to say. And now I have a somewhat embarrassing confession to make ... As I concocted the various examples and as I worked through the various supporting arguments, I began to get an extreme sense of *déjà vu.* Eventually I recalled that some years earlier Hugh Darwen had proposed an article on the same general subject for inclusion in one of our joint "Writings" books; however, I'd rejected his article at the time because I disagreed—again, at that time—with many of the things he had to say. So I searched through my archives and found Hugh's original draft—and discovered to my chagrin that Hugh had raised many of the same issues (though not all), and come to many of the same conclusions (though again not all), as I have in the present chapter. So I guess I owe Hugh an apology, and I hope he'll accept it in good part.

Let me close by summarizing the things I've proposed in this chapter:

- A relational language should allow *<foreign key def>*s of the following form to be specified as part of the definition of a relvar, be it base or virtual:

```
<foreign key def>
    ::=   FOREIGN KEY
          { [ ALL BUT ] <attribute ref commalist>
              REFERENCES <relation exp>
            [ ON DELETE [ NO ] CASCADE ]
            [ ON UPDATE [ NO ] CASCADE ]
```

The specified *<relation exp>* must satisfy the following condition: If it were to be used as the defining expression for some view *V*, then the specified *<attribute ref commalist>* would constitute a key (or at least a superkey) for *V*.

Aside re SQL: SQL (a) doesn't allow a *<foreign key def>* to be part of a view definition; (b) doesn't allow the target *<relation exp>* to be anything but a base relvar name; and (c) doesn't support the ALL BUT option. *End of aside.*

■ A relational language should also allow the source for a *<foreign key def>* to be specified, within a separate constraint definition, by means of an arbitrary *<relation exp>*—though what should be done about any associated foreign key rules in such a case needs more thought.

Aside re SQL: SQL (a) doesn't allow a *<foreign key def>* to be specified within a separate constraint definition, and therefore (b) doesn't allow the source for such a *<foreign key def>* to be specified by means of an arbitrary *<relation exp>* a fortiori. *End of aside.*

■ A relational language should support the relational equality operator, "=". *Note:* Actually *The Third Manifesto* requires the equality operator to be supported for every type.

Aside re SQL: SQL (a) doesn't support the "=" operator for every type; (b) doesn't really support it at all for table types;[30] and (c) even in those cases where it does support it, doesn't do so properly. *End of aside.*

---

[30] Actually, the notion that a table might even have a type in the first place is treated very strangely in SQL anyway. See my book *Type Inheritance and Relational Theory* (O'Reilly, 2016) for a detailed discussion of this issue.

- A relational language should support the relational inclusion operator, "⊆".

  Aside re SQL: SQL doesn't support the foregoing. *End of aside.*

- I do *not* propose support for the *<quantifier>*s EXACTLY ONE OF, AT LEAST ONE OF, and ALL OF.

  Aside re SQL: SQL agrees with me here. *End of aside.*

———— ◆ ◆ ◆ ◆ ◆ ————

One last point. Recall the following constraint from the section "Inclusion Dependencies" earlier in this chapter:

```
CONSTRAINT INDX P { CITY } ⊆ S { CITY } ;
```

It's an inclusion dependency, of course—an IND—and what that IND says is this: *No part can be stored in a city unless there's at least one supplier in that city.*

Now, {CITY} isn't a key for relvar S, and so this IND clearly isn't a foreign key constraint as conventionally understood. But it can be expressed as one! Since we're now allowing the target of a *<foreign key def>* to be specified as an arbitrary *<relation exp>*, we can certainly add the following to the definition of relvar P:

```
FOREIGN KEY { CITY } REFERENCES S { CITY }
```

And since {CITY} is certainly a superkey—actually it's a key as such—for the projection of S on {CITY}, this specification indeed represents a legitimate foreign key constraint.

What's more, of course, analogous remarks apply to INDs of arbitrary complexity. Thus, the proposals of this chapter allow not just conventional foreign key constraints, but INDs of arbitrary complexity, to be expressed by means of special case syntax: specifically, FOREIGN KEY syntax.

Chapter 3

A Little History

History is not what you thought.
It is what you can remember.
—W. C. Sellar & R. J. Yeatman:
1066 and All That (1930)

This chapter began life as an appendix to the paper on which the previous chapter was based, viz., "Inclusion Dependencies and Foreign Keys," Chapter 13 of the book Database Explorations: Essays on The Third Manifesto and Related Topics, by Hugh Darwen and myself (Trafford, 2010). However, what you see here differs from that earlier version in numerous respects—it has been revised, of course, and considerably expanded, and corrected here and there.

Perhaps I should add that the chapter doesn't necessarily have to be read carefully from beginning to end; it's meant to serve more by way of a reference source, and as a survey of what, frankly, is a pretty confused history—a concrete illustration, in fact, of the sad truth that even the best of us can get into muddles and make mistakes.

The foreign key concept is due to Codd, of course, and so is much of the associated terminology; but Codd's definitions changed considerably over the years, and to some extent his terminology did so too. By way of historical review, therefore, I present in this chapter a series of extracts—most of them edited slightly, but never in such a way as to change the original meaning[1]—from Codd's writings on the subject, with critical commentary by myself (all of it with the benefit of considerable hindsight, I hasten to add). Of course, my criticisms

---

[1] Except that I've deleted all mention of missing information and nulls (thereby, incidentally, making the chapter much shorter than it would otherwise be)—Codd believed that foreign keys should be allowed to accept nulls, but I don't. (I used to, but I changed my mind on the matter many years ago. As explained in Chapter 1, in fact, I now reject the whole notion of nulls as usually understood.)

aren't meant to be ad hominem; however, it would be remiss of me—indeed, it would undermine a large part of the point of this book—to overlook shortcomings when they exist, and I won't.

Two further preliminary remarks:

■ First, quotes in this chapter from Codd's writings (like the asides in previous chapters) are set in **Calibri font**—though usually not in bold—to make them stand out.

■ Second, the history isn't as straightforward as it could be. I mean, it's not exactly linear! As a result, I fear you might find what follows a little bewildering, especially on a first reading. If so, then I apologize, but I don't think the fault is entirely mine.

Without further ado, let me now embark on the history as such.

CODD'S 1969 DEFINITIONS

Codd's very first paper on the relational model was "Derivability, Redundancy, and Consistency of Relations Stored in Large Data Banks" (IBM Research Report RJ599, August 19th, 1969). Here's an extended extract from that paper:

> The set of entities of a given entity type can be viewed as a relation, and we shall call such a relation an *entity type relation* ... Normally, one attribute (or combination of attributes) of a given entity type has values which uniquely identify each entity. Such an attribute (or combination) is called a *key* ... A key is *nonredundant* if it is either a simple attribute (not a combination) or a combination such that none of the participating attributes is superfluous in uniquely identifying each entity ... The remaining relations ... are between entity types, and are, therefore, called *inter-entity relations*. An essential property of every inter-entity relation is that its domains include at least two keys which either refer to distinct entity types or refer to a common entity type serving distinct roles.

Comments: It's clearly possible (albeit with hindsight, as I've said) to criticize this extract on numerous grounds. For example:

■ Although it does at least mention the foreign key concept, tacitly—the final sentence talks about "keys" that "refer to entity types"—it doesn't give a name to that concept.[2] It's hard to talk about concepts that have no name.

   Note: Elsewhere I've elevated this rather obvious state of affairs into a principle, *The Naming Principle*. In fact I did briefly mention that principle in the previous chapter, as you might recall, but let me state it again here for the record:

> **Definition (*Naming Principle*):** Everything we need to talk about should have a name.

■ The talk of "entities" and "entity types" is unfortunate, in my opinion; it represents an unpleasant and unnecessary mixing of formal and informal concepts. (Relational concepts are formal; "entities," and concepts related to them, aren't. This point too is something I discussed briefly in the previous chapter, in connection with Example 1.) Indeed, I'm glad to say that when he revised this paper and republished it the following year—see the next section—Codd mostly dropped such talk.

■ It's really relvars, not relations, that have keys (and foreign keys too, sometimes). Of course, it's true that the term *relvar* wasn't introduced until 1998, by Hugh Darwen and myself, in the first edition of our *Manifesto* book—but the concept certainly existed, in the form of "time-varying relations," even in Codd's 1969 paper. This confusion between relations and relvars is one that I believe could and should have been avoided but, sadly, continues to this day.

   To repeat, it's relvars, not relations, that have keys and foreign keys. However, it can make sense to say of some given relation—i.e., of some given relation *value*, say *r*—that it either does or doesn't *satisfy* some key or foreign key constraint. And if it does, we might even say that *r* "has" the key or foreign key in question. But it must be clearly understood that all such talk is very loose.

   Note: In the remainder of this chapter, I'll keep to the term *relation* when quoting from original sources, but I'll use the term *relvar* everywhere

---

[2] On the other hand, it does suggest quite strongly that if relvar *R* "contains" a foreign key *FK*, then *FK* must actually be a key for *R*. Here's what it says, paraphrased: "An inter-entity relation *R* contains at least two keys which refer [etc., etc.]." But "keys" here doesn't mean, as it would certainly mean in other contexts, keys of *R* itself, but rather keys of those relations that *R* "inter-relates."

else (when it's the mot juste, of course).

■   That qualifier "Normally" in Codd'se second sentence is a little puzzling!—suggesting as it does that there might be situations in which no such unique identifier exists. Now, Codd might have injected that qualifier because of the fuzzy context of entities; but in fact he retains it in his 1970 rewrite (see the next section), where he's definitely talking in terms of relations (or relvars, rather) as such, not entities.

■   Keys aren't really attributes, or combinations of attributes, but rather *sets*: subsets of the pertinent heading, to be precise. A lack of understanding of this simple point has led to a great deal of further confusion over the years.

■   At least I'm pleased to see that Codd says, in the extract quoted, that keys consist of attributes, not domains. On the other hand, he doesn't actually define the term *attribute*, and in fact this sentence seems to be the only place in the paper where it's used! Indeed, later he switches, in the very same paper, to saying that keys consist of domains, not attributes. As I'm sure you know, this muddle over attributes vs. domains is something else that's caused a great deal of confusion over the years.

■   The talk of "nonredundant" keys implicitly suggests the possibility of *redundant* keys—i.e., "keys" that aren't keys at all, as we now understand the concept, but proper superkeys. (I remind you from Chapter 1 that a superkey of a given key *K* is a superset of the attributes that make up *K* that's not identical to *K*.)

What's more, a "key" could contain just one "simple attribute" and still be redundant in the foregoing sense! To be specific, any such "key" will certainly be redundant in that sense if the relvar it applies to is constrained never to contain more than one tuple. See Chapter 3, "TABLE_DUM and TABLE_DEE," of my book *Database Dreaming Volume II* (Technics, 2022) for further explanation.

Note: My own preferred term for "nonredundant" in the foregoing sense is *irreducible*, and that's the term I used in the first two chapters of this book. By contrast, Codd uses the term *minimal* (though not in his first few papers, and certainly not before 1988); but I reject that term as not very apt.

■ Of course it isn't necessary for a relvar with foreign keys to have at least two of them! It *is* necessary if the relvar does indeed represent a relationship between two or more other relvars, which is the case that Codd is considering here, but it obviously isn't necessary in all cases; consider, e.g., the usual departments and employees database for an obvious counterexample.

Note: I suspect that what happened here was that Codd got sidetracked by his own talk of "inter-entity relations," which caused him to overlook the obvious point that one "entity" could reference another without itself having to be a separate "inter-entity" construct as such.

■ One good thing about the extract is that it does *not* require a given foreign key to reference a primary key specifically. As should be clear from Chapters 1 and 2, this is a point I do agree with—though of course it's also a point I've changed my mind on, over the years; I used to believe in primary keys rather more than I do now. Please note, therefore, that all subsequent mentions of the term *primary key* in the remainder of this chapter should be understood in the light of these remarks!

■ Finally, the extract doesn't say as much explicitly, but it's clear from context that all of the relations (or relvars) under consideration are supposed to be base relations (or relvars) specifically; i.e., the possibility that other relations (or relvars) might have keys or foreign keys is never addressed. It's also clear from context that, for any particular foreign key, there's supposed to be exactly one referenced relvar. I'll have more to say on this latter issue in the final section of this chapter.

CODD'S 1970 DEFINITIONS

Codd's 1969 paper was the very first one he (or anyone else!) ever published on the relational model. The following year, however, he revised that paper slightly and republished it, under the title "A Relational Model of Data for Large Shared Data Banks," in *Communications of the ACM* (*CACM 13*, No. 6, June 1970)[3]— and it's that revised version that's usually credited with being the seminal paper in the entire relational field, though as you can see that characterization isn't

---

[3] As far as I know this paper and its 1969 predecessor, together with one internal IBM document, were the only publications of Codd's ever to use that rather quaint term *data bank*.

entirely fair to its 1969 predecessor. Anyway, here's the text from the 1970 paper that's the counterpart to the text I've already quoted from its predecessor in the previous section:

> Normally, one domain (or combination of domains) of a given relation has values which uniquely identify each element (*n*-tuple) of that relation. Such a domain (or combination) is called a *primary key* ... A primary key is *nonredundant* if it is either a simple domain (not a combination) or a combination such that none of the participating simple domains is superfluous in uniquely identifying each element. A relation may possess more than one nonredundant primary key ... Whenever a relation has two or more nonredundant primary keys, one of them is arbitrarily selected and called *the* primary key of that relation ... We shall call a domain (or domain combination) of relation *R* a *foreign key* if it is not the primary key of *R* but its elements are values of the primary key of some relation *S* (the possibility that *S* and *R* are identical is not excluded).

Comments: Again it's possible to criticize this text, with hindsight, in a variety of ways:[4]

- The talk of "entities" has gone (good). However, the qualifier "Normally" has been retained—so now there's a suggestion that there might be *relations* (or relvars, rather), instead of "entities," for which no unique identifier exists (?).

- The talk of "attributes" has been replaced by talk of "domains" (bad).

- "Keys" have become *primary* keys (bad). Well, actually there's a muddle here. First, Codd uses the term *primary key* to mean what in his 1969 paper he called simply a key (and I vastly prefer this latter term myself, and use it wherever possble); so a relation, or rather a relvar, can have any number of such "primary" keys. But then he goes on to say that when there are two or more such "primary" keys, we're supposed to choose one and make it "the" primary key! Thus, a relvar might have two primary keys, but one of them

---

[4] Of course, I won't repeat criticisms I've already made in the previous section in connection with the 1970 paper's predecessor. More generally, in fact, I'll try not to criticize any of Codd's writings in this chapter if I've effectively already made the same criticism in connection with some previous paper, in some earlier section—unless there's some additional point to be made, of course.

is supposed to be chosen as being somehow more primary than the other. How the choice is to be made, and how the distinction is to be made subsequently, isn't clear.

■ Unlike primary keys in general, "the" primary key—if there is one, I suppose we have to add, thanks to that "Normally" qualifier—is required to be nonredundant (better: *irreducible*). Note, however, that the system won't usually be able to tell whether a given key is irreducible; thus, irreducibility in this context has to be more by way of a desideratum than a hard and fast requirement.

■ Here again is the final sentence from the extract quoted above:

> We shall call a domain (or domain combination) of relation *R* a *foreign key* if it is not the primary key of *R* but its elements are values of the primary key of some relation *S* (the possibility that *S* and *R* are identical is not excluded).[5]

So the term *foreign key* is now explicitly introduced (good)—but note that foreign keys are now required to reference primary keys specifically (bad).[6] Also, the requirement that a foreign key not be the primary key of its containing relvar is strange, and in fact both unnecessary and undesirable. But at least the definition does explicitly permit "domain combinations" (better: *attribute* combinations); in other words, foreign keys are now explicitly permitted to be composite. (The 1969 paper was silent on this point.) Note too that the definition requires, or at least strongly implies, that there be a *single* corresponding target relation *S*. I'm in sympathy with this requirement.

One last point on the 1970 paper: To say it again, keys and foreign keys aren't really attributes or combinations of attributes, but rather sets—subsets of the pertinent heading, to be precise. And it follows that key and foreign key

---

[5] A definition of the term *foreign key* that was virtually identical to the one in this final sentence, except that it was expressed in terms of attributes instead of domains, was included in the second edition of my book *An Introduction to Database Systems* (Addison-Wesley, 1977). The first edition, I regret to say, didn't discuss foreign keys at all. (Well, that's to say it didn't use that term; however, it most certainly did discuss the concept, on pages 304-305.)

[6] Meaning, of course, "the" primary key, in cases where there's a choice.

values aren't attribute values, either, but tuples of such values. Codd almost but not quite acknowledges these facts in his paper. Well, that's to say, the extract quoted at the beginning of the present section does at least use the term *element* in such a way as to be capable of supporting such an interpretation ... To spell the point out:

■   That extract begins by talking about "elements" of a relation, which it says are *n*-tuples (or just tuples for short).

■   Then it talks about "elements" of foreign keys, which it says are values of the corresponding primary key.[7]

So the question is: Is the term *elements* being used here in two different senses, or are those senses really one and the same? A charitable interpretation would say it's the latter. Though if that interpretation is indeed the correct one, then I have to say too that, sadly, nowhere in any of his writings did Codd ever really acknowledge that fact—with the consequence that, to this very day, there's still widespread confusion (or widespread lack of understanding, at any rate) regarding the true state of affairs.

CODD'S 1979 DEFINITIONS

In 1979 Codd published his paper "Extending the Database Relational Model to Capture More Meaning" (*ACM Transactions on Database Systems 4*, No. 4, December 1979). His main purpose in that paper was to define a set of extensions to the original relational model, to yield what he called the extended model RM/T. Before describing those proposed extensions, however, he first gave a summary of the original model as he saw it at the time, and the following edited extract is taken from that summary:

> With each relation is associated a set of candidate keys. *K is a candidate key* of relation *R* if it is a collection of attributes of *R* with the following time-independent properties.

---

[7] I assume here for simplicity (as indeed I think Codd does throughout the 1970 paper, despite definitions in his own later writings) that a given referencing relvar has precisely one corresponding referenced relvar. Under that assumption, it's legitimate to talk about "the" corresponding primary key. (Of course, I'm also assuming here that the target key is a primary key specifically.)

1. No two rows of *R* have the same *K* component.

2. If any attribute is dropped from *K*, the uniqueness property is lost.

For each base relation one candidate key is selected as the *primary key*. For a given database, those domains upon which the simple (i.e., single attribute) primary keys are defined are called the *primary domains* of that database ... All insertions into, updates of, and deletions from base relations are constrained by the following [rule] ... (Referential integrity:) Suppose an attribute *A* of a compound (i.e., multiattribute) primary key of a relation *R* is defined on a primary domain *D*. Then, at all times, for each value *v* of *A* in *R* there must exist a base relation (say *S*) with a simple primary key (say *B*) such that *v* occurs as a value of *B* in *S*.

Comments:

■ The talk of "domains" has been replaced by talk of "attributes" (good).

■ The talk of "tuples" has been replaced by talk of "rows" (bad). *Note:* My reasons for not regarding this change as an improvement are discussed in detail in my book *SQL and Relational Theory: How to Write Accurate SQL Code*, 3rd edition (O'Reilly, 2015). See also the comments at the very end of the introductory section in Chapter 4.

■ Relvars are now required to have at least one candidate key, instead of at least one primary key; [8] the term *primary key* is now reserved for that particular candidate key that has been chosen, somehow, as being "more equal than the others." Distinguishing candidate keys in general from primary keys in particular is clearly an improvement (at least in clarity, if not in substance).

---

[8] Codd first used the term *candidate key* in his paper "Further Normalization of the Data Base Relational Model," in Randall J. Rustin (ed.), *Data Base Systems: Courant Computer Science Symposia Series 6* (Prentice-Hall, 1972). *Note:* At that time *database* was usually written as two separate words (*data base*)—hence the title of that paper. Though I can't help adding that it's a very bad title anyway, because what's being "further normalized" isn't the relational model as such, but rather relations (more precisely, relvars) in the database. Of course, the fix is easy—just replace "of" by "in" in that title.

■ Keys of all kinds are now explicitly required to be irreducible.

■ The term *foreign key* has disappeared!—though the concept survives, of course, at least implicitly, as part of the referential integrity rule. (Incidentally, I believe the RM/T paper was the first of Codd's writings to mention this latter term.)

■ The definition doesn't actually require foreign keys to be simple (i.e., single attribute), but I believe this was Codd's intention (note that his definition of the referential integrity rule refers only to single attribute primary keys as targets—see below). However, the justification for this change from the 1970 definition is unclear.

■ The referential integrity rule should, but in fact does not, require attribute *B* to be defined on domain *D*. (Presumably this was just an oversight.)

■ The same rule explicitly requires foreign keys to be components of composite primary keys. No justification for this undesirable and unnecessary restriction is given.

■ That same rule also requires foreign keys to consist of exactly one attribute—no more, no less. No justification for this undesirable and unnecessary restriction is given.

■ The *primary domain* concept is new. I note that the primary keys mentioned in the definition of that concept are presumably intended to be primary keys of, specifically, base relations, though the paper doesn't say as much. But in any case I consider the concept as contributing nothing; in fact, I regard it as both undesirable and unnecessary. Indeed, it's easy to see that attributes defined on primary domains aren't necessarily foreign keys, and foreign keys aren't necessarily defined on primary domains (apologies for the slightly loose wording here). Here's an example to illustrate the first of these points.[9] Suppose:

---

[9] Developing an example to illustrate the converse point—viz., that foreign keys aren't necessarily defined on primary domains—is left as an exercise. (In fact, of course, any foreign key involving two or more attributes will suffice to make the point, since primary domains are "simple" by definition.)

a. Base relvar HOLIDAYS has primary key {DATE}, defined on a domain with that same name.

b. Base relvar EMP has an attribute HIREDATE defined on that same domain DATE.

c. HOLIDAYS and EMP are the only relvars in the database.

Then domain DATE is a primary domain, but {HIREDATE} isn't a foreign key.

Note: In his 1988 paper (see the section after next) Codd subsequently agreed with the foregoing position, using an essentially isomorphic example.

■ Note finally that the referential integrity rule no longer requires—if it ever actually did require, I suppose in fairness I have to add—that a given foreign key correspond to just one corresponding referenced relvar. Again, I'll comment on this issue in the final section of this chapter.

CODD'S 1987 DEFINITIONS

The next publication of Codd's to discuss these matters—though they weren't its principal topic—was his paper "More Commentary on Missing Information in Relational Databases (Applicable and Inapplicable Information)," in *ACM SIGMOD Record 16*, No. 1 (March 1987). In that paper, he argues among other things that referential integrity should apply to simple foreign keys only. That is, he apparently allows composite foreign keys, but doesn't require referential integrity to apply to them (?). This position seems to me to introduce an unnecessary element of confusion into what started out as a fairly simple concept. After all, what's the point of saying something's a foreign key if it isn't subject to the referential integrity requirement?[10] Let's examine Codd's arguments.

He begins by giving a definition of referential integrity which he says "corresponds closely" to that in the RM/T paper as discussed in the previous section:

---

[10] More on this rhetorical (?) question in the next section.

(Referential integrity:) Let *D* be a domain from which one or more single attribute primary keys draw their values. Let *K* be a foreign key which draws its values from domain *D*. Every value which occurs in *K* must also exist in the database as a value of the primary key of some base relation.

Comment: I don't really understand this definition. It defines referential integrity in terms of foreign keys; but what's a foreign key? I think it has to be defined in terms of referential integrity! In other words, foreign keys are the mechanism in terms of which referential integrity is defined, and by means of which it's enforced. It's true that the original 1970 definition of foreign key didn't mention referential integrity by name, and likewise the original 1979 definition of referential integrity didn't mention foreign keys by name either; but each of those definitions most certainly involves the other *concept*; thus, I regard the two as being inextricably interwoven.

Codd then goes on to give an example of two databases, each involving a relation R3 with a composite primary key (SNO,PNO) and another relation R4 with a composite attribute (SNO,PNO):

```
R3   ( SNO , PNO , ... )
     PRIMARY KEY ( SNO , PNO )

R4   ( ... , SNO , PNO , ... )
```

In one of the two databases, X say, values of R4.(SNO,PNO) are required to match values of the primary key of R3, whereas in the other database Y they aren't. In database Y, therefore, referential integrity clearly doesn't apply to (the composite) attribute R4.(SNO,PNO), and it seems to me that the attribute in question should therefore not be regarded as a foreign key. But Codd does seem to regard it as a foreign key, but one to which referential integrity doesn't apply (?).

What about database X, where (to repeat) values of R4.(SNO,PNO) *are* required to match values of the primary key of R3? Well, here's what Codd has to say (but note that the italicized comments in brackets are mine, not Codd's):

There are two ways in which this example ... could be handled:

1. Make the referential integrity rule applicable to all PK-FK pairs of keys, whether simple or compound ... [*i.e., treat R4.(SNO,PNO) as a genuine foreign key*].

2. Make the referential integrity rule applicable to simple PK-FK pairs of keys only, and require the [database administrator] to impose a referential constraint on just those compound PK-FK pairs of keys for which the constraint [happens to apply] by specifying a user defined integrity constraint ... [*i.e., don't treat R4.(SNO,PNO) as a foreign key—or rather, treat it as a foreign key, but one to which the referential integrity rule either (a) doesn't apply, or (b) does apply but has to be specified explicitly by means of a "user defined" integrity constraint to that effect (?)*].

Method 2 complies with [the definition of referential integrity in the RM/T paper] and with [the earlier] definition of the foreign key concept. In addition, Method 2 is cleaner than Method 1, because it separates the foreign key concept from the more complicated referential integrity concept. Thus Method 2 is adopted.[11]

Comments:

- "Method 2 complies with the [original] definition in the RM/T paper of referential integrity"? Well, maybe it does—it's hard to tell!—but I think Method 1 complies more closely with the original [1970] definition of foreign key. As already indicated, I think the original definition of referential integrity was deficient in a number of respects anyway. In any case, it's surely more important to come up with a set of rules that are definitive and truly useful, rather than just to preserve earlier definitions for their own sake.

- In what way exactly is Method 2 "cleaner" than Method 1? What exactly is the distinction between the foreign key concept and the referential integrity concept? What use are foreign keys without referential integrity? How do

---

[11] Codd later reversed his position on this point.

you define foreign keys without mentioning referential integrity (the concept, at least, if not the term)? Or vice versa?

Codd then continues:

Referential integrity should be implemented as far as possible as a special case of user defined integrity ... Further, it should be remembered that referential integrity is a particular application of a subset constraint ... Subset constraints may, however, apply between other pairs of attributes also (e.g., nonkeys and keys that are nonsimple).

Comments: Here Codd is appealing to some ideas that he didn't actually publish until the following year (see the next section), so I think I need to inject a little background explanation. His mention of "user defined integrity" in particular has to do with a constraint classification scheme that he went on to describe in detail in that subsequent paper. What follows is a brief description of that scheme, with interspersed comments and criticisms of my own:

- First of all, constraints are either "C-timed" or "T-timed," where C stands for command and T for transaction. (Codd always used the term command—usually inappropriately, in my opinion—for what would more conventionally be called a statement.) Thus, C-timed means immediate checking and T-timed means deferred checking. However, I reject this timing distinction; as explained in Chapter 1, I believe that *all* constraints need to be checked immediately (and there are strong arguments in support of this position on my part, of course).
    I note in passing, just for accuracy's sake, that type constraints in particular are checked "even more immediately" than other constraints—by which I mean, more specifically, that they're checked on invocation of a special operator called a *selector*. Further specifics are beyond the scope of the present discussion; if you want to know more, I refer you to my book *SQL and Relational Theory: How to Write Accurate SQL Code*, 3rd edition (O'Reilly, 2015).

- Second, constraints are divided up into five kinds, viz., D (domain), C (column), E (entity), R (referential), and U (user defined). However, I reject this scheme for several reasons, some but not all of which are explained in the next few paragraphs.

■ Domain constraints correspond, I presume, to what in Chapter 1 I called type constraints. If that presumption on my part is correct, then we don't need to discuss them any further here.

Aside: Actually that presumption on my part *isn't* correct, not entirely. To tell the truth Codd never seems to say anywhere exactly what a domain constraint consists of, but in his book on RM/V2—see the section "Codd's 1990 Definitions" below—he says this: "Three kinds of domain integrity constraints ... are (1) regular data type, (2) ranges of values permitted, and (3) whether or not the ordering comparators greater than (>) and less than (<) are applicable to those values." A proper, careful response to this quote could easily take several pages and would be far too much of a distraction from our main topic, so I won't attempt such a response here. Suffice it to say that:

1. Codd's "regular data type" corresponds to what in *The Third Manifesto* we call a *possible representation*. It has or should have essentially no effect on the type (or domain) being defined.

2. Codd's "ranges of values" correspond to what in *The Third Manifesto* we call a *type constraint*—but it's only one special case.

3. The question of what operators apply to values of type *T* (be they "comparators" or operators of any other kind) is a whole separate question—it has nothing to with the definition of type *T* as such.

But at least it's true that we don't need to discuss Codd's "domain constraints" any further here. *End of aside.*

■ Column constraints are constraints—of course, I'd prefer to call them attribute constraints—that constrain the values that can appear in an individual column (over and above the constraint already imposed by the fact that the column in question is defined to be of a certain type, or domain). For example, values of column STATUS in the suppliers relvar S must be integers, because they're defined to be of type INTEGER—but they might additionally be subject to a "column constraint" that says the integers in question must lie in the range 1 to 100 inclusive.

My objection to column constraints is simply that I see no logical reason to single them out for special treatment in this way, and several reasons not to.

■   Entity and referential constraints are a very different kettle of fish. Of course, they correspond to the entity integrity rule and the referential integrity rule, respectively;[12] but those rules aren't constraints as such but rather what might be called *metaconstraints*, or in other words constraints on constraints. For example, the entity integrity rule—which (a) is vacuous, of course, if we reject nulls (but let's overlook that point, just for the moment), and in any case (b) talks about primary keys specifically, which I don't really believe in either—says, in effect:

> *There must be an individual integrity constraint for each base relvar in the database to the effect that the primary key of that relvar doesn't allow nulls.*

Each such individual constraint can then be regarded, in a sense, as a specific instance of the generic entity integrity rule.

Analogous remarks apply to the referential integrity rule and referential constraints also, of course.

■   As for the final category, "user defined" constraints: Well, "user defined" is certainly a poor choice of name. I mean, it's not helpful—in fact, it's actively misleading—because in the final analysis *all* integrity constraints have to be "user defined" by *some* user. Even referential constraints (and entity constraints too, if you believe in them, which I don't) must be defined by some user—i.e., by means of appropriate key and foreign key specifications—in every individual case (i.e., for every individual database). And as for domain and column constraints, they're certainly defined by some user also.

---

[12] Those rules were introduced in the RM/T paper, which I discussed in the previous section. But I didn't discuss the entity integrity rule in that section, because (as we'll see in a moment) it has to do with nulls.

As noted in Chapter 1, therefore, Hugh Darwen and I just use the one generic term *database constraint*, by which we mean, quite simply, any constraint that's not a type constraint. Then we can usefully distinguish between general metaconstraints such as the referential integrity rule, on the one hand, and specific constraints that apply to specific databases—including in particular specific instances of those metaconstraints—on the other.

Now I return to Codd's own text, which for convenience I'll repeat below in two separate pieces. First:

> Referential integrity should be implemented as far as possible as a special case of user defined integrity.

I don't really know what this statement means. But to the extent I do understand it, though, I reject it; in fact, it seems to conflict with Codd's own classification scheme as I've just described it! Some more specific comments:

■   For reasons already explained in detail in Chapter 2, I certainly feel that special treatment is desirable, in both syntax and implementation, for referential constraints.. But I don't know whether that's what Codd means by "implemented as a special case."

■   I agree that referential constraints are user defined, in the sense that they have to be defined, either implicitly or explicitly, by some suitably authorized user. But (to say it again), surely all integrity constraints have to be defined by some suitably authorized user; thus, the term "user defined integrity" doesn't capture the concept I think Codd might be aiming at—whatever that might be.[13]

■   Moreover, referential constraints, like all constraints, require some suitably authorized user to specify the "violation response" (i.e., the action the system is to take if the constraint is violated). But in the case of referential constraints specifically, certain common responses (CASCADE and NO ACTION) can be identified. In that particular case, therefore, special casing both the constraints as such and those common responses seems desirable, for reasons of both usability and efficiency.

---

[13] In his RM/V2 book—see the final section in this chapter—Codd explicitly defines "user defined integrity constraints" to be "constraints other than those of the domain, column, entity, and referential types." I don't think this definition is very helpful.

> Further, it should be remembered that referential integrity is a
> particular application of a subset constraint ... Subset constraints
> may, however, apply between other pairs of attributes also (e.g.,
> nonkeys and keys that are nonsimple).

As noted in Chapter 2, *subset constraint* is just another name for an
inclusion dependency—a reasonable name, in fact, because, e.g., the inclusion
dependency

```
P { CITY } ⊆ S { CITY }
```

can be read as "The set of part cities is a subset of the set of supplier cities." And
yes, it's true that a referential constraint is a special case. But why we're being
told that this state of affairs "should be remembered" isn't exactly clear. If X is
an attribute of both relvar R_2 and relvar R_1, and if every value of X in R_2 must be
a value of X in R_1, then:

a. If in addition values of X in R_1 are unique, then $\{X\}$ is a key for R_1, and the
    subset constraint is indeed a referential constraint; but so what?

b. If on the other hand values of X in R_1 aren't unique, then the situation is
    quite different (e.g., the insert – update – delete rules are likely to be quite
    different), and the relevance of the point to a discussion of referential
    integrity and foreign keys is unclear.

CODD'S 1988 DEFINITIONS

In 1988 Codd published a paper with the title "Domains, Keys, and Referential
Integrity in Relational Databases" (*InfoDB 3*, No. 1, Spring 1988), which he
clearly intended as a definitive statement on foreign keys and related matters
(though to be honest I don't think it succeeded in meeting that objective). To
quote from the abstract:

> There is at present a great deal of confusion over ... domains, primary
> keys, foreign keys, and referential integrity. This article represents an
> attempt by the inventor of the relational model to replace the confusion ...

by some understanding and to show how full support for domains, primary keys, and foreign keys is essential in providing full support for all five types of integrity in the relational model ... .

All subsequent quotes in this section are taken from that 1988 paper, though I've edited and rearranged them considerably for present purposes.

> (*Referential integrity*:) Let *D* be a primary domain (either simple or composite), and let *K* be a foreign key defined on *D*. Every value of *K* must be equal to some value of the primary key (also defined on *D*) of some base relation.
>
> Full support for foreign keys includes full support for referential integrity. However, it is useful to distinguish between the two concepts, because referential integrity is just one of the five forms of integrity in a relational system.
>
> A DBMS could support primary and foreign key declarations but omit support for referential integrity (i.e., it could provide just partial foreign key support).
>
> The DBMS should not be designed to deduce foreign keys from primary keys and their domains, unless it also allows the database administrator to override its deductions where necessary.

Comments:

■ Once again Codd draws a distinction between the referential integrity and foreign key concepts. Well, I agree that such a distinction can be made—referential integrity defines legitimate states of the database, foreign keys guarantee such states—but I don't see much point in making it. After all, the concepts are surely in lock step with one another. In other words, I don't see how (at least in a relational context) you can have referential integrity without foreign keys, or foreign keys without referential integrity.[14] Thus, I don't find the distinction in question to be particularly useful, or helpful.

■ Consider these two statements from the extract quoted:

---

[14] But see the "*Note:*" paragraph in the very next bullet item!

a. (*Referential integrity:*): ... Every value of [a given foreign key *K*] must be equal to some value of the primary key ... of some base relation.

b. A DBMS could support primary and foreign key declarations but omit support for referential integrity.

Statement a. says, in effect, that if some value of *K* doesn't satisfy the referential integrity requirement, then—by definition!—*K* isn't a foreign key. Statement b. says, in effect, that a foreign key *K* can exist that doesn't satisfy the referential integrity requirement. There seems to be some contradiction here.

Note: After I first wrote the foregoing, a product was announced that (to my amazement) did exactly what Codd's text suggests—i.e., it allowed a foreign key to be declared, but didn't enforce the corresponding integrity constraint![15] The stated intent was to enable users to prepare for some future release of the product in which the constraint might be enforced after all. But I stand by my contention that such a "foreign key" isn't really a foreign key at all, and such a facility doesn't constitute foreign key "support" in any significant sense. After all (to beat the point to death, perhaps), such a simple level of "support" could be achieved via the system's ordinary comment mechanism. Tell me again: What would be the point of supporting the declaration of a foreign key but not enforcing the corresponding integrity requirement?

■ Codd says it's useful to distinguish between referential integrity and foreign keys "because referential integrity is just one of the five forms of integrity in a relational system." Well, first, this "justification" looks like nonsense to me; what on earth does the fact that there are "five forms of integrity" have to with whether or not foreign keys and one of those "five forms" can be disentangled? To me, this looks like a complete red herring. (At the risk of beating the point to death: You might just as well say it's useful to distinguish between being French and holding French citizenship because France is just one of several European jurisdictions.)

---

[15] It occurs to me now, very belatedly, that it might have been Codd's 1988 paper that gave the product in question *carte blanche* to do this.

Second, I've already explained in an earlier section why I don't think much of those "five forms of integrity," anyway.

■ "The DBMS should not be designed to deduce foreign keys from primary keys and their domains, unless it also allows the database administrator to override its deductions where necessary." I agree, but note that this is a change from Codd's original position as implied by his definition of referential integrity in his RM/T paper (see the section before last).

■ The extract quoted begins with a reference to the concept of a primary domain. As a matter of fact the paper generally has quite a lot to say about primary domains. Here are some of the things it says:

> If *D* is a domain on which some primary key *K* is defined, it is often useful to refer to *D* as a primary domain. If *K* is composite, then *D* is a composite primary domain.

> Note that (a) not every component of a composite primary domain is itself a primary domain; (b) not every component of a composite primary key is itself a primary key.

> A column could be defined on a primary domain and yet be neither a primary key nor a foreign key.

I don't propose to analyze this text in detail; as far as I'm concerned, primary domains are a pretty useless concept (as I think the last of the foregoing quotes makes rather obvious), and I have nothing constructive to say about them. But I do want to offer one comment. As I've already indicated elsewhere, I don't think it's useful—in fact, I think it does the cause of genuine understanding a major disservice—to think of a "composite key" as being defined on a "composite domain." Instead, I think it's better just to stay with the idea that each component attribute of such a key is—of course!—defined on its own domain (better: *is of its own type*), and drop the concept of a "composite domain" entirely. Ditto the concept "composite attribute," if it exists (which it must, I suppose, as soon as we permit composite domains).

In fact, I believe what Codd should have done here is recognize that (a) keys are defined as subsets of headings and are thus of some tuple type, and accordingly that (b) key values are tuples. See Chapter 1 for elaboration of these points.

(*Foreign keys*:) A foreign key is a single column or combination of columns of a relation *S*, whose domain *D* is that of a primary key in the database, and each of whose values is required at all times to equal the value of some primary key (with domain *D*) of at least one relation *R*, where relations *R* and *S* are not *required* to be distinct (but are *permitted* to be distinct, and this is the usual case). A foreign key may have *n* corresponding primary keys (where *n* is any integer greater than or equal to 1, and *n* = 1 is the usual case). When *n* > 1, ... any selected foreign key value *may happen to equal* any number of values of the corresponding *n* primary keys, but is *required to equal* at least one of them ... A foreign key within relation *R* is not necessarily a component of the primary key of relation *R*.

Comments:

- The talk of "attributes" in earlier writings has been replaced by talk of "columns." Personally, I don't feel this is an improvement, for reasons discussed in detail in my book *SQL and Relational Theory: How to Write Accurate SQL Code*, 3rd edition, O'Reilly, 2015). See also the comments at the very end of the introductory section in Chapter 4.

- The wording isn't as careful as it might be. For example: "Each [foreign key value] is required ... to equal the value of some primary key." Surely, "the value of some primary key" here should be "some value of the primary key," or perhaps "the value of the primary key in some row"? And why not replace "whose domain *D* is that of a primary key in the database" by "defined on some primary domain *D*"? (Of course, this suggested revision assumes we agree to retain the primary domain concept in the first place, which I don't actually believe we should.)

- At least it's good to see that keys and foreign keys are now explicitly allowed to be "composite"—though as I've said, it would be better to recognize that they're actually of some tuple type. (If the degree of that tuple type is greater than one, then that's the "composite" case; if that degree is one, that's the "simple" case; but what about the case of degree zero? Codd doesn't seem to have a term for that case.)

■ It's also good to see it explicitly stated that foreign keys don't have to be components of the pertinent primary key.

■ But overall, of course, the most interesting thing about the extract quoted is the emphasis it lays on the possibility that *n*—i.e., the number of primary keys corresponding to a given foreign key—might be greater than one. More specifically, the wording "*may happen to equal* any number of values of the corresponding *n* primary keys, but is *required to equal* at least one of them" shows clearly that Codd is talking about the case I referred to in Chapter 2 as AT LEAST ONE OF. Oddly enough, of the three cases I discussed in that chapter, AT LEAST ONE OF is the one that seems hardest to justify intuitively! Once again, see my further remarks on this topic at the end of this chapter.

Finally, there's one more point in the paper under discussion that I want to draw your attention to, though I have no further comment on it. Codd first repeats the example of the two databases X and Y—see the previous section—and then continues as follows:

> Method 2 is undesirable, in that it treats simple and composite keys differently. The relational model therefore now supports Method 1. This represents a change in my position with respect to one paragraph of [the RM/T paper] and one of [the 1987 paper, discussed in the previous section].

CODD'S 1990 DEFINITIONS

In 1990 Codd published his book on what he called The Relational Model Version 2 (RM/V2 for short): *The Relational Model for Database Management Version 2* (Addison-Wesley, 1990).[16] Here's what that book has to say regarding foreign keys:

---

[16] Available online at *https://codeblab.com/wp-content/uploads/2009/12/ rmdb-codd.pdf*. I should add that I've published an extensve and detailed analysis of RM/V2 in its entirety (i.e., not just of its foreign key aspects) elsewhere. See my book *E. F. Codd and Relational Theory, Revised Edition* (Technics, 2021).

The value of the primary key in each row of the pertinent R-table identifies the particular object represented by that row uniquely within the type of objects that are represented by that relation. Everywhere else in the database that there is a need to refer to that particular object, the *same* identifying value drawn from the *same* domain is used. Any column containing those values is called a *foreign key* ... *Referential integrity* is defined as follows: Let *D* be a domain from which one or more primary keys draw their values. Let *K* be a foreign key, which draws its values from domain *D*. Every ... value which occurs in *K* must also exist in the database as the value of the primary key on domain *D* of some base relation.

Comments:

- "R-table" is a new term. However, all Codd means by it is either a relation or a relvar (depending on context) in the familiar relational model sense; the "R-" prefix is intended to stress the point that certain properties commonly associated with tables in general (e.g., top to bottom row ordering, left to right column ordering) don't apply to R-tables.

    But wouldn't it have been better just to "bite the bullet" in the first place and stick to proper relational terminology? I think it would. In fact, I see Codd's introduction of this "R-table" term, this late in the day, as nothing more than a belated recognition of the fact that it was a mistake right at the outset to pretend that we were dealing with plain old tables with plain old rows and columns—i.e., as such things are all generally understood.

- "Everywhere ... there is a need to refer to that particular object, the *same* identifying value drawn from the *same* domain is used." In my opinion this requirement too strong; it might be good practice, but I can certainly imagine situations where the very same "object" is referenced by, say, employee number in some situations and social security number in others.

    Or perhaps how we interpret the requirement depends on what exactly we mean when we say that two "objects" are "the same"? Or not the same? See the discussion of Example 1 (the invoices and shipments example) in the previous chapter.

- "Any column containing those values is called a *foreign key*": So what about foreign keys involving two or more "columns"? In fact, elsewhere in the RM/V2 book Codd does refer to such foreign keys. E.g., on page 175: "A foreign key consists of one or more columns drawing its values from the domain (simple or composite) upon which at least one primary key is defined."

    Note: That "one or more" should really be "zero or more." Again please see Chapter 3, "TABLE_DUM and TABLE_DEE," of my book *Database Dreaming Volume II* (Technics, 2022) for further explanation.

■ I continue to reject the notion of primary domains (which survive in concept in the extract quoted, even if the term doesn't).

    Finally, Codd says that every foreign key value "must also exist in the database as the value of the primary key ... of *some* base relation" (my italics). Again, therefore, Codd is at least allowing—elsewhere in the book, in fact, he explicitly requires—support for the idea that a given foreign key might have two or more corresponding target relvars. As I've said several times already, however (see in particular the discussion of Example 9 in the previous chapter), I reject this notion. Let me briefly remind you of my reasons why.

■ First of all, I don't support it because if the system allows—as I believe it should—foreign key targets to be defined by means of *<relation exp>*s of arbitrary complexity, then support for "two or more target relvars" as such is logically redundant.

■ Second, even if I could be persuaded to support the EXACTLY ONE OF and ALL OF cases, I don't think I'd support the AT LEAST ONE OF case (which as noted earlier seems to be just the case that Codd requires), because I don't think it's useful.

■ Third, it's interesting to note in this connection that Codd himself explicitly insists on there always being just one target relvar in his extended model RM/T—implying, incidentally, that a conventional relational database not designed in accordance with the single target relvar discipline might be difficult to upgrade to conform to that extended model. In other words, I think we should appeal to *The Principle of Cautious Design*! See the section immediately following.

THE PRINCIPLE OF CAUTIOUS DESIGN

Several of the discussions in the foregoing sections—in fact, several of the discussions all through this book so far—have had a slightly philosophical flavor, and here's the reason for this state of affairs:

- When we talk about the relational model, of course we're talking about a formal system.

- The purpose of that formal system is to be useful as a formal representation of certain aspects of the real world—and the real world is *not* a formal system.

- Thus, the process of mapping between the formal relational model and the informal real world is necessarily not formal either, but only intuitive. (A mapping between two systems can be defined formally only if both of those systems are themselves formal in turn.)

- It follows that there must be a certain element of subjectiveness in defining the rules of the formal relational model. Basically, those rules have to be defined in a way that seems, intuitively, to be a good fit with the way the world works. But it's always possible to argue about matters of intuition, of course—and such arguments are, at least partly if not wholly, philosophical arguments.

To take a concrete example, consider the following rule:

A foreign key must always reference exactly one target relvar.

Now, it's obviously possible to think of situations in which it might seem desirable to violate this rule (I discussed a few such situations in Chapter 2). However, it's my opinion that the comparatively minor additional functionality provided by relaxing the rule is outweighed several times over by the additional complexity it causes (complexity, be it noted, not only for the user who wants to "take advantage" of the relaxation of the rule, but rather for everybody). Personally, I've never seen a situation in which there was a genuine need to have a foreign key reference two or more distinct relvars; rather, it has always turned out—in the examples I've seen—that the design of the database wasn't very good, and could be improved in such a way as to avoid the perceived need.

However, given that such matters are indeed somewhat subjective, I would also argue that a good general principle is to stay with the simple version of the rule for as long as possible, waiting until such time as a genuine need to relax it comes along (if it ever does). If and when that happens, then that'll be the time to back off from the original rule. Such an approach will guarantee the maximum simplicity for the maximum time, and will moreover guarantee that extensions (to the model, or whatever else it is we're talking about) are made in an evolutionary, not revolutionary, manner.

The principle just articulated is applicable to the design of other formal systems also, not just the relational model or extensions thereto. I call it *The Principle of Cautious Design*. To spell it out:

> **Definition (*Principle of Cautious Design*):** When we're faced with a design choice, say between option *A* and option *B* (where *A* is upward compatible with *B*), and the full implications of option *B* aren't yet known, then the recommendation is to go with option *A*.

If we're forced at some future time to "open up" our design to permit option *B*, then nothing we'll have done in the past will be incompatible with that "opening up." If on the other hand we go with option *B* initially, and it subsequently becomes apparent that this was a bad decision, we can never "close our design down" again to insist on option *A*. In other words, we should try to avoid situations in which the model—or the language, or the DBMS, or the database, or whatever it is that we're designing—provides certain options that users have to be explicitly told not to exercise.

By way of illustration, consider the case of SQL and duplicate rows. The designers of the SQL language had a choice: Prohibit duplicate rows (option *A*) or permit them (option *B*). And they made the wrong choice—they went for option *B*. As a result, users have to be warned not to "take advantage" of this possibility, for reasons documented in detail in my book *SQL and Relational Theory: How to Write Accurate SQL Code*, 3rd edition (O'Reilly, 2015) and elsewhere. Clearly it would have been preferable if duplicate rows had been prohibited in the first place.

For the record, my original article on *The Principle of Cautious Design* first appeared in a Codd & Date publication—*The Relational Journal for DB2 Users 2*, No. 3, June/July 1990—and was later republished in the book *Relational*

Database Writings 1989-1991, by Hugh Darwen and myself (Addison-Wesley, 1992).

Chapter 4

Deconstructing

My Own Earlier Writings

Second thoughts are best.

—Euripides:
Hippolytus (428 BCE)

Deconstruction is a technique of literary analysis and criticism. The useful verb "to deconstruct" is defined by the Oxford English Dictionary as follows:

> *To undo the construction of, to take to pieces ... to analyze and reinterpret (first appearance 1973)*

It's a back formation from deconstruction, which is defined as—among other things—"a strategy of critical analysis associated with the French philosopher Jacques Derrida (b. 1930), directed towards exposing ... internal contradictions in philosophical and literary language." In other words, the technique of deconstruction operates on the premise that you can judge a writer's intent only by what he or she has actually said, not by what you might possibly think he or she might possibly have wanted to have possibly said, but didn't.

So deconstruction was exactly what I was doing in the previous chapter: I was deconstructing Codd's writings on referential integrity and foreign keys. However—lest I be thought guilty of some kind of prejudice here—I thought it would be an interesting exercise to redress the balance a little by applying the same kind of deconstruction techniques to some of my own early writings on the same subject. To be specific, I propose to analyze a two-part paper that I wrote sometime in the late 1980s and included in my book

*Relational Database Writings 1985-1989 (Addison-Wesley, 1990).
The paper in question had the rather unimaginative title "Referential
Integrity and Foreign Keys," and the two parts had the equally
unimaginative subtitles "Basic Concepts" and "Further
Considerations," respectively.*

*Now, I have to say that reading that paper again after all these
years was a salutary exercise; indeed, it was rather appalling to see
how much I got wrong. But maybe I shouldn't be too embarrassed ...
In his own preface to The Bertrand Russell Dictionary of Mind, Matter
and Morals (ed., Lester E. Denonn), Citadel Press, 1993, Bertrand
Russell—a personal hero of mine—wrote the following:*[1]

> *I have been accused of a habit of changing my opinions ... I am not
> myself in any degree ashamed of [that habit]. What physicist who was
> already active in 1900 would dream of boasting that his opinions had
> not changed during the last half century? ... [The] kind of philosophy
> that I value and have endeavoured to pursue is scientific, in the sense
> that there is some definite knowledge to be obtained and that new
> discoveries can make the admission of former error inevitable to any
> candid mind. For what I have said, whether early or late, I do not
> claim the kind of truth which theologians claim for their creeds. I
> claim only, at best, that the opinion expressed was a sensible one to
> hold at the time ... I should be much surprised if subsequent research
> did not show that it needed to be modified. [Such opinions were not]
> intended as pontifical pronouncements, but only as the best I could do
> at the time towards the promotion of clear and accurate thinking.
> Clarity, above all, has been my aim.*

*Well, I've certainly changed my own opinions over the years with
respect to referential integrity and foreign keys. Pace Russell, though,
I don't think I can honestly claim not to be ashamed of doing so (a
liitle bit, at any rate). The fact is, some of what I wrote in that early
paper was the result of nothing but muddled thinking on my part and
was, frankly, just plain wrong. Nevertheless, I think it can be
instructive to republish those earlier opinions and take a careful
deconstructional look at them, with a view to seeing exactly how and*

---

[1] I've quoted these wonderful remarks before—in the preface to the 8th edition of my book *An Introduction to Database Systems* (Addison-Wesley, 2004) in particular (see reference [13]).

why they were wrong and (just possibly) learning from past mistakes. So what I plan to do is this:

- *I'll repeat the original text of that earlier paper (which I'll refer to from this point forward as "the subject paper")—though I'll tidy that text up a little here and there, where it sems to need it, and I'll omit portions that for one reason or another aren't particularly relevant to the present exercise.*

- *But I'll also add a fair amount of commentary and analysis, in **Calibri font**, just as if I were critiquing a piece of technical writing by some other writer. And I'll make no attempt to spare my own feelings as I'm doing so.*

One final preliminary remark. The subject paper was originally intended as nothing but a private working draft. In other words, I meant it to serve merely as a basis for discussion—discussion with anyone who might be interested, of course, but discussion with Codd, the inventor of the relational model, in particular. It seemed to me at the time that the topic was in urgent need of clarification, and I hoped to persuade Codd of that fact and of the need to produce a definitive statement on the subject: a definitive statement that, I proposed, could be a joint production between him and myself. Well, he did agree that such a statement was needed, but he rejected the idea of collaboration; instead, he wrote a paper of his own, the one I referred to in the previous chapter as "the 1988 paper." In my opinion, however, that 1988 paper unfortunately still failed in all too many ways to serve as that necesary definitive statement, even though it did incorporate a few of my own suggestions and examples (and even though I reviewed the paper in draft form and offered numerous suggestions in connection with it—almost none of which were accepted, however). I therefore decided to tidy up and publish my original working paper (i.e., the subject paper) at the time as my own attempt at clarifying a confused but important area, and that's what I did. Though I have to say now, I wish I'd made a better job of it.

The foreign key and referential integrity concepts originated in a couple of early papers by Codd.[2] They're of paramount importance in the database field. Yet they're surrounded by an extraordinary degree of confusion: confusion in the open literature, confusion in the database community at large, and confusion in the database marketplace. Numerous conflicting definitions and explanations can be found in the literature—in books, papers, reference manuals, trade journals, and various other publications. Clarification is needed, urgently.

So this paper is an attempt at providing such clarification. What it does is this:

■ It surveys some of the various discussions given in Codd's publications on the subject, with analysis and commentary on those discussions by myself, and it outlines my own preferred definitions and approach to the subject.[3]

■ It then goes on to offer much additional discussion and explanation, together with some concrete recommendations for putting the ideas into practice.

I need to inject a few general remarks into the discussion right up front, concerning (a) nulls, (b) primary keys, and (c) relations vs. relvars. First, nulls. When I originally wrote the subject paper, I still believed in nulls. Why? Because at that time I believed more generally that if Codd said something was so, then that something must indeed be so. (I was still a little in awe of him, in other words.) But I came to understand that, actually, he wasn't always right— he was capable of making mistakes, just like anyone else—and nulls in particular were a mistake (probably the worst he made, as far as the relational model was concerned). The truth is, nulls were, and still are, a disastrously bad idea. Thus, along with many other people—people whose opinions I respect—I now firmly reject them and everything to do with them. **Every mention of nulls in the subject paper should thus be taken with a very large pinch of salt.**

---

[2] For the record: The term *foreign key* was first mentioned in reference [8], though in fact the concept (but strangely enough not the term) was discussed in that paper's predecessor, viz., E. F. Codd: "Derivability, Redundancy, and Consistency of Relations Stored in Large Data Banks," IBM Research Report RJ599 (August 19th, 1969). And the term *referential integrity* was first mentioned in reference [10]—but (again rather strangely) this time it was the term *foreign key* that wasn't mentioned, except for a single brief throwaway reference much later on in the paper, in a different context.

[3] But much of the material mentioned in this first bullet is omitted in this republication, since it has been already been covered in previous chapters (especially Chapter 3).

Of course, rejecting nulls doesn't make the problem they're supposed to solve—namely, the "missing information" problem—go away. But there are other and better ways to address that problem. This isn't the place to get into details; you can find a more detailed discussion of the problem, and ways to deal with it (together with references to other, still more detailed discussions), in my book *Fifty Years of Relational, and Other Database Writings* (Technics, 2020).

Second, primary keys. I've explained my position with respect to primary keys in detail in previous chapters (especially Chapter 1), and I'm not going to repeat the arguments here; I just want to make it clear that **you should take every mention in the subject paper of primary keys too with a pinch of salt**—not as large as the one in connection with nulls, perhaps, but large enough. In fact, every time you see a reference to primary keys in the subject paper, it would a good idea if you mentally reworded it to refer to just keys, unqualified, instead.

Third, relations vs. relvars. I wrote the subject paper before I'd fully taken on board the logical difference between relations and relvars—a logical difference that, as I've observed elsewhere, Codd himself never did take on board (or at least, if he did, then he never gave any sign of having done so in any of his writings). As a consequence, the subject paper frequently talks in terms of relations when it would have been better to talk in terms of relvars (or, more often perhaps, in terms of tables when it would have been better to talk in terms of table variables). I won't comment further on this point every time it arises; instead, I'll leave it as an exercise for you to make the necessary adjustments, mentally, as you read. Most of the time, at any rate.

Note: For the purposes of this paper I treat the terms *relation* and *table* as synonymous. Likewise for the terms *attribute* and *column* (and the terms *tuple* and *row* also—but I probably won't use the term *tuple* at all)).

I really wish I hadn't said that! It's true, of course, that thinking of relations, attributes, and tuples as tables, columns, and rows, respectively, can make the ideas a little easier to digest (at first, at any rate)—but at the same time they do the cause of genuine understanding a great disservice. The fact is, there are some serious logical differences between the concepts mentioned. That's to say, a relation isn't exactly a table, an attribute isn't exactly a column, and a tuple isn't exactly a row. Thus, I now feel—with hindsight, of course—that it would have been better to introduce, and embrace, the more precise terms right at the outset. But I didn't do that. So again I'm going to have to ask you to make some appropriate mental adjustments as you read.

EXAMPLES

This section presents a number of introductory examples. The examples make use of a kind of "pseudo SQL" syntax based on one first used in reference [13] and explained in more detail in the section "Foreign Key Rules," later. For present purposes, I'll just take it to be self-explanatory.

One consequence of the fact that I now believe primary keys as such should be downplayed is that the "pseudo SQL" syntax of the subject paper's examples needs a little tweaking. But the tweaking required is a very minor matter in the larger scheme of things, and I don't want to get sidetracked into discussing it in detail, and I propose to ignore it from this point forward.

Note: I omit domain definitions for brevity. Please understand, however, that this omission mustn't be construed as meaning that I think domains aren't important [19]. But I won't be discussing them very much, neither in this chapter nor elsewhere in the book. Let me just remind you, though, that a domain is nothing more nor less than a type (see Chapter1).

Example 1 (Departments and Employees)

```
DEPT    ( DNO , ... )
        PRIMARY KEY ( DNO )

EMP     ( ENO , DNO , ... )
        PRIMARY KEY ( ENO )
        FOREIGN KEY ( DNO ) REFERENCES DEPT
```

I've omitted irrelevant attributes. Sample values:

```
DEPT                EMP

┌───────┬───────┐   ┌───────┬───────┬───────┐
│ DNO   │  ...  │   │ ENO   │ DNO   │  ...  │
╞═══════╪═══════╡   ╞═══════╪═══════╪═══════╡
│ D1    │  ...  │   │ E1    │ D1    │  ...  │
│ D2    │  ...  │   │ E2    │ D1    │  ...  │
│ D3    │  ...  │   │ E3    │ D2    │  ...  │
└───────┴───────┘   │ E4    │ D2    │  ...  │
                    │ E5    │ null  │  ...  │
                    └───────┴───────┴───────┘
```

Points arising:

- First, terminology. Here are some rough definitions of the terms *primary key* and *foreign key* (more precise definitions can be found in the section "A Proposal," later).

  > **Definition (primary key):** Loosely, a primary key is just a unique identifier. A little more precisely: The primary key for a table T is a column PK of T such that, at any given time, no two rows of T have the same value for PK.

  > **Definition (foreign key):** Loosely, a foreign key is a column in one table whose values are values of the primary key of some other table (or possibly the same table). A little more precisely: A foreign key is a column FK of some table T_2 such that, at any given time, every nonnull value of FK in T_2 is required to be equal to the value of the primary key PK in some row of some table T_1. Table T_2 here is the *referencing* table, table T_1 the *referenced* or *target* table. They aren't necessarily distinct.

  Well, OK, I did say these definitions were "rough," but now I think they were probably *too* rough, in several different ways. In fact, you might find it a useful exercise to try and identify, and fix, everything in those definitions that could benefit from such fixing.

- More terminology: Since a given foreign key value obviously represents a reference to the row containing the matching primary key value (the *referenced row* or *target row*), the problem of ensuring that the database doesn't contain any invalid foreign key values is known as the *referential integrity* problem. The constraint that values of a given foreign key must match values of the corresponding primary key is known as a *referential constraint*.

- Referential constraints can be represented diagrammatically as follows:

  ```
  referencing table ──▶ referenced table
  ```

  For example:

  ```
  EMP ──▶ DEPT
  ```

  The arrow means there's a foreign key in the table from which the arrow emerges that refers to the primary key of the table to which the arrow points. Please forgive the slight sloppiness here—"the table from which the arrow emerges" would of course more correctly, albeit more clunkily, be "the table identified by the name from which the arrow emerges" (and similarly for "the table to which the arrow points," of course).
  Note: In some circumstances it might be desirable to label the arrow with the name of the relevant foreign key, but I won't bother to show such labels in the examples in what follows. Actually, "the name of the relevant foreign key" here would more correctly be "the name of the relevant foreign key constraint." The point isn't much discussed in the subject paper, but in fact constraints do always have names (possibly only implicitly)—and in the case of a referential or foreign key constraint in particular, that name is logically distinct from the name(s) of the attribute(s) involved in that foreign key.

- As we'll see later, primary keys in base tables must always have "nulls not allowed." In the example, therefore, neither DEPT.DNO nor EMP.ENO can accept nulls. Well, yes, but I reject nulls anyway.

- By contrast, foreign keys are sometimes allowed to accept nulls. (No, they're not!) In the example, the department number for employee E5 is null (meaning the department for employee E5 is unknown, perhaps, or maybe that employee E5 simply doesn't have a department for some reason). The example needs a fix of some kind. Perhaps the easiest would be just to remove the row for E5.

■ Note that, although of course every value (**nonnull by definition**) of a given foreign key is required to appear as a value of the corresponding primary key, the converse isn't so—that is, the primary key corresponding to some given foreign key might contain a value that doesn't currently appear as a value of that foreign key. In the example, the department number D3 appears in table DEPT but not in table EMP (department D3 currently has no employees).

For the remaining examples in this section I'll leave it as an exercise to choose a set of sample values to illustrate the various points discussed.

Example 2 (Courses, Offerings, and Enrollments)

```
COURSE       ( CNO , ... )
             PRIMARY KEY ( CNO )

OFFERING     ( CNO , ONO , ... )
             PRIMARY KEY ( CNO , ONO )
             FOREIGN KEY ( CNO ) REFERENCES COURSE

ENROLLMENT   ( CNO , ONO , ENO , ... )
             PRIMARY KEY ( CNO , ONO , ENO )
             FOREIGN KEY ( CNO , ONO ) REFERENCES OFFERING
```

Example 2—courses, offerings, and enrollments, where the ENROLLMENT table represents enrollments of employees (ENO) in offerings (ONO) of courses (CNO)—illustrates a number of additional points:

■ Keys, both primary and foreign, can be composite (i.e., multicolumn). Of course, a foreign key will be composite if and only if the primary key it matches is composite also. These observations miss, and in fact obscure, the real point, which is that keys are *always* sets of attributes (even if the set in question contains just one attribute). But I'll stay with the "composite" terminology for now, and come back to discuss these matters in detail later.

■ In addition to the foreign keys shown, column ENROLLMENT.CNO can also be regarded as a foreign key, referencing table COURSE. I'll discuss this point further in a later section.

- It's not necessarily the case that every component of a composite key (either primary or foreign) is itself a foreign key. Specifically, columns OFFERING.ONO, ENROLLMENT.ONO, and ENROLLMENT.ENO in the example aren't foreign keys. (Of course, ENROLLMENT.ENO in particular could become a foreign key, if an employees table were to be added to the database.)

- Table OFFERING illustrates the point that the same table can be both a referenced (or target) table and a referencing table—there's a referential constraint *to* table OFFERING from table ENROLLMENT, and a referential constraint *from* table OFFERING to table COURSE, as the following diagram indicates:

$$ENROLLMENT \longrightarrow OFFERING \longrightarrow COURSE$$

It's convenient to introduce the term *referential path*. Let tables T_n, T_{n-1}, ..., T_2, T_1 be such that there's a referential constraint from table T_n to table T_{n-1}, a referential constraint from table T_{n-1} to table T_{n-2}, ..., and finally a referential constraint from table T_2 to table T_1:

$$T_n \longrightarrow T_{n-1} \longrightarrow T_{n-2} \longrightarrow \cdots \longrightarrow T_2 \longrightarrow T_1$$

Then the chain of arrows from T_n to T_1 represents a referential path from T_n to T_1 (and that path is of length $n-1$). More precisely: There's a referential path, of length $n-1$, from T_n to T_1 if and only if (a) T_n references T_1 directly (in which case the path is of length one, of course), or (b) T_n references some T_{n-1} directly and there's a referential path from T_{n-1} to T_1. In the example, there are referential paths from ENROLLMENT to OFFERING, from OFFERING to COURSE, and from ENROLLMENT to COURSE. In fact, there are two distinct referential paths from ENROLLMENT to COURSE—one direct, of length one, and one via OFFERING, of length two:

As I've said, I'll come back and discuss this kind of situation further in a later section.

Example 3 (Suppliers and Parts)

```
S  ( SNO , SNAME , STATUS , CITY )
   PRIMARY KEY ( SNO )

P  ( PNO , PNAME , COLOR , WEIGHT , CITY )
   PRIMARY KEY ( PNO )

SP ( SNO , PNO , QTY )
   PRIMARY KEY ( SNO , PNO )
   FOREIGN KEY ( SNO ) REFERENCES S
   FOREIGN KEY ( PNO ) REFERENCES P
```

This is the well known suppliers and parts example, described in detail in reference [13] and elsewhere. It illustrates the point that a single table—table SP in the example—can include two or more distinct foreign keys:

```
S  ◀──  SP  ──▶  P
```

It also happens in the example that the combination of the two foreign keys serves as the primary key of the containing table. (I'm assuming here that there can't be two or more shipments—i.e., SP rows—for the same supplier and same part.) However, it's not necessarily the case that every component of a composite primary key is a foreign key, as we've already seen from Example 2. Nor is it necessarily the case that every foreign key is a component of a composite primary key, as we've seen from Example 1.

Example 4 (Self-Referencing)

```
EMP ( ENO , ... , SALARY , MNO , ... )
    PRIMARY KEY ( ENO )
    FOREIGN KEY ( MNO ) REFERENCES EMP
```

The MNO value in a given EMP row in this example is the employee number of the manager of the employee identified by the ENO value in that same EMP row.[4] Thus, the example illustrates the point that the referenced table and the referencing table aren't necessarily distinct; i.e., a foreign key can reference

---

[4] When I originally wrote the subject paper I hadn't fully taken on board the obvious fact that a foreign key attribute and the matching target key attribute need, formally, to be the very same attribute, and thus in particular to have the same name (implying that some attribute renaming will sometimes be necessary). This comment applies to several of the examples here and in later sections.

the primary key of its own containing table. For obvious reasons, such a table is said to be *self-referencing*. Note that, by definition, a self-referencing table such as EMP here is the sole table involved in a referential path of length one (a path from the table directly to itself):

```
EMP
```

By the way, the foreign key in this example (MNO) will probably have "nulls allowed"—no, it won't!—because at least one employee, namely the president of the company, has no manager (unless, of course, the president acts as his or her own manager). Note too that if the president's manager *is* shown as null, then that null will presumably be of the "value doesn't exist" variety, not the "value unknown" variety.

Example 5 (Referential Cycle)

```
DEPT ( DNO , ... , MNO , ... )
     PRIMARY KEY ( DNO )
     FOREIGN KEY ( MNO ) REFERENCES EMP

EMP  ( ENO , DNO , ... )
     PRIMARY KEY ( ENO )
     FOREIGN KEY ( DNO ) REFERENCES DEPT
```

A self-referencing table such as EMP in Example 4 is actually just a special case of a more general situation: namely, one in which there's a *cycle* of referential constraints. Such a cycle arises whenever there's a referential path from some table to itself. The present example shows a cycle involving two tables: Table EMP includes a foreign key (DNO) referencing table DEPT, and table DEPT includes a foreign key (MNO) referencing table EMP. In other words, there's a referential path from each table to itself (in each case, via the other table):

```
EMP   DEPT
```

In general, of course, cycles can involve any number of tables (i.e., can be of any length n where $n \geq 1$, and $n = 1$ is the self-referencing case).[5] The general picture of a cycle is thus as follows:

$$T_n \longrightarrow T_{n-1} \longrightarrow T_{n-2} \longrightarrow \ldots \longrightarrow T_2 \longrightarrow T_1 \longrightarrow T_n$$

As suggested in the discussion of the self-referencing case (Example 4 above), it's likely that at least one foreign key in a cycle will have "nulls allowed" (no, it won't)—likely, but not absolutely necessary, if integrity checking is deferred (but it mustn't be). See the section "Foreign Key Rules," later.

Example 6 (Bill of Materials)

```
P    ( PNO , ... )
     PRIMARY KEY ( PNO )

PP ( MAJOR_PNO , MINOR_PNO , QTY , ... )
     PRIMARY KEY ( MAJOR_PNO , MINOR_PNO )
     FOREIGN KEY ( MAJOR_PNO ) REFERENCES P
     FOREIGN KEY ( MINOR_PNO ) REFERENCES P
```

This is the well known "bill of materials" example: Table P is a master list of parts, and table PP shows which parts (MAJOR_PNO) contain which other parts (MINOR_PNO) as components. Each part can contain any number of components and each part can be a component of any number of parts, so there's a many to many relationship between parts and parts; hence the need for a separate table (PP) to represent that relationship. The example thus illustrates the point that a single table can include two or more foreign keys, all referencing the same target table.

---

[5] The notion of length can be a little confusing in the presence of cycles. The cycle in the example is of length two, because the path from EMP to itself involves two referential constraints, one from EMP to DEPT and one from DEPT back to EMP again. (Similarly for the path from DEPT to itself, of course.) As you can see, therefore, the cycle in the example, of length two, involves two paths (two "subpaths," if you like), each of which is of length one.

In an example like this one, incidentally, there are once again several referential paths (all of them of length one, in this particular case) from the referencing table to the target table. To repeat, this issue will be discussed further in a later section.

Note: The situation illustrated by the bill of materials example is sometimes confused (but shouldn't be) with that illustrated by the previous example (the referential cycle example). There's no cycle here.

Example 7 (Employees and Programmers)

```
EMP   ( ENO , ... , JOB , ... )
      PRIMARY KEY ( ENO )

PGMR ( ENO , ... , LANG , ... )
      PRIMARY KEY ( ENO )
      FOREIGN KEY ( ENO ) REFERENCES EMP
```

This final example illustrates the point that a foreign key can also be the primary key of its containing table. Table EMP lists all employees, and table PGMR lists just those employees that are programmers; thus, every employee appearing in PGMR must also appear in EMP (but the converse is false). So the primary key of table PGMR is also a foreign key, referring to the primary key of table EMP. Note that the two tables can be regarded as representing, respectively, an entity subtype (programmers) and the corresponding entity supertype (employees). In fact, the example is typical of the way entity subtypes and supertypes would be represented in a relational database [17]. This use of subtype and supertype terminology to explicate situations such as the one at hand is deprecated, somewhat. See Example 9 in Chapter 2 for further discussion.

As an aside, let me point out that there's another integrity constraint that also needs to be maintained in this example—a given employee must be represented in table PGMR if and only if the value of EMP.JOB for that employee is "Programmer." However, this constraint isn't a referential constraint as such. See references [14] and [21] for a discussion of integrity constraints in general.

———— ◆ ◆ ◆ ◆ ◆ ————

The foregoing examples and discussion illustrate the general point that absolutely any column can be a foreign key; furthermore, of course, any column can become (or indeed cease to be) a foreign key as the database evolves over time. I now proceed to examine some of Codd's writings on such matters. But I've already done this and more in Chapter 3, so I'll omit the next four sections of the subject paper here.

A PROPOSAL

My own preferred definitions are as follows.

Primary Keys

In order to define the primary key concept precisely, it's necessary first to define a more primitive notion, viz., "candidate key." Attribute *CK* (possibly composite) of relation *R* is a *candidate key* for *R* if and only if it satisfies the following two time-independent properties:

1. *Uniqueness*: At any given time, no two rows of *R* have the same value for *CK*.

2. *Minimality*: If *CK* is composite, no component of *CK* can be eliminated without destroying the uniqueness property.

First, I now prefer the term *irreducibility* to the term *minimality* in this context. More to the point, though, I'd prefer to drop the candidate key concept altogether and regard the foregoing as a formal definition of just a *key*, unqualified. Other mentions of "candidate" keys in the subject paper would then have be adjusted accordingly, of course. Also, the opening clause of this subsection notwithstanding, I'm not sure it's possible to define the primary key notion *precisely*. A primary key is just a key that's been singled out—not, in general, according to any formal criteria—for special syntactic treatment. That's all.

From the set of candidate keys for a given relation, exactly one is chosen as the *primary* key for that relation; the remainder, if any, are called *alternate* keys [13]. An alternate key is thus a candidate key that's not the primary key. (I don't disagree that it might be desirable in practice to choose one key as primary, but the reasons for doing so will be purely pragmatic—a matter of possibly convenient shorthand, that's all. In fact, the SQL standard does exactly this. By contrast, **Tutorial D** doesn't support the primary key notion at all.) Note that:

- In practice it's the primary key that's the really important one. (I no longer agree with this statement.) Candidate keys and alternate keys are merely concepts that necessarily arise during the process of defining the more important concept "primary key." (Though alternate keys can occasionally be significant also. See reference [22] for further discussion of this point.) The text in parentheses here is just more evidence in support of the position that "primary" keys shouldn't be distinguished semantically from "alternate" keys, but rather that "primary" and "alternate" keys are better all treated, at least semantically, as just keys (i.e., as all equal to one another, semantically if not syntactically).

- The rationale by which the primary key is chosen, in cases where there's a choice, is beyond the scope of the relational model as such. In practice the choice is usually straightforward. But informal, and necessarily so.

Foreign Keys

Attribute *FK* (possibly composite) of base relation R_2 is a foreign key if and only if it satisfies the following two time-independent properties: (Replace "Attribute *FK* (possibly composite)" by "Subset *FK* of the heading.")

1. Each value of *FK* is either wholly null or wholly nonnull. Since I now reject nulls entirely, this first requirement can be deleted. So can the qualifier "nonnull" in the second requirement (see the paragraph immediately following), and indeed everywhere it appears.

2. There exists a base relation R_1 (not necessarily distinct from R_2) with primary key *PK* such that each nonnull value of *FK* is identical to the value of *PK* in some row of R_1. Since I now reject primary keys—at least as anything more than just a possibly convenient syntactic shorthand—the qualifier "primary" can be deleted.

R_1 and R_2 are known as the *referenced* (or *target*) relation and the *referencing* relation, respectively.

Discussion

1. My definition of primary key is intended to be equivalent to Codd's [12]; the only point that seems to need any elaboration here is the requirement that candidate (and hence primary) keys satisfy the minimality property. The purpose of that requirement is merely to ensure that, for example, the composite attribute S.(SNO,CITY) in the suppliers relation S isn't considered as a candidate key for that relation (i.e., because CITY is irrelevant for unique identification purposes).

  Note: As Codd points out in reference [12], the fact that a given candidate key CK_1 satisfies the minimality requirement doesn't mean that another candidate key CK_2 can't exist that involves fewer components; it's entirely possible, for example, that CK_1 involves three simple attributes and CK_2 only two. Note too that if relation R were to include a foreign key for which the corresponding "primary key" failed to satisfy the minimality requirement, then relation R would probably not be in third normal form [9].

2. Attributes $R_1.PK$ and $R_2.FK$ in the definition of foreign key should be defined on the same domain (**better:** *be of the same type*).[6] *Note:* Actually, this point is implied by the definition of domain [12,19]; I deliberately didn't call it out explicitly, however, because a system can provide a useful level of support for foreign keys without necessarily having to provide full support for domains as well. I do agree that full support for foreign keys would require full support for domains as well.

The next paragraph refers to "composite" domains and keys (and implicitly composite attributes also), but it would be better to avoid such terminology, and in particular to recognize that key values are *tuples*. I leave the detailed fixes as an exercise.

3. As the definitions indicate, both primary and foreign keys are allowed to be composite. (Of course, a foreign key will be composite if and only if its matching primary key is composite. This fact is implied by the fact that the foreign key and its matching primary key must be defined on the same domain—

---

[6] Better still: *be the very same attribute*.

the domain being composite in the case under consideration—but is probably worth calling out explicitly.) However, I do believe as suggested earlier that composite keys need to be treated with care. Once again, see later for further discussion.

4. I agree with Codd that nulls shouldn't be allowed in primary keys (at least in base tables). **No, they shouldn't be allowed** *anywhere*. As previously noted, Codd refers to this requirement as "entity integrity." For convenience, let me spell it out again here:

> **Definition (entity integrity):** The entity integrity rule states that no attribute that participates in the primary key of a base relation is allowed to accept nulls.

See later for further discussion. **Actually not.**

5. In contrast to the previous point, I believe both types of null (or "mark" [11])—namely, "value unknown" and "property doesn't apply"—should be legal for foreign keys, in general. **No, they shouldn't be allowed** *anywhere*. In fact, I suspect that the "property doesn't apply" type is likely to be needed more often than the "value unknown" type in this context.
Note: Other types of null might also be required (in this context as well as others). **No. It's true, speaking rather loosely, that if entities of type** *B* **are generally supposed to reference entities of type** *A*, **then, first, there might be some entities of type** *B* **for which such a reference makes no sense; second, for the entities of type** *B* **in question, there might be several different reasons why such a reference makes no sense ("value unknown," "property doesn't apply," possibly others too; see Chapters 12 and 13 of my book** *Database Dreaming Volume I*, **Technics, 2022, for a detailed discussion of some of those "several different reasons"). But these facts don't necessarily mean the system has to support different kinds of nulls, or indeed any kind at all, nor that foreign keys have to "accept" such nulls.**

6. The expression "wholly null or wholly nonnull" in the definition of foreign key is explicitly intended to exclude the possibility that a multiattribute foreign key value might have some components null and others nonnull (because—as I've suggested several times already—I believe this latter possibility leads to

undesirable and unnecessary complexity). **Yes indeed.** Once again, see later for further discussion.

7. Reference [10] introduces the concept of "primary domains," but I don't find it to be particularly useful—at least, not in this context; it might be useful in other contexts, such as database design. **Not demonstrated.** I've therefore excluded it from my proposed definitions. **Good.**

8. Note that the foreign key definition is framed explicitly in terms of base relations. Extensions to handle derived relations (views in particular) can be added at a later time if desired. **OK, I was appealing here, tacitly but I think validly, to *The Principle of Cautious Design*. But now we have a much better idea of the kinds of extensions we need (see Chapters 1 and 2), and I now regard them as an intrinsic part of the definition accordingly.**

> *Note*: I've deliberately been ignoring the question of foreign keys for views in particular (**OK—see above**). The topic is interesting (**yes**), and important for view updating purposes (**yes, somewhat**), but it isn't directly relevant to referential integrity as such. (**Yes it is! I suppose I was thinking, when I wrote the subject paper, that referential integrity—and indeed all kinds of integrity— applied to the base data only. After all, if the base data is correct, then derived data will be correct too, a fortiori. But what I hadn't fully taken on board at the time was *The Principle of Interchangeability*—see Chapter 1. I've since seen the error of my ways; I mean, I now realize that there are several good reasons why it's important to be able to define integrity constraints for derived data too.**)

9. I deliberately require there to be a single target relation for each foreign key. (**This is still my position, except that now of course I'd frame it in terms of relvars, not relations.**) I feel this is a justifiable simplification at this stage of development. If someone comes along subsequently with a genuine requirement for one of the three cases discussed earlier, then there are two ways we could go:

a. We could extend the foreign key definition accordingly.

b. We could leave the foreign key definition alone and insist that the situation be treated as a particular kind of "general" integrity constraint (i.e., a constraint that's handled by means of a general integrity language such as that described in references [14] and [21], instead of by means of special case syntax).

Method b. complies with my preferred definition of foreign key: It's simpler, and it has the virtue of encouraging clean database designs. Moreover, Method b. doesn't preclude the adoption of Method a. at a later time. To elaborate briefly on this latter point: If Method b. is adopted now, then Method a. can be adopted subsequently if desired, when all the ramifications are thoroughly understood. What's more, if Method a. does subsequently prove desirable, it'll be a compatible extension—existing programs and databases won't thereby be invalidated. I therefore vote for Method b.
  Note: This vote of mine for Method b. can be seen as an application of *The Principle of Cautious Design.* **Yes indeed.**

10. Finally, I do *not* propose a definition for referential integrity that's separate from the concept of foreign key. **Good.** I don't find such a separation either useful or desirable. However, both terms need to be explained, since both appear in the existing literature. I therefore propose the following definition:

> **Definition (referential integrity):** The referential integrity rule states that the database must never contain any unmatched foreign key values (where an unmatched foreign key value is a nonnull foreign key value for which there doesn't exist a matching value of the primary key in the relevant target relation).

FOREIGN KEY RULES

In reference [15] I extended the basic idea of referential integrity by introducing a set of *foreign key rules*, which specified what the DBMS should do if a user attempted to perform an update that, if just blindly executed, would violate some referential constraint. The general intent of those rules was to enable the DBMS to maintain the integrity of the data either (a) by rejecting such an attempted update, or (b) by accepting it but performing some appropriate compensatory action on some other part of the database. Here are the rules I proposed:

■ A nulls rule (ALLOWED or NOT ALLOWED)

■ A delete rule (RESTRICTED or CASCADES or NULLIFIES)

■ An update rule (RESTRICTED or CASCADES or NULLIFIES)

NULLIFIES, of course, I no longer believe in at all (and all mention of NULLIFIES in what follows should be deleted; I'll reinforce this point here and there in what follows, but I won't keep on saying it). As for CASCADES and RESTRICTED: Per Chapter 2, I now prefer the keywords (or spellings) CASCADE and NO ACTION, respectively, but otherwise I still support them.

The following explanation of these rules is based on that given in reference [13], which uses the familiar suppliers and parts database as a basis for its explanations and examples.

First of all, note that the referential integrity rule as given in the previous section is framed purely in terms of database states. Any state of the database that fails to satisfy the rule is by definition incorrect; but how exactly are such incorrect states to be avoided? The rule itself doesn't say.

One possibility, of course, would be for the system to reject any operation that, if executed, would result in an illegal state. Sometimes, however, a preferable alternative would be for the system to accept the operation but to perform certain additional compensatory actions, if necessary, in order to guarantee that the overall result is still a legal state. For example, if the user asks to delete the row for supplier S1 from relation S, it should be possible to get the system to delete the shipment rows for supplier S1 from relation SP as well, without any further action on the part of the user (assuming that such a "cascade delete" effect is indeed what's wanted).

It follows that, for any given database, it should be possible for the user—in this context, probably the database designer [17]—to specify which operations should be rejected and which accepted, and, for those that are accepted, what compensatory actions if any should be performed by the system. For each foreign key, therefore, the database designer needs to answer three questions, as follows:

1. Can that foreign key accept nulls? For example, does it make sense for a shipment to exist for which the supplier is unknown? The answer in this particular case is probably no. But in other situations the answer might

well be different; for example, in the case of the departments and employees database, it might well be possible for some employee to be currently assigned to no department at all. **Delete this paragraph!**

2. What should happen on an attempt to delete the target of a foreign key reference?—for example, an attempt to delete a supplier for which there exists at least one matching shipment? For definiteness, let's consider this case explicitly. In general there are at least three possibilities:

    a. RESTRICTED (NO ACTION) The operation is "restricted" to the case in which there are no such matching shipments, and is rejected otherwise.

    b. CASCADES (CASCADE) The operation "cascades" to delete those matching shipments also.

    c. NULLIFIES (Drop this option.) The foreign key is set to null in all such matching shipments and the supplier is then deleted (of course, this case won't apply if the foreign key doesn't accept nulls in the first place).

3. What should happen on an attempt to update the primary key (**better: *referenced key***) of the target of a foreign key reference?—for example, an attempt to update the supplier number for a supplier for which there exists at least one matching shipment? For definiteness, again, let's consider this case explicitly. In general there are at least the same three possibilities as for DELETE:

    a. RESTRICTED (NO ACTION) The operation is "restricted" to the case in which there are no such matching shipments, and is rejected otherwise.

    b. CASCADES (CASCADE) The operation "cascades" to update those matching shipments also.

    c. NULLIFIES (Drop this option.) The foreign key is set to null in all such matching shipments and the supplier is then

updated (of course, this case won't apply if the
foreign key doesn't accept nulls in the first place).

For each foreign key in the design, therefore, the designer should specify,
not only the attribute or attribute combination constituting that foreign key and
the target relation referenced by that foreign key, but also the answers to the
foregoing three questions (i.e., the three rules that apply to that foreign key).
Hence the following syntax proposal for a FOREIGN KEY clause (part of a base
table definition)—

```
FOREIGN KEY ( foreign-key ) REFERENCES target
          NULLS [ NOT ] ALLOWED
          DELETE OF target effect
          UPDATE OF target-primary-key effect
```

—where *effect* is RESTRICTED or CASCADES or NULLIFIES. (Drop NULLS
[NOT] ALLOWED, and replace *target-primary-key* by *target-key*.)
Added later: The foregoing was originally written in 1981 or thereabouts
[15]. Some additional comments are appropriate at this time:

1. It's important to understand that, from a logical point of view, database update
operations are always atomic (all or nothing), even if under the covers they
involve several row updates on several tables because of, e.g., a CASCADES
delete rule (possibly even several such rules). Yes, this is important, and it
should have received more emphasis in the original text.

2. Note that there's no explicit insert rule. Instead, INSERTs on the referencing
table (also UPDATEs on the foreign key in the referencing table) are governed
by the combination of (a) the nulls rule and (b) the basic referential integrity rule
itself, i.e., the requirement that there be no nonnull unmatched foreign key
values. In other words, taking suppliers and parts as a concrete example:

- An attempt to INSERT a shipment (SP) row will succeed only if (a) the
  supplier number in that row exists as a supplier number in table S (or is
  null, if nulls are allowed) *and* (b) the part number in that row exists as a
  part number in table P (or is null, if nulls are allowed).
  Note: Actually, of course, columns SNO and PNO in table SP must
  have "nulls not allowed," because they're components of the primary key
  of that table. This comment applies to the next bulleted paragraph as well.

■ An attempt to UPDATE a shipment (SP) row will succeed only if (a) the supplier number in the updated row exists as a supplier number in table S (or is null, if nulls are allowed) *and* (b) the part number in the updated row exists as a part number in table P (or is null, if nulls are allowed).

Note also that the foregoing applies to the referencing table, whereas the delete and update rules apply to the referenced table. Thus, to talk about an insert rule as such (i.e., as if such a rule were somehow similar to the existing delete and update rules) might be a little confusing.

3. Let T_2 and T_1 be, respectively, a referencing table and the corresponding referenced table—

$$T_2 \longrightarrow T_1$$

—and let the delete rule for the referential constraint be CASCADES. Then a DELETE on a given row of table T_1 will imply a DELETE on corresponding rows (if any) of table T_2. Now let table T_2 in turn be referenced by some other table T_3:

$$T_3 \longrightarrow T_2 \longrightarrow T_1$$

Then the effect of the implied DELETE on rows of T_2 is exactly the same as if an attempt had been made to delete those rows directly; i.e., it depends on the delete rule specified for the referential constraint from T_3 to T_2. If that implied DELETE fails (because of the delete rule from T_3 to T_2 or for any other reason), then the entire operation fails and the database remains unchanged. And so on, recursively, to any number of levels.

4. The remarks of the previous paragraph apply to the CASCADES update rule also, mutatis mutandis, if the foreign key in table T_2 is part of (or has any columns in common with) the primary key (**better:** *target key*) of that table.

5. Consider the following referential cycle:

$$T_n \longrightarrow T_{n-1} \longrightarrow T_{n-2} \longrightarrow \ldots \longrightarrow T_2 \longrightarrow T_1 \longrightarrow T_n$$

Clearly, either (a) at least one foreign key in this cycle must have nulls allowed, or (b) some constraint checking can't be done at the time of the individual update but must instead be deferred to some later time, such as COMMIT time (end of transaction). For if neither (a) nor (b) applies, there'll be no way to insert a row into any of the tables involved. **But there's another solution—a better one— that requires neither nulls nor COMMIT-time checking! See the discussion of multiple assignment in Chapters 1 and 2.**

For reasons such as the foregoing (and possibly other reasons also, beyond the scope of the present discussion), integrity constraints—i.e., integrity constraints in general, not just referential constraints—need to be divided into two categories, immediate and deferred:

- *Immediate* means the constraint is checked as part of the processing of each and every update statement that might violate it. Immediate constraints are required to be satisfied at statement boundaries. The system is responsible for ensuring that this requirement is met.

- *Deferred* means such immediate checking doesn't occur; instead, the checking is deferred to some later time (e.g., COMMIT time, or perhaps even later). **No. I now reject deferred checking as logically incorrect[7]—all checking should be immediate, and the rest of the text of this point 5. should be deleted.**

For integrity constraints in general, additional research is certainly needed to identify all of the requirements and implications of deferred checking in full detail. For referential constraints specifically, however, deferred checking simply means that if table T_2 contains a foreign key FK referring to the primary PK of table T_1, then a nonnull value can be introduced into column $T_2.FK$ (via an INSERT or UPDATE on table T_2) that doesn't currently exist as a value in column $T_1.PK$. Of course, it'll still be an error if any such unmatched values still exist in column $T_2.FK$ by the time the checking is performed, whenever that happens to be.

In order to cater for the foregoing, we need to introduce an extension to the FOREIGN KEY clause to allow the checking time to be specified, e.g., as follows:

---

[7] "Perhaps even later" is even more wrong!—if the notion of *degrees of wrongness* can even be said to make any sense.

```
FOREIGN KEY ( foreign-key ) REFERENCES target
          CHECK checking-time
          NULLS [ NOT ] ALLOWED
          DELETE OF target effect
          UPDATE OF target-primary-key effect
```

In this syntax, *checking-time* is either IMMEDIATE or AT COMMIT. *Note*: Other possible checking times might conceivably be introduced at some future point. No! IMMEDIATE is the only one that makes logical sense.

From this point forward, I'll assume for simplicity that all referential constraint checking is immediate, barring any explicit statement to the contrary— i.e., I'll assume CHECK IMMEDIATE is the default.

6. The nulls rule (nulls allowed or not allowed) will require some refinement if the relational model and/or relational products are ever extended to incorporate distinct kinds of null—for example, if "value unknown" is ever formally distinguished from "property doesn't apply." Of course, an analogous remark applies to every aspect of the model that involves nulls—e.g., the entity integrity rule, the outer join operation, etc. Delete this paragraph.

7. The SQL standard committees are currently (1988) proposing a set of extensions to the SQL standard somewhat along the lines sketched above [5], and IBM in particular has recently incorporated some but not all of the proposed functionality into Version 2.1 of DB2 and Version 2.2 of SQL/DS [2,3,6,7]. But the standard and IBM versions both suffer from an unfortunate excess of complexity, owing in part to the fact that they're defined at too low a level of abstraction (row at a time instead of set at a time). See Chapters 5 and 6 for a brief sketch of the standard version and the IBM version, respectively.

8. Of course, the RESTRICTED – CASCADES – NULLIFIES options for the foreign key delete and update rules don't exhaust the possibilities; they merely represent a set of cases that are commonly required in practice. (NULLIFIES is perhaps required less often than the other two. How about never?[8]) In principle, however, there could be an arbitrary number of possible responses to, e.g., an attempt to delete a particular supplier. For example:

---

[8] Sorry, this is a bit of an in joke—Codd once wrote a paper called "How about Recently?" (*Proc. International Conference on Databases: Improving Usability and Responsiveness*, Haifa, Israel, August 2nd-3rd, 1978).

- A conversation could be held with the end user.

- Information could be written to some archive file.

- The shipments for the supplier in question could be transferred to some other supplier.

It'll never be feasible to provide declarative syntax for all conceivable responses. In general, therefore, *effect* in the syntax above should be extended to include the possibility of invoking a user defined procedure (this possibility was overlooked in reference [15]).

Note: The proposals of reference [5] in fact do include at least one additional explicitly defined "effect," namely PENDANT, which can be characterized informally as "last one out turns off the light"—for example, deleting the last employee in a given department causes the department to be deleted also. However, the PENDANT rule seems to lead to a very great deal of additional complexity. My own feeling is that the whole area of additional possible "effects" stands in need of further research. **Yes!**

9. For reasons beyond the scope of the present discussion—see reference [24] for further specifics—it might be the case that some tables won't permit direct DELETE operations at all (i.e., DELETE NOT ALLOWED will be specified as part of the definition of the table in question). If T_1 is such a table and $T_2.FK$ is a foreign key that references it, then any delete rule for that foreign key would be completely irrelevant and should thus not be specified at all.

10. In a similar vein—see the discussion of surrogate keys later—some primary keys might not permit UPDATE operations at all (i.e., UPDATE NOT ALLOWED will be specified as part of the definition of the primary key in question). If $T_1.PK$ is such a primary key and $T_2.FK$ is a foreign key that references it, then any update rule for that foreign key would be completely irrelevant and should thus not be specified at all.

Part II of the subject paper began with the following list of issues to be discussed:

- Why every table should have exactly one primary key (I no longer agree with this position—see further comments below)

- Why foreign keys should match primary keys, not alternate keys (I no longer agree with this position either—again, see further comments below)

- Why foreign keys aren't pointers (OK)

- Why key definitions should be special cased (OK)

- Why conterminous referential paths should be treated with caution (OK)

- Why primary key values in base tables shouldn't be wholly or partly null (first, replace "primary key" by just "key"; second, delete "in base tables"; third, no "value" can be null anyway—it's a contradiction in terms; fourth, I reject nulls 100% anyway, so actually *nothing* can "be null," be it either wholly or partly)

- Why composite foreign key values shouldn't be partly null (first, I no longer much care for that composite vs. noncomposite terminology; second, I reject nulls 100% anyway, so actually *nothing* can "be null," be it either wholly or partly)

- Why overlapping keys should be treated with caution (OK)

- Why noncomposite keys are a good idea (I no longer much care for that composite vs. noncomposite terminology)

- Why a single target table is a good idea (OK)

The foregoing list was followed by an explanation of *The Principle of Cautious Design*. I omit that explanation here, except for just this one sentence:

> *The Principle of Cautious Design* is directly relevant to almost all of the discussions to follow.

Yes, it is, even in those cases where I've changed my mind—like the first two items above, in fact!—since I first wrote the subject paper, back in the 1980s. Indeed, in most of those cases, it was adherence to *The Principle of Cautious Design* that allowed me to do that—change my mind, I mean—without getting into serious "backward compatibility" issues.

The one exception to the foregoing happy state of affairs is, of course, ***nulls***. I originally supported nulls, and now I don't. Well, I know I'm not the only person to have changed his or her mind on that particular topic. Along with all those other people I wish, now, that nulls had never been invented, and never incorporated into SQL, and never implemented in DBMS products. But it's too late for all that, of course. So what we have to do, as I've said, is simply do our best to ensure that users are educated about the problems and are thereby motivated to avoid nulls like the plague they are.

Of course, it's quite difficult, if not impossible, to avoid nulls in SQL 100%. Even if you make the sensible decision never to have any nulls in your database as such, there are situations where SQL actually generates nulls, dynamically. For example, if you ask for the sum of a set of numbers, and that set happens to be empty, then SQL gives a null. (It should give zero, of course, but it doesn't.) As a consequence, you have to include tests and repairs and workarounds in your SQL code to make sure that such "generated" nulls are always immediately replaced by a genuine value, or otherwise removed, before they have a chance to do any further damage. But such matters are beyond the scope of this discussion; if you want to know more—in particular, if you want some concrete recommendations in this regard—then I refer you once again to my book *SQL and Relational Theory: How to Write Accurate SQL Code*, 3rd edition (O'Reilly, 2015).

There's one more point I want to make before we start getting into details: Several of the issues raised in what follows are somewhat complex in nature, and the reader might be forgiven for concluding that referential integrity is a complicated topic. However, while I might agree with that conclusion, I would also argue, strongly, that the complexities in question are inherent (for the most part, at any rate). In other words, the complexities in question aren't ones that are introduced by the relational foreign key and referential integrity concepts as such; rather, they're complexities that are intrinsic to the way the world is. Indeed, a good case can be made that the relational concepts allow us to articulate certain real world problems in a precise manner, thereby giving us a good basis for addressing those problems. The discussions in the rest of this paper should be seen in this light. This is all still basically true.

WHY EVERY TABLE SHOULD HAVE EXACTLY ONE PRIMARY KEY (?)

To repeat, this is one of the issues I've changed my mind on—but I think it's worth taking a look at the original text of the pertinent section nevertheless. First, however, let me state for the record exactly what I do now believe in this connection:

> Every relvar has at least one key. For a base relvar, at least one key must be explicitly declared. For a derived relvar, the system might or might not be able to determine the pertinent key(s) for itself, but in any case it should be possible to declare keys explicitly. For any relvar, one key might perhaps be designated as "primary"—but if it is, it's merely a matter of pragmatic convenience and has no semantic significance.
>
> Given the foregoing, I suppose we have to retain, though downplay, the term *alternate key*; I mean, if we're allowed to choose one key as primary, then we need a term to refer to the ones not so chosen. By contrast, the term *candidate key* is no longer needed—a "candidate" key is just a key, period.

I've argued in favor of this position (i.e., that every table should have exactly one primary key) at some length elsewhere [16], and I don't want to repeat all the details here. The argument is essentially as follows:

- Entities are identifiable, by definition (i.e., they have identity). True.

- The relational model requires entity identifiers (like everything else) to be represented by values. True.

- Primary key values serve, precisely, as the necessary representations. Replace "primary key values" by "key values" and this sentence becomes true; otherwise it's only partly true.

The foregoing argument shows why each table (each base table, at least) should certainly have at least one unique identifier—i.e., at least one key, in relational terms. (It also shows by implication why base tables, at least, don't permit duplicate rows [20].) The next question is, of course, what if some table has two or more such identifiers? Here the argument goes as follows:

- Suppose some given table does have two or more unique identifiers. (By "table" here, I originally meant a base relvar specifically—but a derived relvar also can have two or more keys, of course.)

- Then not distinguishing one of those identifiers as primary (i.e., treating them all as interchangeable) leads to unnecessary complexity. **Not necessarily true. Reference [22] gives some counterexamples.**

To paraphrase an example first given by Codd in reference [12], a relational system that failed to distinguish one of the identifiers as primary would be like a memory addressing scheme that failed to provide a single, unique way of addressing individual memory cells—the point being, of course, that primary keys *are* the addressing mechanism (the row level addressing mechanism, that is) in the relational model. **No, it's keys in general that are the addressing mechanism. The memory addressing analogy is specious.**

Now, it's sometimes argued that synonyms (i.e., two or more different names for the same thing) are normal and natural in the real world **(true)**, and hence that having to distinguish one identifier as primary is artificial **(certainly true in some cases)** and unduly restrictive **(possibly true in some cases)**. I would respond to this argument as follows:

- It's certainly true that synonyms exist in the real world, and hence we certainly do need a way of dealing with them in our formal database systems. **OK.**

- However, it's also true that synonyms can cause confusion in the real world. And it's obviously desirable to try to avoid such confusion, most especially within our disciplined—or would-be disciplined—database systems. **OK.**

■ Inside the database, therefore, "one name for one thing" is a good principle,
even if we can't persuade people to adhere to that principle outside the
system. **A good principle, yes—but not necessarily one to be followed in
cases where there are good reasons not to.** (In fact, using *surrogates*—
i.e., identifiers with no inherent meaning—is often an even better principle.
True. I'll return to this point later.)

In general, of course, the database will also need to include special
conversion tables, mapping the variety of external identifiers that apply to some
entity to that entity's single internal identifier (in other words, the corresponding
primary key). **Not necessarily. There might not be any need for the system as a
whole to be aware that two distinct identifiers actually refer to the same real
world entity.** And in some cases it *might* be desirable to conceal that internal
identifier from users by means of the system's view mechanism—though it's true
that this technique might lead to performance and/or updatability problems, given
the limitations of most current implementations. On the whole, it's probably
better to expose the internal identifiers to the user. **All true.**

Added later: Recently, Codd unfortunately seems to have been shifting his
position, or at least using a different set of terms, in connection with the primary
key question. Given that certain relational operations can generate tables
containing primary key values that are either wholly or partly null—**not in "my"
relational model, they can't!**—Codd now suggests that the term *primary key* be
reserved for tables (perhaps just base tables?) for which it can be guaranteed that
the primary key has "nulls not allowed"; for tables (perhaps views?) for which
such a guarantee can't be made, he suggests that the term *weak identifier* be used
instead [12].

In my opinion this change should be resisted. The term *primary key* has
been used with its original meaning in countless places—books, papers,
specifications, database designs, manuals, etc., not to mention products and
presentations and discussions—ever since Codd first defined it in reference [8].
To change it now can only cause confusion. In fact, Codd himself uses it with its
original meaning in the very paper in which he introduces the "weak identifier"
term, when he says that "each relation [has] *exactly one* primary key" [12]. In
what follows, I'll continue to use "primary key" in its original sense. **Yes, I will,
but that "original sense," to me, isn't as significant as I once thought it was. To
say it again, the distinction between keys in general and primary keys in
particular is merely a matter of syntax (or pragma), not one of semantics.**

Note: Codd also states in that same reference [12] that it's "completely unnecessary" for a primary key to be "declared or deduced" for any relation that's not a base relation or a view or a snapshot.[9] I disagree with this position also; there are good reasons why it's highly desirable for the system to be able to deduce the primary key of the result of *any arbitrary relational expression.* (OK, except that "the primary key" should be replaced by "the keys.") See the paper "The Keys of the Kingdom" in my book *Relational Database Writings 1985-1989* (Addison-Wesley, 1990).[10]

WHY FOREIGN KEYS SHOULD MATCH PRIMARY KEYS, NOT ALTERNATE KEYS (?)

As you know by now, this is another issue I've changed my mind on—I now believe a foreign key should be allowed to match any key, not necessarily one that's been singled out as "primary"—but again I think it's worth taking a look at my original text nevertheless.

An alternate key is a candidate key that's not the primary key of the table in question. For example, the PERSON table might have two candidate keys, SSNO (social security number) and LICNO (driver's license number); if we choose SSNO as the primary key, then LICNO would be an alternate key. *Note:* Actually, as we'll see below, it might be the case that SSNO and LICNO both have nulls allowed and hence not be usable as the primary key. (Well, I'd rather put it this way: Not everyone has a social security number, and not everyone has a driver's license; so any design that assumes the opposite is bad by definition, and the example intuitively fails.) But let's ignore this point for the moment.

Now, it's sometimes suggested that foreign keys should be permitted to match, not necessarily the primary key, but rather any candidate key in the target table. For example, one table T_1 might have a foreign key matching the primary key PERSON.SSNO, and another table T_2 might have a foreign key matching the

---

[9] A snapshot is a named derived table, like a view; unlike a view, however, a snapshot is "real," not virtual (like a base table, in fact). Snapshots aren't very important so far as we're are concerned here, and I propose to ignore them from this point forward.

[10] Hugh Darwen is the author of that paper, but he wrote it using the pen name "Andrew Warden." But in any case a more recent paper by Hugh is more relevant—"The Role of Functional Dependence in Query Decomposition," in our joint book *Relational Database Writings 1989-1991* (Addison-Wesley, 1992).

alternate key PERSON.LICNO. In fact, the currently proposed extensions to the SQL standard [4,5] explicitly permit such a possibility. Good for the standard! The IBM products DB2 and SQL/DS [2,3]—to their credit—don't. I was wrong. It's not particularly to their credit after all. But it's not a big deal.

The argument against this position is essentially the same as the argument against "two or more primary keys" and is thus subject to the same criticisms; indeed, allowing a foreign key to match an alternate key is just one specific aspect of allowing "two or more primary keys." Briefly, allowing "two or more primary keys"—in particular, allowing a foreign key to match an alternate key— doesn't seem to provide a useful level of additional functionality, and it certainly does cause additional complexity. (The proposed SQL extensions [4,5] bear eloquent witness to this claim.)

I no longer completely agree with the remarks in the foregoing paragraph. To be specific:

1. If there aren't any primary keys but only keys, unqualified, then obviously a foreign key must be allowed to reference a key that hasn't been defined as primary.

2. Even if primary keys are defined, there are still situations where allowing a foreign key to reference a key not defined as primary seems appropriate and desirable.

3. (Re my suggestion that the proposed SQL extensions cause additional complexity:) I'm no longer sure this is true. First of all, the SQL language is pretty complex anyway. Second, I'm not convinced that allowing a foreign key to reference any key complicates the language any more than requiring it to match a primary key does. Third, the SQL standard documentation, like the SQL language itself, is pretty complex too!—but I don't think it's fair to lay *all* of the blame for that documentary complexity at the feet of the language the documents are trying to describe. Rather, I think part of the blame has to be laid at the feet of the people who write the documents in question. The plain truth is, those documents are badly organized and, in places, quite badly written. I've given plenty of examples of these shortcomings in other books of mine; see, e.g.,

Chapters 1-2 and 4-5 of my book *Stating the Obvious, and Other Database Writings* (Technics, 2020).

The rest of my original text in this section strikes me as unclear—and that's being charitable to my earlier self!—and thus not worth repeating or commenting on here, so I'll omit it.

WHY FOREIGN KEYS AREN'T POINTERS

Critics have been known to suggest that foreign keys are nothing more than pointers in disguise (pointers, of course, being prohibited in the relational model). The following list—which is probably incomplete—of logical differences between the two concepts shows why that suggestion is incorrect.

- Foreign keys are logical, pointers are physical. More precisely: Foreign keys are defined at the relational (logical) level, pointers are defined at the storage (physical) level. The suggestion that foreign keys are pointers in disguise thus stems from a basic confusion over levels of abstraction; foreign keys are a higher level abstraction than pointers. (It's true that pointers might be used to implement foreign keys—though in practice they almost never are, at least in today's mainstream SQL products—but they're by no means the only possible implementation.)

- Pointers identify stored records (more precisely, locations in storage); foreign keys identify entities. Well, a little more accurately: Pointers (pointer values, that is) are addresses of stored records, foreign key values are references to tuples.

- Foreign keys usually have inherent "real world" meaning—i.e., they can be understood outside the system—whereas pointers certainly don't and can't. Contrast, for example, the foreign key value D4 (a department number, referring to a certain specific department), which does have meaning outside the system, vs. a pointer to a stored record for that department, which probably consists of some obscure disk address.

- Foreign keys don't change their value if the target to which they refer moves to another location. (In fact, of course, the relational model has no notion of "location" in this sense, anyway.)

- Foreign keys can be composite, pointers can't. Or rather: Foreign key values are tuples, pointer values are scalars.

- Pointers have physical performance connotations, foreign keys don't.[11]

- Pointers are a special data type, one that's quite different from the conventional "real data" data types. As a consequence, they require special operators of their own—e.g., CONNECT, DISCONNECT, and RECONNECT (these examples are taken from CODASYL [1]). Foreign keys, by contrast, are simply conventional data, and they're represented in terms of conventional data types; thus, they don't require special operators. Instead, functions analogous to CONNECT, DISCONNECT, and RECONNECT are performed by the conventional data manipulation operators INSERT, DELETE, and UPDATE.

- Pointers also require special "referencing" and "dereferencing" operators, which foreign keys don't. To elaborate briefly: Given a variable *V*, the referencing operator applied to *V* returns a pointer to *V*; conversely, given a variable *P* containing a pointer, the dereferencing operator applied to *P* returns the variable the pointer in *P* points to.

- Pointers *point*: That is, they have directionality, and they have a single, specific target. Foreign key values, by contrast, are regular data values: A given foreign key value is simultaneously connected, logically speaking, to all references to the entity in question, no matter where in the database those references happen to be. For example, the department row for department D4 is logically connected to all rows for employees in that department, and each of those employee rows is logically connected to all of the others and to the pertinent department row as well. In other words,

---

[11] Even if they involve some level of indirection (which they might), they'll still have such connotations— because if they don't, there's no reason to have them in the first place! *Note:* I note in passing that, unlike foreign keys, object IDs in the OO world *are* "pointers in disguise" (at least to a first approximation), and so my criticisms in this section of pointers in general apply to object IDs in particular.

foreign key values, like all attribute values in a relational database, are "multiway associative."

Furthermore, all references to the same entity are represented in a relational database in the same way (i.e., by the same value), and hence are easily recognizable by both the system and users. This point might not be 100% valid, if the same "entity type" can have two or more distinct keys.

■ Adding a new foreign key to an existing table and adding a new pointer-based access path to existing stored data are very different operations—the first might be comparatively trivial, the second will almost certainly require a physical database reorganization. Similarly for dropping foreign keys vs. dropping pointers, of course.

■ Pointers are implementation dependent: Their properties and behavior depend at least in part on the underlying hardware and/or operating system and/or DBMS. In particular, they're likely to be machine local; for example, in a distributed system, a pointer probably won't be able to point from one machine to another. Foreign keys aren't implementation dependent in any such sense at all.

■ Pointer values are addresses, foreign key values aren't. Since variables have addresses and values don't—because variables have location in time and space and values don't—it follows that pointers, by definition, point to variables, not values. By contrast, foreign keys "point to" tuples, which are values, not variables (excuse my sloppy wording here). *Note:* It follows from the foregoing state of affairs that pointers actually do much more violence to the relational model than is usually realized. See reference [25] for an elaboration of this point.

■ Pointers are subject to the well known "dangling references" problem; foreign keys aren't. (In this regard, see the epigraph to Chapter 2.)

■ My book *Type Inheritance and Relational Theory* (O'Reilly, 2016) shows that pointers and a good model of type inheritance are logically incompatible. It also shows that the same criticism doesn't apply to foreign keys.

- Finally, recall that foreign key constraints are a special case of inclusion dependencies; so even if it's argued that a foreign key is "something like" a pointer, inclusion dependencies in general most certainly aren't.

WHY KEY DEFINITIONS SHOULD BE SPECIAL CASED

I still stand by the general message of this section, but (a) everything having to do with primary keys should be revised to talk in terms of just keys, unqualified, and (b) everything having to do with nulls should be deleted.

A full function database management system needs to be able to support the definition and enforcement of integrity constraints of arbitrary complexity. Several languages have been proposed for the declaration of such constraints; see, for example, reference [21]. (The languages in question are sometimes referred to as "assertion / trigger languages" [23], where "assertion" refers to the constraint as such and "trigger" refers to the procedure the system is to execute if the constraint is violated.) And since primary and foreign key constraints are just special cases of integrity constraints in general, it follows that primary and foreign key constraints must at least be capable of being expressed in any such general language. Here, for example, is a definition of the primary key constraint for table S (suppliers), expressed in the hypothetical integrity constraint language described in reference [21].[12] *Note:* SX and SY here are range variables, both ranging over table S.

```
CREATE INTEGRITY RULE S_PK
    ON INSERT SX.SNO ,
       UPDATE SX.SNO :
    CHECK FORALL SX ( NOT IS_NULL ( SX.SNO ) AND
                      FORALL SY ( IF SX.SNO = SY.SNO
                                  THEN SAME ( SX , SY ) ) )
    ELSE REJECT ;
```

But this formulation is pretty clumsy! The special case syntax

```
PRIMARY KEY ( SNO )
```

---

[12] It's relevant to the thesis of this book to point out that the definition shown actually *doesn't* define a primary key as such, it just defines a key.

(part of the definition of table S) is preferable for several reasons:

- It's better for the user, because it's more user friendly.

- It's better for the system, because it allows the system to recognize the special case more easily and hence implement it in a special case (more efficient) way—which is clearly desirable for a constraint that's so important and fundamental.

- It enables the system to recognize and understand the associated semantics more easily. For example, the system needs to understand the semantics of primary keys (also foreign keys, sometimes) in order to be able to do view updating correctly. Likewise, the optimizer also needs to understand the semantics of primary keys (also foreign keys, sometimes) in order to be able to perform certain kinds of optimization.

Now, the foregoing example and discussion have to do with primary key constraints specifically. But analogous points apply, with perhaps even more force, to foreign key constraints also. By way of illustration, here's a "general constraint language" declaration—again based on an example in reference [21]—of the foreign key constraint from SP.SNO in the shipments table SP to the primary key S.SNO in the suppliers table S, with NULLS NOT ALLOWED and RESTRICTED update and delete rules. (The CASCADES and NULLIFIES cases are much worse, by the way!) *Note*: SX and SPX here are range variables, ranging over tables S and SP, respectively.

```
CREATE INTEGRITY RULE SP_S_FK
    ON INSERT SPX.SNO ,
        UPDATE SPX.SNO ,
        UPDATE SX.SNO ,
        DELETE SX :
    CHECK FORALL SPX ( NOT IS_NULL ( SPX.SNO ) AND
                        EXISTS SX ( SX.SNO = SPX.SNO ) )
    ELSE REJECT ;
```

Here's the special case syntax equivalent (part of the definition of SP):

```
FOREIGN KEY ( SNO ) REFERENCES S
        NULLS NOT ALLOWED
```

(I'm assuming the default referential action is always RESTRICTED.)

There's another point to be made under the general heading of special casing, viz.: The foreign key concept is occasionally criticized on the grounds that it's too rigid. For example, why does the target row have to exist before a referencing row can exist? In the case of suppliers and parts, for example, why shouldn't it be possible to insert a shipment row at any time, and have the system automatically create appropriate entries in the suppliers and parts tables if they don't already exist?

I would respond to this criticism by invoking *The Principle of Cautious Design* once again. Provided the system does support a general constraint language such as the one proposed in referenc [21], then *any* constraint can always be expressed (albeit in a somewhat clumsy manner, in some cases). The question of which specific ones are given special case treatment thus becomes a judgment call on the part of the DBMS (and language) designer. The objective is to strike a healthy balance between two somewhat conflicting objectives:

a.   On the one hand, it's desirable to special case those constraints that occur frequently in practice, for the reasons sketched earlier in this section.

b.   On the other hand, it's also desirable not to clutter up the interface with an excessive number of special cases, for all the usual reasons (too much to learn, teach, document, remember, implement, etc., etc.).

In the particular case under consideration (the ability to insert a referencing row before the corresponding referenced row), I would argue that the desirability of special casing isn't clear, since it seems to me that the need for such a rule doesn't arise very often in practice. (By contrast, the desirability of special casing primary and foreign keys as previously discussed is surely beyond doubt.) Following *The Principle of Cautious Design*, therefore, I would argue against special casing such a rule at this time.

WHY CONTERMINOUS REFERENTIAL PATHS SHOULD BE TREATED WITH CAUTION

As with the previous section, I still stand by the general message of what follows, but everything having to do with primary keys should be revised to talk in terms of just keys, unqualified, and everything having to do with nulls should be deleted.

As we've seen, it can sometimes happen that there are two or more distinct referential paths from some table T_n to some other table T_1. Two examples were given earlier in this chapter:

a. The courses – offerings – enrollments example, in which there were two distinct paths from table ENROLLMENT to table COURSE:

b. The bill of materials example, in which there were two distinct paths from table PP to table P:

Since they have the same start and end points, let's agree to describe the distinct paths in such examples as *conterminous*. As the title of the section indicates, conterminous paths need to be treated with a certain amount of care. Let me elaborate.

Note first that the two examples are actually different in kind:

a. In the first example, the fact that there's a direct path from ENROLLMENT to COURSE is really just a logical consequence of the fact that there are paths from ENROLLMENT to OFFERING and from OFFERING to COURSE. In other words, if *e*, *o*, and *c* represent an ENROLLMENT row, an OFFERING row, and a COURSE row, respectively, and if *e* references *o* and *o* references *c*, then *e* will necessarily reference *c* directly as well. Hence, if the system enforces the referential constraints from ENROLLMENT to OFFERING and from OFFERING to COURSE, the direct constraint from ENROLLMENT to COURSE will be enforced automatically.

    Since the situation just described is essentially just an extension of the situation that arises in connection with the familiar concept of transitive functional dependence [9], I'll refer to a referential constraint such as the direct constraint from ENROLLMENT to COURSE in this example as *transitive* (via OFFERING).

b. In the second example, the two paths are quite independent of one another. There are no transitive constraints.

The two cases a. and b. both need careful treatment, though case a. is more straightforward than case b. The easiest way of dealing with case a. is simply not to declare the transitive constraint; as already explained, that constraint will be enforced automatically anyway, so long as the constraints that imply it are enforced. If it *is* declared, though, then care must be taken to ensure that the associated delete and update rules are defined in such a way as to be compatible with the delete and update rules defined for the constraints that imply it. For example, if the delete rules from ENROLLMENT to OFFERING and OFFERING to COURSE are both CASCADES, it wouldn't make much sense to say the delete rule from ENROLLMENT to COURSE is RESTRICTED. As far as the system is concerned, in fact, declaring the transitive constraint has the effect (conceptually) of converting case a. into case b., since the system won't be aware of the fact that the transitive constraint is in fact transitive, and in fact will presumably have to behave as if it isn't.

Now let's take a closer look at case b.

At this point the subject paper went on to discuss this case in detail. However, most of that discussion is subsumed by the discussion of the same example near the end of Chapter 2, so I'll omit it here. (Another portion of the original discussion in the subject paper had to do with DB2 specifically, and I've moved that material to Chapter 6.)

WHY PRIMARY KEY VALUES IN BASE TABLES SHOULDN'T BE WHOLLY OR PARTLY NULL

There's nothing in this section from the subject paper that's worth preserving— not even by way of an object lesson.

WHY COMPOSITE FOREIGN KEY VALUES SHOULDN'T BE PARTLY NULL

Several of the usual criticisms arise here:

- "Composite" values of any kind are better (and more simply) understood as tuples.

- Null isn't a value, so the idea that *any* "value" might be either partly or wholly null is a contradiction in terms.

- More to the point, I reject nulls anyway, so the idea that *anything* might be either partly or wholly null is in fact meaningless.

Like the previous section, therefore, this section could be removed without loss (except for some tiny nuggets of information concerning DB2, SQL/DS, and the SQL standard). However, I've let it stand pretty much unchanged (i.e., with essentially no further commentary), mainly because it can serve as a kind of Awful Warning regarding just a few of the infinitely many practical problems that nulls can lead to.

As explained previously, foreign keys, unlike primary keys (primary keys in base tables, at any rate), sometimes do have to be allowed to be null. If the foreign key in question is composite, however, it's my position that every individual value of that foreign key should either be wholly null (i.e., all components null) or wholly nonnull (i.e., all components nonnull), and not a mixture (i.e., some components null and others nonnull). The basic argument is, again, that foreign key values (like primary key values) are entity identifiers, and a partly null identifier doesn't make much sense. (A wholly null identifier, by contrast, does make sense in this context—it means, e.g., that the corresponding entity is unknown, or that no such corresponding entity exists. For example, an EMP row with a null DNO might be legal—it would represent an employee for whom the department is unknown, or perhaps an employee who for some reason simply doesn't have a department.)

Now, it's sometimes argued that a partly null foreign key value could also make sense. For example, in the courses – offerings – enrollments database, a (CNO,ONO) foreign key value of (C99,null) in an ENROLLMENT row could mean that we know that the employee in question is enrolled in some offering of course C99, but we don't know which one. (For the sake of the example I choose to overlook the point that the foreign key in question is actually part of the primary key of the containing table, and hence that nulls wouldn't be allowed anyway.)

As a matter of fact, the currently proposed extensions to the SQL standard [4,5] do explicitly permit such a possibility; so too do the IBM products DB2 and SQL/DS [2,3]. However, it's my feeling that such a possibility doesn't really provide a useful level of additional function, and it certainly does lead to a very great deal of complexity. In fact, a perceived "need" for partly null foreign key values tends to suggest that the database designer has done a poor design job and hasn't pinpointed the proper entities. Let me explain why I feel this way.

The first point is that, as previously explained, not all components of a composite foreign key are necessarily foreign keys themselves. For example, in the composite foreign key ENROLLMENT.(CNO,ONO), CNO *is* a foreign key itself (perhaps just an implicit one), but ONO isn't. We might therefore agree that a (CNO,ONO) value of (C99,null) is valid, provided at least that course C99 does exist—but what about a value of (null,O99)? It's probably an error, if no course has an associated O99 offering; but if it *is* an error, exactly what kind of error is it? What constraint is being violated? It's certainly not a referential constraint, because (to repeat) ENROLLMENT.ONO isn't a foreign key.

Next, consider the following example (where LOC stands for "location"):

```
DEPT ( DNO , LOC , ... )
     PRIMARY KEY ( DNO , LOC )

EMP  ( ENO , ..., DNO , LOC , ... )
     PRIMARY KEY ( ENO )
     FOREIGN KEY ( DNO , LOC ) REFERENCES DEPT
```

Suppose columns EMP.DNO and EMP.LOC both have "nulls allowed," and suppose the two tables contain the following rows (irrelevant columns omitted):

DEPT	DNO	LOC
	D1	NYC

EMP	ENO	DNO	LOC
	E1	D1	null
	E2	null	NYC

Also, assume until further notice that the update rule for the foreign key EMP.(DNO,LOC) is RESTRICTED. Now let's examine the question "Can the existing DEPT row be updated to (D2,SFO)?"

a. Suppose the answer is yes. Then it follows that the two existing EMP rows can't be considered as matching the existing DEPT row (for otherwise the update wouldn't be permitted). And after the update, *no component of the foreign key values in those two EMP rows matches anything at all!* Thus, we're forced to the conclusion in this case that a partly null foreign key value *must always be legal*, regardless of the values of the nonnull components. Furthermore, after the update:

   1. There's no possible UPDATE (other than a "no op") that can legally be applied to LOC in the E1 row, except for one that sets LOC to SFO *and simultaneously sets DNO to D2*.

   2. There's no possible UPDATE (again, other than a "no op") that can legally be applied to DNO in the E2 row, except for one that sets DNO to D2 *and simultaneously sets LOC to SFO*.

   In other words, columns EMP.DNO and EMP.LOC aren't truly independent of one another. So what does a partly null foreign key value even mean in this case? E.g., what does it mean to say that the location for employee E2 is New York, if there's no department in New York?

b. So it looks as if the answer (i.e., to the question "Can the existing DEPT row be updated to (D2,SFO)?") must be no. Thus it must be the case that the two EMP rows are considered as matching the existing DEPT row after all. In which case, if the DEPT table additionally includes a row (D2,NYC), the EMP row for E2 must be considered as matching that DEPT row as well—i.e., it must be considered as matching both DEPT rows, the one for D1 and the one for D2. But for a given EMP row there's supposed to be exactly one corresponding DEPT row; so we have a contradiction.

Note: Case a. above corresponds to the way in which the proposed SQL standard actually works [4,5]. The same goes for DB2 and SQL/DS [2,3] also.

Now suppose by contrast that the relevant update rule is CASCADES. In this case, updating the DEPT row to (D2,SFO) will succeed. But does that update cascade to update anything in table EMP?

a.   If the answer is no, then it must be the case that the two existing EMP rows aren't considered as matching the existing DEPT row. This possibility was examined under the discussion of RESTRICTED above (paragraph a.).

b.   If the answer is yes, then it must be the case that the two EMP rows *are* considered to match the existing DEPT row. This possibility was examined under the discussion of RESTRICTED above (paragraph b.). However, there's now a subsidiary question: What effect does that cascade have? Specifically, is the EMP row (E1,D1,null) updated to (E1,D2,null) or to (E1,D2,SFO)? Whichever it is, why? (And similarly for the EMP row (E2,null,NYC), of course.)

Consideration of the case of the NULLIFIES update rule is left as an exercise. Consideration of the effect of attempting to delete the existing DEPT row under the various possible delete rules is also left as an exercise—except that it's worth mentioning that the possibilities quickly become very complex indeed, in the general case, if distinct foreign keys are allowed to overlap (see the next section).

The foregoing discussion gives some idea of the kind of complexity that can arise from the possibility that foreign key values might be partly but not wholly null—and please note that I certainly don't claim that the discussion above was exhaustive and covered all possible problems. My recommendation, that foreign key values not be allowed to be partly null, enables such complexities to be avoided, while (in my opinion) representing no significant loss of functionality.

Of course, I haven't yet answered the question "What if there's (apparently) a genuine business requirement to have a partly null foreign key value?" For example, what if there's (apparently) a genuine requirement to be able to record the fact that some employee is enrolled in some offering of course C99, but we don't currently know which one? The following design for the courses – offerings – enrollments database represents one possible approach to this problem, an approach that doesn't flout the principle that foreign key values shouldn't be partly null:

```
COURSE      ( CNO , ... )
            PRIMARY KEY ( CNO )

OFFERING    ( XNO , CNO , ONO , ... )
            PRIMARY KEY ( XNO )
            ALTERNATE KEY ( CNO , ONO )
            FOREIGN KEY ( CNO ) REFERENCES COURSE

ENROLLMENT  ( XNO , ENO , ... )
            PRIMARY KEY ( XNO , ENO )
            FOREIGN KEY ( XNO ) REFERENCES OFFERING
```

XNO here is a surrogate identifier for OFFERING (see later in this chapter for further discussion of surrogates), and the combination (CNO,ONO) is now an alternate key for that table. (Note that, as explained earlier, there's no prohibition against alternate key values being either wholly or partly null.) The composite foreign key (CNO,ONO) in the ENROLLMENT table is now replaced by the "simple" (noncomposite) foreign key XNO. In the following set of sample values, employee E1 is shown as being enrolled in offering O1 of course C1 and an unknown offering of course C99:

COURSE

CNO	...
C1	...
C99	...

OFFERING

XNO	CNO	ONO
X1	C1	O1
X2	C99	null

ENROLLMENT

XNO	ENO
X1	E1
X2	E1

WHY OVERLAPPING KEYS SHOULD BE TREATED WITH CAUTION

Much of what this section has to say I still agree with, except that (a) the text referring to primary keys needs to be cleaned up, (b) the same applies to some extent to the text referring to composite keys, and (c) everything to do with nulls should be deleted. I've added some comments.

The relational model does permit composite keys, of course, and several examples of such keys have already been shown. However, it's a good idea to be very sparing in the use of such keys (see the next section). And if composite keys are used nonetheless, then they should be treated as much as possible as if they weren't composite after all: in other words, as if they were indivisible, except possibly for retrieval purposes. In fact, the position taken in the previous section—viz., that composite foreign key values shouldn't be allowed to be partly null—is a consequence of this more general recommendation. And another is: If possible, don't let composite keys overlap. That's what the present section is all about.

First let me make that "nonoverlapping" recommendation a little more precise:

a.   Let *FK1* and *FK2* be two foreign keys in the same table *T*.[13] Then there shouldn't exist three distinct columns *C1*, *C*, and *C2* in table *T* such that *C1* is part of *FK1* and not *FK2*, *C2* is part of *FK2* and not *FK1*, and *C* is part of both *FK1* and *FK2*:

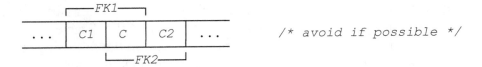

b.   Let *PK* and *FK* be primary key and a foreign key, respectively, in the same table *T*. Then there shouldn't exist three distinct columns *P*, *C*, and *F* in table *T* such that *P* is part of *PK* and not *FK*, *F* is part of *FK* and not *PK*, and *C* is part of both *PK* and *FK*:

In other words, it's acceptable to have one primary or foreign key totally included in another, or coextensive with another (see several examples earlier), but it's not a good idea to have two such keys such that each has both (a) some column in common with the other and (b) some column not so in common.

Why is such nonoverlapping desirable? The fundamental reason is that overlapping obviously implies a loss of independence, in the sense that changing a value in a common column in one of the keys in question will necessarily cause a change in value of all of the overlapping keys also. In other words, overlapping gives rise to side effects—and side effects can lead to unnecessary complexity, as

---

[13] The reason I depart from my usual practice here, writing, e.g., *FK1* instead of *FK*₁, is merely typographical.

we all know only too well. Consider the following example (the PROJ table represents projects; JNO is project number, LOC is location, and irrelevant columns are omitted as usual):

```
DEPT ( DNO , LOC , ... )
     PRIMARY KEY ( DNO , LOC )

PROJ ( LOC , JNO , ... )
     PRIMARY KEY ( LOC , JNO )

EMP  ( ENO , ... , DNO , LOC , JNO , ... )
     PRIMARY KEY ( ENO )
     FOREIGN KEY ( DNO , LOC ) REFERENCES DEPT
     FOREIGN KEY ( LOC , JNO ) REFERENCES PROJ
```

The (DNO,LOC) foreign key in table EMP means the employee in question (ENO) works for the indicated department at the indicated location, while the (LOC,JNO) foreign key in that same table means the same employee works on the indicated project at the indicated location.

The first point, of course, is that for the design shown for table EMP to be even feasible, there must be another constraint in effect, to wit:

If employee e works for department d at location l_1 and works on project j at location l_2, then l_1 and l_2 must be the same.

Even if this constraint does currently hold, of course, there's no guarantee that it'll always do so in the future. Thus, the design shown above for table EMP isn't a very good one, because it assumes the opposite (i.e., that the constraint *will* always hold). Surely it would be better to include two distinct columns, DLOC and JLOC say, in the EMP table; then if it's in fact true that for any given employee the DLOC and JLOC values must be the same, then that constraint can be separately stated and enforced—and subsequently dropped, if need be.

Next, suppose that, despite the argument just given, we do in fact stay with the overlapping key design, and suppose the tables contain the following rows (irrelevant columns omitted again):

DEPT

DNO	LOC
D1	NYC

EMP

ENO	DNO	LOC	JNO
E1	D1	NYC	J1

PROJ

LOC	JNO
NYC	J1

Then:

- **(Delete this paragraph.)** First, if the recommendation of the previous section (no partly null foreign key values) is accepted, then it won't be possible, within a given row, for one of the two foreign keys—i.e., EMP.(DNO,LOC) and EMP.(LOC,JNO)—to be null and the other not. Certainly, therefore, if one has "nulls not allowed," then so must the other. And if they both have "nulls allowed," then another constraint, to the effect that each is null if and only if the other is too, will need to be stated and enforced as well. As indicated earlier, therefore, there's clearly a lack of independence between the two foreign keys.

- **(Delete this paragraph.)** Second, suppose again that the "no partly null foreign key values" recommendation is accepted, and suppose nulls are in fact allowed for the two foreign keys. Consider the effect of a NULLIFIES delete rule for the foreign key EMP.(DNO,LOC). A DELETE for the DEPT row (D1,NYC) will accordingly set DNO and LOC in the EMP row for E1 to null. *The DELETE should therefore set JNO to null in that row as well*—because JNO can't be nonnull if LOC is null. In other words, the DELETE should produce a side effect, and that side effect is clearly necessary as we've just seen—yet it's also undesirable, because it means that project information is lost for certain employees. (As mentioned earlier, side effects are generally undesirable.)

- Detailed consideration of the update rules and other delete rules is left as an exercise for the reader. Note, however, that if we agree that every LOC value appearing in EMP must appear in both DEPT and PROJ, then there's another constraint to maintain: viz., that every LOC value in DEPT must also appear in PROJ and vice versa. (For there'd be little point in having a LOC value in one and not in the other, because no EMP could have that LOC value.) Is it really likely that DEPT.LOC and PROJ.LOC are so totally interdependent in this manner? It begins to look once again as if the database design is bad—bad in the sense that it can't be an accurate model of reality.

I turn now to a more complicated example, the point of which is to show that overlapping keys might sometimes be desirable, but that (as claimed at the beginning of the section) they certainly do need careful treatment. The database concerns suppliers (S), parts (P), and projects (J):

```
S ( SNO , ... )
   PRIMARY KEY ( SNO )

P ( PNO , ... )
   PRIMARY KEY ( PNO )

J ( JNO, ... )
   PRIMARY KEY ( JNO )
```

The following table SP indicates which suppliers are capable of supplying which parts (and please note that this isn't quite what we usually take table SP to mean, in the usual suppliers and parts example):

```
SP ( SNO , PNO )
    PRIMARY KEY ( SNO , PNO )
    FOREIGN KEY ( SNO ) REFERENCES S
    FOREIGN KEY ( PNO ) REFERENCES P
```

Analogously, tables PJ and JS indicate, respectively, which parts are capable of being supplied to which projects and which projects are capable of being supplied by which suppliers:

```
PJ ( PNO , JNO )
    PRIMARY KEY ( PNO , JNO )
    FOREIGN KEY ( PNO ) REFERENCES P
    FOREIGN KEY ( JNO ) REFERENCES J

JS ( JNO , SNO )
    PRIMARY KEY ( JNO , SNO )
    FOREIGN KEY ( JNO ) REFERENCES J
    FOREIGN KEY ( SNO ) REFERENCES S
```

Finally, table SPJ indicates which suppliers actually supply which parts to which projects:

```
SPJ ( SNO , PNO , JNO )
    PRIMARY KEY ( SNO , PNO , JNO )
    FOREIGN KEY ( SNO , PNO ) REFERENCES SP
    FOREIGN KEY ( PNO , JNO ) REFERENCES PJ
    FOREIGN KEY ( JNO , SNO ) REFERENCES JS
```

As you can see, table SPJ has three foreign keys, each of which overlaps the other two. For example, the combination SPJ.(SNO,PNO) is a foreign key that references table SP (because, clearly, a particular value for (SNO,PNO) can appear in table SPJ only if the indicated supplier is capable of supplying the indicated part—i.e., only if the (SNO,PNO) value in question appears in table SP). Points arising:

- All of the foreign keys in this example—the ones already discussed and the ones mentioned in the next bullet item below—must obviously have NULLS NOT ALLOWED, because every such foreign key is in fact a component of the primary key of table SPJ.

- Columns SNO, PNO, and JNO in table SPJ can also be regarded as foreign keys, referencing tables S, P, and J, respectively. However, there's no need to declare those foreign keys explicitly, since the corresponding referential constraints are transitive.

- Observe that there are several conterminous paths in this example. For example, there are two paths from SPJ to S, one via SP and one via JS. The complete referential diagram looks something like this (I've shown the table names in boxes for clarity):

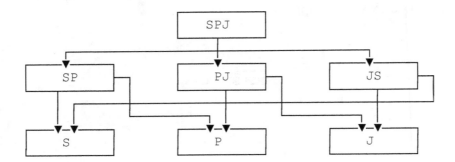

- Now we have some additional integrity constraints to maintain, over and above the foreign key constraints. For example, every SNO value appearing in table S must also appear in table SP (because it makes no sense to have a supplier who's not allowed to supply any parts). This isn't a foreign key constraint, though, because it's not the case that for every SNO value in table S there must be exactly one corresponding row in table

SP.[14] We can express it as follows, using the hypothetical integrity language of reference [21] once again:

```
CREATE INTEGRITY RULE S_SP
    AT COMMIT :
    CHECK FORALL S ( EXISTS SP ( SP.SNO = S.SNO ) ) ;
```

Note that the checking must be done "AT COMMIT" (i.e., it must be deferred), for otherwise there'd be no way to insert a new supplier into table S, nor to delete the last SP row for a given supplier (etc., etc.). **No! We don't need COMMIT-time ("deferred") checking. What we do need, as explained in Chapter 1, is support for multiple assignment. Thus, the "AT COMMIT:" specification should be removed from the foregoing "integrity rule" definition.**

Analogous deferred constraints (**delete "deferred"**) S_JS, P_SP, P_PJ, J_PJ, and J_JS must also be defined and maintained, of course (**remove the "AT COMMIT:" specifications**):

```
CREATE INTEGRITY RULE S_JS
    AT COMMIT :
    CHECK FORALL S ( EXISTS JS ( JS.SNO = S.SNO ) ) ;

CREATE INTEGRITY RULE P_SP
    AT COMMIT :
    CHECK FORALL P ( EXISTS SP ( SP.PNO = P.PNO ) ) ;

CREATE INTEGRITY RULE P_PJ
    AT COMMIT :
    CHECK FORALL P ( EXISTS PJ ( PJ.PNO = P.PNO ) ) ;

CREATE INTEGRITY RULE J_PJ
    AT COMMIT :
    CHECK FORALL J ( EXISTS PJ ( PJ.JNO = J.JNO ) ) ;

CREATE INTEGRITY RULE J_JS
    AT COMMIT :
    CHECK FORALL J ( EXISTS JS ( JS.JNO = J.JNO ) ) ;
```

■ Now consider the foreign key SP.SNO (corresponding to the referential constraint from table SP to table S). What's the delete rule? It obviously

---

[14] Actually it's an inclusion dependency (IND). In fact, it's an *equality* dependency (EQD)—the set of SNO values in S and the set of SNO values in SP must be equal. But the constraint to be shown in just a moment represents only that IND, not the full EQD. *Exercise:* So how could the full EQD be represented?

can't be NULLIFIES. Can it be CASCADES? If it is, symmetry dictates that the delete rule for the foreign keys SP.PNO, PJ.PNO, PJ.JNO, JS.JNO, and JS.SNO must all be CASCADES also. Similarly for RESTRICTED, mutatis mutandis. Analogous remarks apply to the update rules for these foreign keys also.

■ What about the foreign key SPJ.(SNO,PNO)? What's the delete rule here? Again NULLIFIES is clearly not possible, but RESTRICTED and CASCADES both seem to be acceptable. Again symmetry suggests that whatever the answer is, it should be the same for foreign keys SPJ.(PNO,JNO) and SPJ.(JNO,SNO) also. Similar remarks apply to the update rule—except that, once again, an update rule of CASCADES will cause possibly undesirable side effects.

To conclude the discussion of this example, I sketch below an alternative design that avoids the overlapping primary and foreign keys. (Tables S, P, and J are the same as before and aren't explicitly shown.)

```
SP  ( SPNO , SNO , PNO )
    PRIMARY KEY ( SPNO )
    ALTERNATE KEY ( SNO , PNO )
    FOREIGN KEY ( SNO ) REFERENCES S
    FOREIGN KEY ( PNO ) REFERENCES P

PJ  ( PJNO , PNO , JNO )
    PRIMARY KEY ( PJNO )
    ALTERNATE KEY ( PNO , JNO )
    FOREIGN KEY ( PNO ) REFERENCES P
    FOREIGN KEY ( JNO ) REFERENCES J

JS  ( JSNO , JNO , SNO )
    PRIMARY KEY ( JSNO )
    ALTERNATE KEY ( JNO , SNO )
    FOREIGN KEY ( JNO ) REFERENCES J
    FOREIGN KEY ( SNO ) REFERENCES S

SPJ ( SPJNO , SPNO , PJNO , JSNO )
    PRIMARY KEY ( SPJNO )
    ALTERNATE KEY ( SPNO , PJNO , JSNO )
    FOREIGN KEY ( SPNO ) REFERENCES SP
    FOREIGN KEY ( PJNO ) REFERENCES PJ
    FOREIGN KEY ( JSNO ) REFERENCES JS
```

The primary keys SPNO, PJNO, JSNO, and SPJNO are surrogates (see the next section). Constraints S_SP, S_JS, P_SP, P_PJ, J_PJ, and J_JS remain as before.

I'd like to make one more point. As noted near the beginning of the section, it *is* generally acceptable to have two keys that "overlap" in the sense that one key is totally included in the other. However, if the two keys in question are both foreign keys, there's still some need for caution. Consider the following example (an edited and simplified (?) version of the courses – offerings – enrollments example):

```
C ( CNO )
  PRIMARY KEY ( CNO )

O ( CNO , ONO )
  PRIMARY KEY ( CNO , ONO )

E ( CNO , ONO , ENO )
  FOREIGN KEY ( CNO )           REFERENCES C
  FOREIGN KEY ( CNO , ONO ) REFERENCES O
```

In table E, foreign key CNO is totally included in foreign key (CNO,ONO). There are two cases to consider:

a.   CNO in table O is also a foreign key (referring to table C).

b.   CNO in table O isn't a foreign key.

Case a. is essentially the original courses – offerings – enrollments example and is perfectly acceptable (modulo earlier discussions). Case b., however, is rather strange. Case b. apparently permits a row (*c,o*) to appear in table O without a corresponding row (*c*) in table C. *Note carefully, however, that the row (c,o) can't in turn have a corresponding row (c,o,e) in table E.* For if such a row (*c,o,e*) did appear in table E, then row (*c*) would have to appear in table C after all, because E.CNO is a foreign key referring to table C. Hence the row (*c,o*) in table O has no logical connection with *either* of the other two tables. I suppose such a combination of circumstances *might* occur in practice, but it doesn't seem very likely. So I don't say such a case is impossible; however, I do say that if it arises (or seems to arise) in practice, then at the very least it should cause the designer to reflect a while, with a view to deciding whether such a design is truly appropriate.

WHY NONCOMPOSITE KEYS ARE A GOOD IDEA (?)

Much of what this section has to say I still agree with, except that (a) the text referring to primary keys needs to be cleaned up, and (b) the text referring to nulls should be deleted. Also, I've added some new material following the original text.

As I've already suggested several times, I tend to feel that composite keys are generally to be avoided (even though I've given several examples of such keys, for tutorial reasons if nothing else). Thus, every time a composite key arises during the database design process, it's a good idea to consider carefully whether it might not be better to introduce a new, noncomposite column to act as the key instead. In the case of shipments, for example (table SP), it might be worth introducing a new SHIPNO column ("shipment number") as the primary key. (SP.(SNO,PNO) would then be an alternate key.) In this section I present some of the arguments in favor of such an approach. *Note:* Some of the following arguments have been presented elsewhere (see, e.g., reference [17]).

   The first and most obvious point is that all of the problems discussed in the last two sections simply don't arise if keys are always noncomposite. **(Not true!)** In fact, an argument can be made that those problems (like so many others) all stem from a confusion over levels of abstraction. For consider: From an abstract point of view, foreign keys are nothing more than references from one entity to another; thus, (a) the possibility of such references overlapping, and (b) the possibility of such references being partly null, simply don't arise. It's only because (a) foreign keys happen to be represented by columns, and (b) those columns happen to be allowed to be composite, that such questions even occur in the first place. **(I would rephrase the foregoing sentence, thus: It's only because (a) key values, and therefore foreign key values, are tuples, and (b) those tuples can be of degree greater than one, that such questions even occur in the first place.)** In other words, the complications of the last two sections arise only because of a confusion between an abstract concept, on the one hand, and the concrete realization of that concept in the relational model, on the other.

   A more pragmatic point is that composite keys can be clumsy, in the sense that they can lead to cumbersome WHERE clauses (e.g., in joins). For example:

```
SELECT  *
FROM    OFFERING , ENROLLMENT
WHERE   OFFERING.CNO = ENROLLMENT.CNO
AND     OFFERING.ONO = ENROLLMENT.ONO
```

Such clumsy formulations don't represent any kind of fundamental problem, of course, but they can be awkward and tedious for the user. Thus, it would be nice if the system allowed composite columns (*hmmm ...*) to be given noncomposite names [19], so that the above join could be simplified to (e.g.)

```
SELECT  *
FROM    OFFERING , ENROLLMENT
WHERE   OFFERING.XNO = ENROLLMENT.XNO
```

(where XNO stands for the combination of CNO and ONO). Unfortunately, few systems today provide any support for such composite column naming (again, *hmmm ...*). Instead, therefore, it might be desirable to introduce XNO as a noncomposite primary key for OFFERING and as a corresponding noncomposite foreign key in ENROLLMENT, thus:

```
OFFERING   ( XNO , CNO , ONO , ... )
           PRIMARY KEY ( XNO )
           ALTERNATE KEY ( CNO , ONO )

ENROLLMENT ( XNO , ENO , ... )
           .....
           FOREIGN KEY ( XNO ) REFERENCES OFFERING
```

As you can see, the combination (CNO,ONO) now serves as an alternate key for OFFERING and has been removed entirely from ENROLLMENT. One consequence of this revised design—not the only one, of course—is that it simplifies the formulation of the join.

Another problem with composite keys is that they can lead to redundancy—redundancy, that is, at the logical level. (They might or might not lead to redundancy at the physical level.) For example, if offering 3 of course 86 has 20 students enrolled, then the fact that course 86 *has* an offering 3 appears 21 times in the composite-key design—once in an OFFERING row and 20 times in 20 ENROLLMENT rows. Again, therefore, it might be better to introduce a new, noncomposite key XNO (say) for the OFFERING table and then to use XNO in the ENROLLMENT table, as suggested above. This revised design has the effect of eliminating the redundancy. (Though in fairness it must be pointed out that so long as the system enforces referential integrity, redundancy of the kind described shouldn't be a problem at the logical level.)

Next: If we assume there's a one to one correspondence between rows (rows in base tables, that is) and stored records—as is in fact the case in most implementations at the time of writing—then:

- Introducing the noncomposite key XNO as above will probably have the additional advantage that it'll reduce disk space requirements.

- On the other hand, there's a disadvantage also: namely, that more joins will now be needed. For example, the query "List course numbers for courses attended by employee E5" will now require a join, whereas previously it didn't. It's true that a view could be defined to conceal the join from the user, but of course the join would still be there; furthermore, most current products would probably not allow that view to be updated. Also, of course, the join will probably represent a performance penalty (under my stated assumption that there's a one to one correspondence between rows and stored records).

- A related point (again under my stated assumption) is as follows: With the original (composite key) design, it would be possible to index the ENROLLMENT table on CNO, and hence to get good performance for a query such as "List employees who have attended course C5." With the revised design, such an index would probably not be possible (at least in current products).

Another argument against composite primary keys is that the column combination in question might lose its uniqueness property. Consider the suppliers and parts database, for example, where we've been assuming that, at any given time, there can't be more than one shipment for a given supplier and given part. Under that assumption, the composite column SP.(SNO,PNO) of the shipments table does possess the uniqueness property and so can be used as the primary key. But suppose now that the business rules are changed, so that (e.g.) there can now be more than one shipment for a given supplier and a given part, just not on the same date. Now the previous assumption is no longer valid, and the combination (SNO,PNO) can no longer serve as the primary key (we need to introduce a new SHIPDATE column, and specify the combination (SNO,PNO,SHIPDATE) as the primary key). Such a change is likely to be extremely disruptive for existing users and existing applications. But if we'd already introduced a noncomposite key—SHIPNO, say—in our original design, it's at least possible that there'd be less disruption.

Analogously, the column combination that was previously being used as the primary key might lose its "nulls not allowed" status. Arguments similar to those of the previous paragraph apply in this case also.

Next: Introduced keys such as XNO and SHIPNO in the examples above don't have to have any intrinsic meaning. For example, the program that creates OFFERINGs can simply maintain a counter, increasing that counter by one to generate a new XNO value each time a new OFFERING is created. One consequence of this lack of intrinsic meaning is that *there'll never be any need to update column OFFERING.XNO at all*, which means in turn that any update rule for the foreign key ENROLLMENT.XNO would be completely irrelevant and thus needn't be specified.

Columns such as XNO and SHIPNO, whose sole function is to represent the existence of some entity, are sometimes referred to as *surrogates* [10]. In addition to all of the advantages listed above, surrogates offer another very important benefit, which is precisely that (as just stated) they have no intrinsic meaning—their *only* purpose is to stand for the entity they represent. It's an unfortunate fact that database designers love to encode all kinds of meaning into primary keys, and that such encoding can lead to horrendous problems of a very practical nature [17]. Surrogates avoid such problems. Thus, I tend to feel there are strong arguments in favor of the use of surrogates, even if the entities in question already have noncomposite keys anyway.[15]

Another argument in favor of surrogates is provided by the example discussed briefly in an earlier section involving social security numbers (SSNO) and driver's license numbers (LICNO). Suppose we initially have two distinct "person" tables (used in two distinct applications), one with primary key SSNO and the other with primary key LICNO. Suppose now that it's required to coalesce these previously separate tables in some manner, perhaps by replacing them by their outer union [10]. Since some persons have a social security number but no driver's license and some the opposite, neither of SSNO and LICNO can serve as the primary key for the resulting table. Hence the coalescing is bound to be disruptive for both existing applications. By contrast, if the two original tables had had surrogate primary keys, then the coalesced table

---

[15] In fact, a good case could be made that familiar real world identifiers such as "employee number," "social security number," "part number," "driver's license number," etc., etc., are all in fact nothing but surrogates anyway.

could retain the same primary key, and it is at least possible that those existing applications could continue to work unchanged.

See reference [17] for further discussion of surrogates.

The message of the foregoing paragraphs might still be broadly valid—though I confess I'm more than a little skeptical—but the text of those paragraphs needs a lot of work. In particular the mention of outer union should definitely be dropped!

A year or two after I first published the subject paper I published another paper on a related topic, with the title "Composite Keys." That paper first appeared in *InfoDB 5*, No. 3 (Fall 1990), but was subsequently incorporated into my book *Relational Database Writings 1989-1991* (Addison-Wesley, 1992). What follows is a heavily edited version of one section from that paper. Basically, what it does is offer some counterarguments to the arguments presented above—counterarguments, that is, to the position that composite keys should be avoided.

I begin with an example, a minor variation on the courses – offerings – enrollments database. Here's the referential diagram:

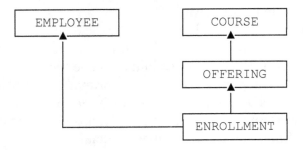

Each employee has an employee number (ENO) and an employee description (ED); each course has a course number (CNO) and a course description (CD); each offering has an offering number (ONO), unique within course, and an offering description (OD); and each enrollment has an employee number (ENO), unique within offering, and an enrollment description (ND).

Here now is the "obvious" relational version of this database, not using surrogates (and also, incidentally, avoiding all mention of primary keys as such):

```
EMPLOYEE     ( ENO , ED )
             KEY ( ENO )

COURSE       ( CNO , CD )
             KEY ( CNO )

OFFERING     ( CNO , ONO , OD )
             KEY ( CNO , ONO )
             FOREIGN KEY ( CNO ) REFERENCES COURSE

ENROLLMENT   ( CNO , ONO , ENO , ND )
             KEY ( CNO , ONO , ENO )
             FOREIGN KEY ( CNO , ONO ) REFERENCES OFFERING
             FOREIGN KEY ( ENO ) REFERENCES EMPLOYEE
```

And here by contrast is a version that does use surrogates—where, to spell the point out, by "surrogates" I mean keys whose values are generated by the system (and whose existence is concealed, in all likelihood, from the end user). *Note:* I follow reference [10] in distinguishing surrogate columns by giving them names that end with the special character "%" (percent).

```
EMPLOYEE     ( E% , ENO , ED )
             KEY ( E% )
             KEY ( ENO )

COURSE       ( C% , CNO , CD )
             KEY ( C% )
             KEY ( CNO )

OFFERING     ( O% , C% , ONO , OD )
             KEY ( O% )
             KEY ( C% , ONO )
             FOREIGN KEY ( C% ) REFERENCES COURSE

ENROLLMENT   ( N% , O% , E% , ND )
             KEY ( N% )
             KEY ( O% , E% )
             FOREIGN KEY ( O% ) REFERENCES OFFERING
             FOREIGN KEY ( E% ) REFERENCES EMPLOYEE
```

Now consider the problem of inserting a new ENROLLMENT tuple. Regardless of which version of the database we're using (i.e., with or without surrogates), the user will have to provide the relevant employee number, course number, offering number, and enrollment description. With the first design (without surrogates), the insert procedure is straightforward:

```
INSERT
INTO    ENROLLMENT ( CNO , ONO , ENO , ND )
VALUES ( given CNO , given ONO , given ENO , given ND ) ;

IF SQLCODE = foreign key violation THEN ... ;
```

The system's foreign key enforcement mechanism will then take care of ensuring that the given CNO, ONO, and ENO values are all at least plausible, in the sense that everything they reference does at least exist somewhere else in the database.

What about the design with surrogates? Here the insert procedure has to look something like this:

```
/* check that the given ENO is valid */
SELECT E%
INTO    temp E%
FROM    EMPLOYEE
WHERE   ENO = given ENO ;

IF SQLCODE = data not found THEN ... ;

/* check that the given CNO is valid */
SELECT C%
INTO    temp C%
FROM    COURSE
WHERE   CNO = given CNO ;

IF SQLCODE = data not found THEN ... ;

/* check that the given ONO is valid */
SELECT O%
INTO    temp O%
FROM    OFFERING
WHERE   C% = temp C%
AND     ONO = given ONO ;

IF SQLCODE = data not found THEN ... ;

/* obtain a surrogate for the new enrollment */
temp N% := SURROGATE_GENERATOR ( ... ) ;

/* now do the INSERT */
INSERT
INTO    ENROLLMENT ( N% , O% , E% , ND )
VALUES ( temp N% , temp O% , temp E% , given ND ) ;
```

Points arising:

1. The validity of the given data values is now being checked by the user (or by the user's application code, I should rather say) instead of by the system. The usefulness of the system's foreign key enforcement mechanism is thus severely undermined.

2. To rub salt into the wound, the system will very kindly perform foreign key checks on the offering and employee surrogates on the INSERT! Those checks aren't very likely to fail.

3. The code is obviously longer, more tedious to write, more error prone, harder to debug, and harder to maintain, than it was before.

4. The code will also almost certainly perform worse than before.

5. The point isn't fully illustrated by the example, but the design with surrogates will also involve additional overhead (in terms of both space and time) in ensuring that the key constraints on EMPLOYEE.ENO, COURSE.CNO, OFFERING.(C%,ONO), and ENROLLMENT.(O%,E%) are maintained.

Now consider the question of retrieving the descriptive information (ND) for some specific enrollment. In both designs, again, the end user will have to provide the appropriate course number, offering number, and employee number. With the first design (without surrogates), the retrieval procedure will then consist of a single SQL SELECT from the ENROLLMENT table, like this:

```
SELECT  ND
FROM    ENROLLMENT
WHERE   CNO = given CNO
AND     ONO = given ONO
AND     ENO = given ENO ;
```

With the second design (with surrogates), by contrast, it has to look something like this (still a single SELECT, of course, but a much more complex one, involving among other things a four-way join):

```
SELECT  ND
FROM    ENROLLMENT , EMPLOYEE , OFFERING , COURSE
WHERE   CNO = given CNO
AND     ONO = given ONO
AND     ENO = given ENO
AND     ENROLLMENT.E% = EMPLOYEE.E%
AND     ENROLLMENT.O% = OFFERING.O%
AND     OFFERING.C% = COURSE.C% ;
```

Points arising:

1. The code is obviously longer, more tedious to write, more error prone, harder to debug, and harder to maintain, than it was before.

2. The code will almost certainly perform worse than before.

I'll leave detailed consideration of UPDATE and DELETE operations as an exercise for you. The basic point is clear, though: Surrogates might solve some problems, but they have problems of their own.

WHY A SINGLE TARGET TABLE IS A GOOD IDEA

The discussion in this section of the subject paper was essentially identical to the discussion of Example 9 in Chapter 2, and I therefore omit it here.

SOME OPERATIONAL CONSIDERATIONS

In this section I very briefly consider a few operational aspects of the referential integrity concept. I have no critical comments on this section.

■ It must be possible to create and destroy foreign key constraints dynamically. If an attempt is made to create a new constraint over existing tables, the system must check that the new constraint is satisfied by existing data values before accepting it and recording it in the system catalog. That check can be done either at the time the constraint is defined (this is the SQL/DS approach [3]) or at some later time (this is the DB2 approach [2]);

if it's done at a later time, the constraint must remain in some kind of "not yet effective" state until that time.

■ Referential integrity clearly has implications for point in time recovery operations. Basically, point in time recovery must recover logically related data as a unit (for otherwise the restored data probably won't be consistent). Reference [18] addresses this issue by introducing the notion of a *referential structure*—informally, just a set of tables that are interconnected via referential constraints. More precisely, a referential structure consists of a set *RS* of tables such that:

    a. Every table in *RS* either references or is referenced by some table in *RS* (possibly the same table).

    b. No table not in *RS* either references or is referenced by any table in *RS*.

    c. No proper subset of the tables in *RS* satisfies conditions a. and b. (This condition is necessary in order to prevent, e.g., the collection of tables T_2, T_1, U_2, U_1, with the only foreign key references being from T_2 to T_1 and from U_2 to U_1, being considered a referential structure.)

Then point in time recovery needs to operate in terms of such referential structures. In particular, utilities will be needed to dump and restore such structures as a unit.

■ Let T_1 be a base table. Creating another base table T_2 that has a foreign key referencing table T_1 can have the effect of constraining the operations that can legally be performed on table T_1. For example, a previously acceptable DELETE against T_1 might now fail, if the delete rule for the foreign key in T_2 is RESTRICTED.

In order to prevent such unpleasant surprises, therefore, it seems appropriate to require the creator of the foreign key in table T_2 to hold some suitable authorization before he or she is allowed to create that foreign key. In SQL/DS, for example [3,7], the owner of table T_1 would have to grant the creator of table T_2 the REFERENCES privilege on table T_1. (By contrast, in SQL/DS a user who deletes a row in table T_1 and thereby deletes or updates one or more rows in table T_2—by virtue of a

CASCADES or NULLIFIES delete rule—doesn't require any particular authorization on table T_2.)

- Finally, consider locking. In implementing update operations against tables that are part of some referential structure, the system must follow an appropriate set of locking protocols in order to guarantee that it's not possible, for example, for user B to insert a shipment (SP row) that references a supplier (S row) that user A is halfway through deleting. The details are beyond the scope of this chapter; however, some idea of what's involved can be found in a paper by Alur [6], and I refer you to that paper for further discussion.

CONCLUDING REMARKS

In this chapter I've surveyed the question of referential integrity and related matters in considerable detail. I've tried to be reasonably comprehensive, but I make no claim that the treatment is in any way exhaustive. Indeed, I know it isn't; for example, there are certainly some unsolved problems, as I've indicated at one or two points in the text. I'll close by mentioning another such problem (a challenge for the reader): What are the implications for referential integrity of distributed database technology? This is a problem that's likely to acquire considerable practical significance over the next few years. Actually I don't know that it ever did. I could be wrong.

ACKNOWLEDGMENTS

First and foremost, I'm grateful to Ted Codd for inventing the basic concepts on which this chapter is based—namely, the concepts of the relational model (the foreign key and referential integrity concepts in particular), which have contributed immeasurably to our overall understanding of data and database systems and have provided the foundation for a wealth of interesting and important developments in the database field. My various critical remarks are intended merely to clarify those concepts, not to suggest in any way that there's something fundamentally wrong with them. I'm also grateful to numerous friends and colleagues, especially Nagraj Alur, Charley Bontempo, Hugh Darwen, Nat Goodman, Sharon Weinberg, and Colin White, for many helpful discussions. But the opinions expressed are my own, of course, and all errors, of either omission or commission, are my own also.

REFERENCES

1. Data Base Task Group (DBTG) of CODASYL Programming Language Committee: Final Report (April 1971).

2. IBM Corporation: Programming Announcement IBM DATABASE 2 (DB2) Version 2 (April 19th, 1988).

> What I'm referring to in this book as DB2—which was the original product name, or at least an official abbreviation for the official product name—is now officially known as "Db2 for z/OS" [*sic lowercase b*]. The version current at the time of writing is Version 13. See the annotation following the next reference for a little more more detail.

3. IBM Corporation: Programming Announcement Structured Query Language / Data System (SQL/DS) Version 2 Release 2 (June 21st, 1988).

> What I'm referring to in this book as SQL/DS—which was the original product name, or at least the official abbreviation for the official product name—is now officially known as something else, I can't recall exactly what. *Note:* The history of product name changes for SQL/DS in particular, but in fact for all of the DBMS products in IBM's so called "DB2 family," is far too complicated and baroque for ordinary mortals either to remember or to understand, and I refuse to be sucked into attempting to explain it here. The specifics can be found on Wikipedia, if you're interested.

4. ISO/TC97/SC21/WG3 / ANSI X3H2: Database Language SQL Addendum-1. Document ISO DBL AMS-10 / ANSI X3H2-87-205 (1987).

5. ISO/IEC JTC1/SC21/WG3 / ANSI X3H2: ISO-ANSI (working draft) Database Language SQL2. Document ISO DBL CPH-2b / ANSI X3H2 88 210 (April 1988).

"SQL2" became a standard in 1992, at which time it was officially labeled *SQL:1992*. Hugh Darwen and I published a user's guide to that version: viz., *A Guide to the SQL Standard* (4th edition, Addison-Wesley, 1997). *Note:* Like IBM's SQL products (see the annotation to references [1] and [2] above), the SQL standard has gone through numerous versions. The most recent version for which any kind of user's guide exists (so far as I'm aware) is SQL:1999—see Jim Melton and Alan R. Simon, *Understanding the New SQL: A Complete Guide* (Morgan Kaufmann, 2002).

6. Nagraj Alur: "IBM DATABASE 2 and Referential Integrity," *InfoDB 3*, No. 1 (Spring 1988).

7. Nagraj Alur: "Primary and Foreign Key Support in SQL/DS," *InfoDB 3*, No. 3 (Fall 1988).

8. E. F. Codd: "A Relational Model of Data for Large Shared Data Banks," *Communications of the ACM 13*, No. 6 (June 1970).

This was Codd's first generally available publication on the relational model. But it was heavily based on—in fact, in most respects it was essentially identical to—an IBM research report by Codd that was published the previous year: "Derivability, Redundancy, and Consistency of Relations Stored in Large Data Banks," IBM Research Report RJ599 (August 19th, 1969). *Note:* That research report was subsequently republished in *ACM SIGMOD Record 38*, No. 1 (March 2009).

9. E. F. Codd: "Further Normalization of the Data Base Relational Model," in *Data Base Systems*, Courant Computer Science Symposia Series 6 (Prentice-Hall, 1972).

10. E. F. Codd: "Extending the Database Relational Model to Capture More Meaning," *ACM Transactions on Database Systems 4*, No. 4 (December 1979).

This was the paper that introduced the extended relational model RM/T.

11. E. F. Codd: "Missing Information (Applicable and Inapplicable) in Relational Databases," *ACM SIGMOD Record 15*, No. 4 (December 1986);

"More Commentary on Missing Information in Relational Databases (Applicable and Inapplicable Information)," *ACM SIGMOD Record 16*, No. 1 (March 1987).

12. E. F. Codd: "Domains, Keys, and Referential Integrity in Relational Databases," *InfoDB 3*, No. 1 (Spring 1988).

13. C. J. Date: *An Introduction to Database Systems: Volume I*, 4th edition (Addison-Wesley, 1985).

> This book is currently in its 8th edition, and now incorporates much of the material (on integrity in particular) from reference [14]—for which reason that "Volume I" qualifier in the title has now been dropped.

14. C. J. Date: *An Introduction to Database Systems: Volume II* (Addison-Wesley, 1982).

15. C. J. Date: "Referential Integrity," *Proc. 7th International Conference on Very Large Data Bases* (September 1981); revised version in C. J. Date, *Relational Database: Selected Writings* (Addison-Wesley, 1986).

> This, I'm rather embarrassed to admit, was the paper that first proposed (a) NULLS [NOT] ALLOWED on a foreign key definition; (b) the CASCADES, RESTRICTED, and NULLIFIES delete and update rules; and (c) the quantifiers EXACTLY ONE OF, AT LEAST ONE OF, and ALL OF. The only part of all this that I still support is CASCADES vs. RESTRICTED, or rather (the syntax I now prefer) CASCADE vs. NO ACTION.

16. C. J. Date: "Why Every Relation Should Have Exactly One Primary Key," in C. J. Date, *Relational Database: Selected Writings* (Addison-Wesley, 1986).

> Another paper I'm now rather embarrassed about. I was still very much under Codd's influence when I wrote it! Here's a quote: "I have discussed the arguments that follow in some detail with Dr Codd ... and he is in full support of my position." Just about the only part of the paper I find myself still in agreement with is the following (lightly edited here):
>
> > If we can agree on the "exactly one primary key" requirement now, there's always the possibility of extending to two or more such keys (if desirable)

at some future time. And note moreover that this argument doesn't apply in the opposite direction: Once we're committed to a standard that says systems must allow two or more keys, a system that permits only one will forever be nonconforming. Requiring support in a proposed standard for any number of keys at this time therefore seems inappropriate—and also rather unwise, since as yet we don't fully understand all the implications of such support.

So in other words I was appealing to *The Principle of Cautious Design* once again. However, I hadn't yet formulated that principle, back in 1986; as noted at the end of Chapter 3, my original article on it first appeared a few years later in a Codd & Date publication—*The Relational Journal for DB2 Users 2*, No. 3, June/July 1990—and was later republished in C. J. Date and Hugh Darwen, *Relational Database Writings 1989-1991* (Addison-Wesley, 1992).

17. C. J. Date: "A Practical Approach to Database Design," in C. J. Date, *Relational Database: Selected Writings* (Addison-Wesley, 1986).

18. C. J. Date: "Primary and Foreign Key Support in DB2," *InfoDB 3*, No. 3 (Fall 1988).

Everything in this paper is now included in the book *A Guide to DB2*, 4th edition, by Colin White and myself (Addison-Wesley, 1993).

19. C. J. Date: "What Is a Domain?", in *Relational Database Writings 1985-1989* (Addison-Wesley, 1990).

This paper is actually not too bad, considering how long ago it was written. However, better coverage of the material can be found in several other publications by myself, the following included:

    a.   Chapters 1, 2, and 22 of *Type Inheritance and Relational Theory* (O'Reilly, 2016)

    b.   Chapters 1 and 2 of *SQL and Relational Theory: How to Write Accurate SQL Code*, 3rd edition (O'Reilly, 2015)—slightly less formal than the previous, but also less complete

    c.   Chapter 11 ("A Type Is a Type Is a Type") of *Database Dreaming Volume I* (Technics, 2022)—an analysis of Codd's attempt (in my opinion, his misguided attempt) in reference [12] to show that domains and types aren't the same thing after all

20. C. J. Date: "Why Duplicate Rows Are Prohibited," in *Relational Database Writings 1985-1989* (Addison-Wesley, 1990).

    Like the previous paper, this one too isn't bad, considering how long ago it was written. But most if not all of what it has to say is now included in my book *SQL and Relational Theory: How to Write Accurate SQL Code*, 3rd edition (O'Reilly, 2015).

21. C. J. Date: "A Contribution to the Study of Database Integrity," in *Relational Database Writings 1985-1989* (Addison-Wesley, 1990).

    In contrast to the previous two references, this paper now shows its age, rather badly. I suppose it wasn't *too* bad for its time, but I wrote it well before I'd formulated, and realized the implications of, *The Principle of Interchangeability*. As a result, it suffers from the implicit assumption that constraints apply to base data only. And it therefore goes on to propose a classification scheme for constraints that, when carefully analyzed, doesn't really make much sense. (Though I still think it makes much better sense than Codd's scheme, which I discussed briefly in Chapter 3.)

22. C. J. Date: "A Note on One to One Relationships," in *Relational Database Writings 1985-1989* (Addison-Wesley, 1990).

    Like references [19] and [20], this paper also isn't too bad, considering when it was written. But I don't think I really understood its message myself at the time—at least, not completely. (Part of that message is that choosing one key and making it primary isn't always feasible.) However, perhaps I can at least claim that it was this paper, in part, that set me thinking—set me on the path, in fact, to my current position regarding keys in general vs. primary keys in particular.

23. K. P. Eswaran and D. D. Chamberlin: "Functional Specifications of a Subsystem for Data Base Integrity," *Proc. 1st International Conference on Very Large Data Bases* (September 1975).

24. B.-M. Schueler: "Update Reconsidered," in G. M. Nijssen (ed.), *Architecture and Models in Data Base Management Systems* (North-Holland, 1977).

This was the first paper, so far as I know, to argue that storage nowadays is (almost) free, and hence that nothing should ever be deleted.

25. C. J. Date: "Don't Mix Pointers and Relations!", in *Database Dreaming Volume II* (Technics, 2022).

Chapter 5

Case Study:

Keys and Foreign Keys

in the SQL Standard

The great thing about standards is, there are so many of them.

—Anon.

This chapter is based on material from a variety of earlier books of mine, including in particular (a) A Guide to the SQL Standard, 4th edition (coauthored with Hugh Darwen, Addison-Wesley, 1997); (b) SQL and Relational Theory: How to Write Accurate SQL Code, 3rd edition (O'Reilly, 2015); and (c) Stating the Obvious, and Other Database Writings (Technics, 2020). It's intended to supplement, not replace, the SQL coverage in earlier chapters. Note: The name SQL should be understood throughout this chapter as referring to the standard version of that language in particular—meaning, more specifically, SQL:1992 and later versions. However, please note too that I've made no attempt to ensure the treatment is 100% up to date and covers the most recent version—what follows is meant as a case study, not a reference text.

Key and foreign key constraints are, of course, just special cases of constraints in general. So what does that phrase "constraints in general" mean, in SQL? Well, a constraint in SQL is basically

a. Just a boolean expression (or something logically equivalent to such an expression)—that part of the definition is OK—that's

b. Required not to evaluate to FALSE.

And it's part b. that causes the trouble; most people would surely expect it to say just "Required to evaluate to TRUE," not "Required not to evaluate to FALSE," but it doesn't. And the reason it doesn't is, of course, nulls—or, more precisely, nulls and their associated three-valued logic (3VL). So now I'm afraid we're going to have to take a closer look at such matters.

Of course, I've made my position clear in earlier chapters regarding nulls in general—in fact, I've done my best to say as little about them as possible. But in the present context they just can't be avoided. The fact is, nulls show up all over the place in SQL, and typically, when they do, they leave havoc in their wake. The section immediately following elaborates.

THREE-VALUED LOGIC AND NULLS

Note: When we talk about nulls, we're forced to talk about three-valued logic (3VL) as well—but which particular 3VL would that be? The point doesn't seem to be widely appreciated, but actually there are many different 3VLs, and which one SQL is supposed to adhere to seems to be defined only implicitly at best. For example, consider the operator called logical implication, which for present purposes I'll denote by the symbol "$\Rightarrow$" (thus, the expression $p \Rightarrow q$ can be read as p IMPLIES q, or IF p THEN q if you prefer). Here's an example: If p is "It's raining" and q is "The streets are getting wet," then I presume we can agree that $p \Rightarrow q$ is TRUE. But what about the expression $p \Rightarrow p$, for arbitrary p? Well, that's surely TRUE, right? But then what if the truth value of p happens to be "the third truth value" UNKNOWN? In that case it turns out that $p \Rightarrow p$ is TRUE in some 3VLs but UNKNOWN in others. What about SQL? Well, we don't know! SQL has no direct support for the "$\Rightarrow$" operator. So all we can do is assume that $p \Rightarrow q$ is equivalent to NOT p OR q—an equivalence that's valid in 2VL, and also valid in some 3VLs but not in all. (Simplifying considerably, therefore, we might say SQL's 3VL is such that UNKNOWN $\Rightarrow$ UNKNOWN is UNKNOWN, not one in which UNKNOWN $\Rightarrow$ UNKNOWN is TRUE. But there's a certain amount of guesswork going on here as you can see.

There's a lot more that could be said on these matters, but this book isn't the right place for it; for further specifics I refer you to Chapter 18, "Why Three- and Four-Valued Logic Don't Work," of my book Date on Database: Writings 2000-2006 (Apress, 2006). So for the remainder of this section I'm just going to assume that the phrase "SQL's 3VL" is capable of a precise interpretation, without getting sucked any further into trying to say just what that interpretation might be.

The fact that we have to say, in SQL, not that a constraint must evaluate to TRUE but rather that it mustn't evaluate to FALSE is just one weirdness we encounter immediately when we start to delve into this topic. But there's another one we have to deal with, too, which is as follows:

- In 3VL, if x is null or y is null or both, then the comparison $x = y$ evaluates not to TRUE and not to FALSE, but rather to UNKNOWN ("the third truth value").

- But that's not the weirdness—it's just something we have to accept (assuming we accept nulls and 3VL in the first place, of course). No, the weirdness is as follows:

    In SQL, any comparison—more generally, any boolean expression— that ought logically to return UNKNOWN actually returns a null instead.

    Technically, we could perhaps say that the expression does return UNKNOWN, but then that UNKNOWN immediately gets implicitly converted, or *coerced*, to a null.

    Note clearly that UNKNOWN really is a genuine value—it's a truth value (a 3VL truth value), just as the more familiar TRUE and FALSE are. By contrast, null isn't a value at all; indeed, that's the whole point about null. (Which is why that phrase *null value*, so commonly heard in SQL contexts, is deprecated, of course—it's a contradiction in terms.[1]) So the coercion just referred to is actually a little weird in itself, because it's coercing something

---

[1] In this connection you might enjoy the following "definition" from the SQL standard (I've quoted this in other writings too, but I think it bears repeating here): "**null value:** A special value that is used to indicate the absence of any data value." OK, so null is a value that means there isn't a value.

that's a value to something that isn't. But the bigger weirdness is doing that coercion in the first place, and thereby treating "the third truth value" as something other than what it is.

By the way, this particular weirdness—this logical mistake, rather—can be traced all the way back to Codd himself. In his paper "Extending the Database Relational Model to Capture More Meaning" (*ACM Transactions on Database Systems 4*, No. 4, December 1979), we find the following:

> [We] shall concern ourselves with only the "value at present unknown" type of null and denote it by ω ... We use the same symbol ω to denote the unknown truth value, because truth values can be stored in databases and we want the treatment of all unknown or null values [*sic*] to be uniform.

The problem with this position is that the truth value UNKNOWN in 3VL just *isn't* what Codd here calls a "null value"—instead, as I've already said, it's a regular value, a truth value, just like TRUE and FALSE are truth values.

Now let me get back for a moment to the first weirdness: viz., the fact that SQL doesn't regard a constraint as violated if it evaluates to UNKNOWN. Logically, of course, we should say in such a situation that *we don't know* whether the constraint is violated; however, just as SQL regards UNKNOWN as FALSE when it evaluates a WHERE clause, so it regards UNKNOWN as TRUE when it checks a constraint (speaking a little loosely in both cases). As a result, updates will sometimes succeed when they really shouldn't. Let me illustrate.

First, note that, more or less by definition, constraints generally take the form NOT EXISTS (*something*), where that *something* is an expression that denotes data that, if it did exist, would violate the constraint in question. Note further that, since we obviously want the constraint not to be violated, we want that *something* to evaluate to an empty result. So consider the following example. Suppose there's a business rule to the effect that all red parts must be stored in London. Here's one way to formulate the corresponding constraint in SQL:[2]

```
CREATE ASSERTION IC35 CHECK
      ( NOT EXISTS
           ( SELECT *
             FROM    P
             WHERE   COLOR = 'Red'
             AND     CITY ≠ 'London' ) ) ;
```

---

[2] For some unknown reason SQL calls constraints "assertions." Also, I've taken the liberty of using the "not equals" symbol "≠" in the example (proper SQL syntax would use "<>" instead).

Incidentally, note the constraint name IC35 ("integity constraint 35") here. Constraints in SQL, including key and foreign key constraints in particular, can always at least optionally be named in SQL. However, I won't bother to show such names in my examples from this point forward unless there's some specific point to be made in connection with them.

Now consider an attempt to INSERT a row into table P in which the COLOR is red but the CITY is null. Well, the best we can say about that row, logically, is that *we don't know* whether it violates the rule (viz., that all red parts must be stored in London). But look what happens if we evaluate the SQL constraint shown above for that particular row:

■ The boolean expression in the WHERE clause becomes

```
COLOR = 'Red' AND NULL ≠ 'London'
```

which evaluates to TRUE AND UNKNOWN, which reduces to UNKNOWN.

■ The SELECT expression thus becomes

```
SELECT * FROM P WHERE UNKNOWN
```

which returns an empty result, because that UNKNOWN gets coerced to a FALSE.

■ The existence test thus becomes

```
EXISTS ( empty table )
```

which returns FALSE. So the NOT EXISTS invocation becomes NOT FALSE, which of course is TRUE, and the constraint is thereby "satisfied."

Having said all that, I now need to own up a little ... The fact is, I deliberately mischaracterized the problem, slightly, when I first mentioned it above. What I said was that SQL doesn't regard a constraint as violated if it evaluates to UNKNOWN. In the case just discussed, though, the constraint evaluates not to UNKNOWN but to FALSE. But it *should* have evaluated to UNKNOWN! After all, "don't know" is a perfectly respectable answer—and in the case at hand it's the right answer—to a question such as "Is every red part in London?" To spell the point out in detail:

■ In 3VL, an existentially quantified expression—i.e., an expression of the form EXISTS (*x*)—will sometimes legitimately return UNKNOWN. And if EXISTS (*x*) returns UNKNOWN, then so does NOT EXISTS (*x*), because, in 3VL, NOT UNKNOWN is still UNKNOWN.[3]

■ So an EXISTS invocation in 3VL sometimes returns UNKNOWN. *But such an invocation in SQL never does.*

It follows that EXISTS in SQL is *not* a faithful implementation of the existential quantifier of 3VL, and hence that—claims to the contrary notwithstanding—SQL doesn't really support 3VL (not fully, at any rate).

But my main purpose in this chapter isn't to discuss three-valued and nulls (at least, no more than I have to); the foregoing discussion could be regarded as no more than a rather lengthy aside, were it not for the fact that, once you let nulls into the picture, they crop up seemingly everywhere, no matter how how hard you try to avoid them. As we'll see!

It's also not my main purpose here to discuss constraints in SQL in general (again, any more than I have to). What I really want to do is talk about key and foreign key constraints specifically. So let me now try and do that. It'll be interesting to see how far we get before nulls and 3VL force their way back into the discourse again.

BASE TABLE CONSTRAINTS

There's another preliminary I need to get out of the way, though. SQL has a feature according to which any constraint that can be formulated by means of a separate CREATE ASSERTION statement can alternatively be specified as part of the definition of some base table—in other words, as a *base table constraint*. For example, consider the following CREATE ASSERTION, which represents the constraint "No supplier with status less than 20 is allowed to supply part P6":

---

[3] This state of affairs might seem a little counterintuitive—after all, "not unknown" in ordinary parlance just means "known." But if you don't whether some part is in London, you also don't know whether that part is *not* in London. In 3VL, therefore, NOT UNKNOWN is defined to be the same as UNKNOWN.

```
CREATE ASSERTION IC82 CHECK
     ( NOT EXISTS ( SELECT *
                    FROM    S NATURAL JOIN SP
                    WHERE   STATUS < 20 AND PNO = 'P6' ) ) ;
```

This constraint could alternatively be stated as part of the definition of base table SP (shipments), like this:[4]

```
CREATE TABLE SP
     ( ... ,
       CONSTRAINT IC82 CHECK   /* "base table" constraint */
     ( NOT EXISTS ( SELECT *
                    FROM    S NATURAL JOIN SP
                    WHERE   STATUS < 20 AND PNO = 'P6' ) ) ;
```

Or base table P (parts):

```
CREATE TABLE P
     ( ... ,
       CONSTRAINT IC82 CHECK   /* "base table" constraint */
     ( NOT EXISTS ( SELECT *
                    FROM    S NATURAL JOIN SP
                    WHERE   STATUS < 20 AND PNO = 'P6' ) ) ;
```

Or in fact absolutely *any base table whatsoever*, in the entire database!—regardless of whether the base table concerned has anything to do, logically speaking, with the constraint in question.

To repeat, then, any constraint that can be formulated by means of CREATE ASSERTION can alternatively be specified as part of some CREATE TABLE (or some ALTER TABLE)—and a constraint that's formulated as part of CREATE TABLE or ALTER TABLE is called a base table constraint.[5] Don't let the terminology fool you, though—in SQL, explicitly declared constraints *always* apply to base tables specifically (with one minor and rather strange exception, to be discussed briefly in footnote 7). Though I should add that if table *T'* is derived in some way from table *T* (it might be a view, for example), then *T'* might well be subject to certain *implicit* constraints that are derived from the ones that apply to *T*. For example, if base table S (suppliers) is subject to the

---

[4] For some unknown reason SQL calls constraints "constraints," not assertions, when they're specified in this alternative style.

[5] SQL calls it just a table constraint, unqualified, because SQL almost always takes the term *table* to mean a base table specifically and forgets about other kinds of tables. In fact, of course, the very keyword TABLE in CREATE TABLE and ALTER TABLE refers to a base table specifically. Note the several violations of *The Principle of Interchangeability* involved in this state of affairs.

constraint that {SNO} is a key, then the view LS (London suppliers, defined to be that restriction of S where the city is London) is subject to that constraint too.

Now, this alternative "base table" style is perhaps useful for constraints that mention just one base table, because (a) which table definition the constraint definition should be made part of is "obvious" in such a case, and moreover (b) the formulation of the constraint can be made a little simpler too. By way of illustration consider the constraint "Supplier status values must be in the range 1 to 100, inclusive." Here's a CREATE ASSERTION formulation:

```
CREATE ASSERTION ... CHECK
    ( NOT EXISTS ( SELECT *
                   FROM   S
                   WHERE  STATUS < 1 OR STATUS > 100 ) ) ;
```

And here's a formulation as part of the CREATE TABLE for table S (i.e., as a base table constraint):[6]

```
CREATE TABLE S
    ( ... ,
        CONSTRAINT ... CHECK ( STATUS ≥ 1 AND STATUS ≤ 100 ) ) ;
```

But there's a trap here (yet another weirdness, in fact): The fact is, any base table constraint, as such, for base table *T* is automatically regarded as satisfied if *T* is empty—even if it's of the form "*T* mustn't be empty"! (Or even if it's of the form "*T* must contain −5 rows"—or the form "1 = 0," come to that.) The reason for this particular weirdness is as follows. To say base table *T* is to satisfy constraint *C* is to say there doesn't exist a row in *T* that violates *C*—loosely:

```
NOT EXISTS ( SELECT * FROM T WHERE NOT ( C ) )
```

And if *T* is empty, the EXISTS invocation returns FALSE (regardless of what form *C* takes), and so the expression overall returns TRUE.

AN IMPORTANT CLARIFICATION

To review briefly, in the relational world:

---

[6] Here I've taken the liberty of using the "greater than or equal" and "less than or equal" symbols "≥" and "≤" (proper SQL syntax would use ">=" and "<=", respectively).

- Every relvar is subject to at least one key constraint.

- Every relation satisfies at least one key constraint.

- Some relvars are subject to certain foreign key constraints.

- Some relations satisfy certain foreign key constraints.

And everyone in my intended audience should thoroughly understand these four points by now, even if they didn't do so before. But the problem is, in this chapter we're not in the relational world, we're in the SQL world—and it's quite difficult, in the SQL world, to talk about such things as key and foreign key constraints with any degree of precision. There are at least two reasons for this state of affairs, both of which should also be familiar to you by now:

- First, SQL doesn't make a clear distinction between relvars and relations (or "tablevars" and tables, I suppose I should say, in this context).

- Second, SQL doesn't fully support *The Principle of Interchangeability* (of base relvars and others).

It seems to me, therefore, that in order to make the discussions in the rest of this chapter (concerning keys and foreign keys in SQL, I mean) as clear and precise as they need to be, there are some things I'm going to have to get a little bit formal about, and that's the point of the present section. I apologize ahead of time if you think what follows is making a mountain out of a molehill, but I think I have to include it. I apologize also if you think I'm being unnecessarily repetitious; but I want to make myself absolutely as clear as I can. Please bear with me.

To say it again, what I've been calling a base table constraint is a constraint that's specified as part of a CREATE TABLE or ALTER TABLE statement. To elaborate:

■ I've already said that any constraint that can be formulated by means of CREATE ASSERTION can alternatively be specified as a base table constraint.

■ In fact, the converse is true too: Any constraint that can be formulated as a base table constraint can alternatively be formulated using CREATE ASSERTION.

■ However (and this is important), there are certain constraints that, when they're formulated as base table constraints, make use of special syntax that *can't* be used—I mean, it's not available for use, and might not make sense if it were—if the constraint were to be formulated using CREATE ASSERTION instead.

■ And as I'm sure you were expecting, SQL provides such special "base table constraint only" syntax for use in formulating key and foreign key constraints in particular.

■ For simplicity, let's ignore foreign keys for the moment and concentrate just on keys. In connection with keys, SQL provides the following two special syntactic constructs, either or both of which can be used exactly as shown in CREATE TABLE or ALTER TABLE, but neither of which can be used exactly as shown in CREATE ASSERTION:

```
UNIQUE ( column name commalist )
PRIMARY KEY ( column name commalist )
```

I repeat for emphasis: These constructs are "base table constraint only" syntax—they can appear in CREATE TABLE or ALTER TABLE but not in CREATE ASSERTION.

■ For the rest of this chapter, then:

   a. I'll limit my use of the term *key definition* to refer, specifically, to a definition of either of the foregoing two syntactic forms—even though they're both defined to be shorthand for something that can be expressed more longwindedly using CREATE ASSERTION.

b. I'll limit my use of the term *key* to mean something that's defined by a key definition, in the foregoing specialized sense of that term.

In other words, for the purposes of the rest of this chapter, I'm *not* going to regard something as a key if it's defined by CREATE ASSERTION, even if that CREATE ASSERTION definition is logically equivalent to some UNIQUE or PRIMARY KEY base table constraint definition.

To say it again in different words: For the rest of this chapter, keys are something that only base tables can have, and then only if the keys in question been defined by that special UNIQUE or PRIMARY KEY syntax in CREATE TABLE or ALTER TABLE.

■ Turning now to foreign keys: In connection with foreign keys, SQL provides the following special syntactic construct, which can be used exactly as shown in CREATE TABLE or ALTER TABLE, but can't be used exactly as shown in CREATE ASSERTION:

```
FOREIGN KEY ( column name commalist )
REFERENCES base table name [ ( column name commalist ) ]
        [ MATCH { SIMPLE | PARTIAL | FULL } ]
```

I repeat for emphasis: This construct is "base table constraint only" syntax—it can appear in CREATE TABLE or ALTER TABLE but not in CREATE ASSERTION.

■ For the rest of this chapter, then:

a. I'll limit my use of the term *foreign key definition* to refer, specifically, to a definition of the foregoing form—even though it's defined to be shorthand for something that can be expressed more longwindedly using CREATE ASSERTION.

b. I'll limit my use of the term *foreign key* to mean something that's defined by a foreign key definition, in the foregoing specialized sense of that term.

In other words, for the purposes of the rest of this chapter, I'm *not* going to regard something as a foreign key if it's defined by CREATE

ASSERTION, even if that CREATE ASSERTION definition is logically equivalent to some FOREIGN KEY base table constraint definition.

To say it again in different words: For the rest of this chapter, foreign keys are something that only base tables can have, and then only if the foreign keys in question have been defined by that special foreign-key-defining syntax in CREATE TABLE or ALTER TABLE.

Finally: It follows from all of the above that as far as SQL is concerned, key constraints and foreign key constraints are always base table constraints specifically.

KEYS

Note: For the purposes of this section I assume you've read and fully digested the material of the previous section, "An Important Clarification."

So, at last, to SQL keys as such. Note first of all that:

- Only base tables can have keys, in SQL.[7] (I've already said this, of course, but I say it again here because I don't want the point to be overlooked).

- Even for base tables, keys are optional. (Of course, any table that doesn't have a key will thereby allow duplicate rows.)

- Key constraint checking in SQL is always immediate, never deferred.[8]

Syntactically speaking, then, a key constraint in SQL is a base table constraint, meaning it's specified as part of a CREATE TABLE statement (usually) or an ALTER TABLE statement (possibly). And as we now know, such a constraint can take either of the following forms:

---

[7] I remind you that in fact, in SQL, only base tables can be subject to explicitly declared constraints of any kind whatsoever—with one slightly strange exception called the CHECK option, which has to do with views and is beyond the scope of the present chapter (or indeed this book). For an exhaustive discussion of the CHECK option, see Chapter 2 ("Assignment") of my book *Stating the Obvious, and Other Database Writings* (Technics, 2020).

[8] As explained in Chapter 1, SQL does support deferred checking for some constraints, despite the arguments in that same chapter to the effect that such checking is never logically correct.

```
UNIQUE ( column name commalist )

PRIMARY KEY ( column name commalist )
```

A given base table can have any number (possibly zero) of key constraints of the first form and/or at most one of the second form.

The first form (UNIQUE) is logically equivalent to the following "check constraint"—

```
CHECK ( UNIQUE ( SELECT column name commalist FROM T ) )
```

—where *T* is the name of the base table to which the key constraint applies, of course.[9] Thus, SQL's definition of uniqueness for keys is identical to its definition of uniqueness in the context of its UNIQUE operator. That operator in turn is defined as follows: The expression

```
UNIQUE ( table expression )
```

returns TRUE if the result of evaluating the specified table expression contains no two distinct rows, r_1 and r_2 say, such that the comparison $r_1 = r_2$ evaluates to TRUE; otherwise it returns FALSE. (It never returns UNKNOWN.) Note carefully, however, that $r_1 = r_2$ doesn't evaluate to TRUE if either of r_1 or r_2 is null or contains any null components;[10] hence, e.g., if column *C* of table *T* contains just 1, 2, 3, NULL, and NULL, then the expression UNIQUE (SELECT *C* FROM *T*) will return TRUE. (In other words, just as EXISTS in SQL sometimes returns FALSE when UNKNOWN would be more logically correct, so UNIQUE sometimes returns TRUE when UNKNOWN would be more logically correct. It might have been more helpful, though obviously clunkier, if the keyword had been not UNIQUE but UNIQUE_EXCEPT_FOR_NULLS.)

Getting back to keys, then: It follows from the foregoing that if we specify the key constraint

---

[9] That hypothetical CHECK constraint could be specified as part of the CREATE TABLE or some ALTER TABLE statement for table *T* or in a separate CREATE ASSERTION statement—or, in fact, as part of a CREATE TABLE or ALTER TABLE for absolutely any table in the database. But for it to be truly "logically equivalent" to a key constraint (as such) for table *T*, it needs to be part of the CREATE TABLE, or ALTER TABLE, for table *T* as such.

[10] See how quickly nulls get back into the picture? Seems like you just can't keep them out. Note in particular here that the statements "row *r* is null" and "row *r* contains null components" aren't equivalent—not even if *r* contains no component that *isn't* null. See Chapter 1, "Equality," of the book mentioned in footnote 7, *Stating the Obvious, and Other Database Writings* (Technics, 2020).

```
UNIQUE ( K )
```

—assuming here for simplicity that K consists of just a single column—then column K can contain any number of values, all of which must be distinct, together with any number of nulls. More generally, let K be a key for base table T; let K involve any number of columns; and let k_2 be a new value for K that some user is attempting to introduce into T via an INSERT or UPDATE operation.[11] That INSERT or UPDATE will be rejected if k_2 is the same as some value for K, k_1 say, that already exists in some row of T. What then does it mean for two values k_1 and k_2 to be "the same"? It turns out that no two of the following statements are equivalent:

1. k_1 and k_2 are the same for the purposes of a comparison condition

2. k_1 and k_2 are the same for the purposes of key uniqueness

3. k_1 and k_2 are the same for the purposes of duplicate elimination

Statement 1 is defined in accordance with the rules of three-valued logic; Statement 2 is defined in accordance with the rules for the UNIQUE operator; and Statement 3 is defined in accordance with the definition of duplicates.[12] For example, let K, k_1, and k_2 be as above; let K again consist of just one column, for simplicity; and let k_1 and k_2 both be null. Then, believe it or not, Statement 1 gives UNKNOWN, Statement 2 gives FALSE, and Statement 3 gives TRUE.

Note: It is at least the case, however, that (a) if Statement 1 gives TRUE, then Statement 2 gives TRUE, and (b) if Statement 2 gives TRUE, then Statement 3 gives TRUE.

I turn now to the second form of key constraint in SQL (viz., PRIMARY KEY):

```
PRIMARY KEY ( column name commalist )
```

---

[11] My apologies—the "new value" mentioned in this sentence, and the "values" mentioned elsewhere in this paragraph, might not be values at all but rather nulls. It's *very* difficult to talk about these matters coherently.

[12] So now I have to explain how SQL defines duplicates! Simplifying considerably, x and y are *duplicates* in SQL if and only if they're either both nonnull and equal, or both null. Note, therefore, that if x and y are duplicates, it doesn't follow that $x = y$ gives TRUE! It also doesn't follow that if UNIQUE (SELECT * FROM T) gives TRUE, then SELECT * FROM T and SELECT DISTINCT * FROM T give results of the same cardinality.

This form is logically equivalent to the following check constraint—

```
CHECK ( UNIQUE ( SELECT column name commalist FROM T )
        AND C₁ IS NOT NULL
        AND C₂ IS NOT NULL
        AND ...
        AND Cₙ IS NOT NULL )
```

—where C_1, C_2, ..., C_n are all of the columns mentioned in the specified column name commalist.[13] Note, therefore, that:

■ While keys in general do permit nulls in SQL, primary keys don't.

■ The complications described above regarding keys and nulls don't apply to a key that's explicitly been designated as primary. In particular, Statements 1, 2, and 3 above are all equivalent if K is a primary key.

FOREIGN KEYS

Note: For the purposes of this section I assume you've read and fully digested the material of the earlier section "An Important Clarification."

As we've seen, it's only base tables that can have keys in SQL, and the same is true for foreign keys also. That is, a foreign key constraint in SQL is a base table constraint, syntactically speaking, meaning that:

■ It's specified as part of a CREATE TABLE statement (usually) or an ALTER TABLE statement (possibly).

■ The referencing table and the referenced table must both be base tables specifically.

   Here then is the syntax for a foreign key definition in SQL, now shown complete—

---

[13] Footnote 9 applies here also.

```
FOREIGN KEY ( column name commalist )
    REFERENCES base table name [ ( column name commalist ) ]
              [ MATCH { SIMPLE | PARTIAL | FULL } ]
              [ ON DELETE response ]
              [ ON UPDATE response }
```

—where the possible *responses* (also known as *referential actions*) are as follows:

```
NO ACTION | RESTRICT | CASCADE | SET DEFAULT | SET NULL
```

In the following explanations I limit myself to points that might not be immediately obvious—though perhaps I should explicitly remind you first that rows and tables in SQL have a left to right ordering to their fields and columns, respectively.

- The columns mentioned explicitly in the column name commalist in the first line of the foreign key definition as shown above constitute the foreign key.

- The optional column name commalist in the second line of the foreign key definition as shown above must be the same, except possibly for the sequence in which the columns are listed, as the column name commalist in some key definition for the referenced table.

- Omitting that second column name commalist is equivalent to specifying one that's identical to the one in the primary key definition for the referenced table (the referenced table must possess a defined primary key in this case).

- The columns mentioned explicitly or implicitly in the second line of the foreign key definition as shown above constitute the corresponding referenced or target key.

- The foreign key and the referenced key must contain the same number of columns, n say. For all i ($1 \leq i \leq n$), the ith column of the foreign key corresponds to the ith column of the referenced key.

- For all i ($1 \leq i \leq n$), the ith column of the foreign key and the ith column of the referenced key must be of the same data type—not just compatible data

types, observe, but (unusually for SQL) *exactly the same* data type.[14]
However, corresponding columns don't have to have the same name.

■ The optional MATCH specification has to do with nulls (see further
discussion below).

■ The optional ON DELETE and ON UPDATE clauses can appear in either
order. Omitting either is equivalent to specifying such a clause with the
NO ACTION option. The semantics of the various options were discussed
briefly in Chapter 2.

■ The definer of a given foreign key needs the REFERENCES privilege on
the referenced key (not on the table that contains that key, observe).

■ Foreign key constraint checking is always immediate, never deferred.

The MATCH Specification

A foreign key definition of the form

```
FOREIGN KEY ( fk ) REFERENCES T [ ( k ) ]
                MATCH { SIMPLE | PARTIAL | FULL }
```

is defined to be equivalent to the following CHECK constraint:[15]

```
CHECK ( ( fk ) MATCH [ SIMPLE | PARTIAL | FULL ]
                            ( SELECT k FROM T ) )
```

Note: I was tempted at this point to leave it at that—leave it as an exercise
for you, I mean, to figure out the detailed semantics of foreign key definitions in
SQL. But I decided on reflection that that wouldn't be very nice of me, and so
I'll have a go at it myself. (It's relevant to mention that the standard itself takes
some 20 highly detailed pages to perform this task—not counting, of course, all
of the references within those pages to other parts of the document, which also
need to be read and absorbed in order to fully understand referential constraints
in SQL.)

---

[14] This strict rule was indeed the case with SQL:1992 but was relaxed in later versions of the standard.

[15] Footnote 9 applies here also.

To begin with, the foregoing specification is defined as you can see in terms of the SQL MATCH operator. That operator in turn is a boolean operator that (like the SQL UNIQUE operator) always returns either TRUE or FALSE, never UNKNOWN. The syntax is:

```
rx MATCH [ UNIQUE ] [ SIMPLE | PARTIAL | FULL ] ( tx )
```

Here *rx* and *tx* are expressions denoting a row *r* and a table *t*, respectively, such that for all *i* the types of the *i*th field of *r* and the *i*th column of *t* are comparable.[16] (Again I remind you that rows and tables have a left to right ordering to their fields and columns, respectively, in SQL.) Thus, there are six cases to consider, depending on (a) whether the UNIQUE option is omitted or specified and (b) whether SIMPLE, PARTIAL, or FULL is specified (omitting this latter option entirely is equivalent to specifying SIMPLE). The following table summarizes the six cases:

	SIMPLE	PARTIAL	FULL
omitted	Case 1	Case 2	Case 3
UNIQUE	Case 4	Case 5	Case 6

Note first that PARTIAL and FULL effectively both degenerate to SIMPLE, and if specified can therefore effectively be ignored, if either (a) *r* and *t* are both of degree one or (b) every component of *r* has "nulls not allowed" (or both). More generally, however, the rules are as follows:

- *Case 1* (no UNIQUE, SIMPLE): The result is TRUE if either (a) any field of *r* is null[17] or (b) *t* contains at least one row, *r'* say, such that *r* = *r'* is TRUE; otherwise the result is FALSE.

- *Case 2* (no UNIQUE, PARTIAL): The result is TRUE if either (a) every field of *r* is null or (b) *t* contains at least one row, *r'* say, such that each

---

[16] The notion of two types being "comparable" is explained in the standard but the details are quite complex, and I omit them here.

[17] Note that here and throughout these rules, wherever condition (a) holds—i.e., whenever either "any field of *r* is null" (for Cases 1 and 4) or "every field of *r* is null" (for Cases 2, 3, 5, and 6)—we effectively have a situation (and in fact not the only one, in SQL) in which *x* = *y* gives TRUE if *x* is null or *y* is null or both.

nonnull field in *r* is equal to its counterpart in *r'*; otherwise the result is FALSE.

■ *Case 3* (no UNIQUE, FULL): The result is TRUE if either (a) every field of *r* is null or (b) every field of *r* is nonnull and *t* contains at least one row, *r'* say, such that *r* = *r'* is TRUE; otherwise the result is FALSE.

■ *Case 4* (UNIQUE, SIMPLE): The result is TRUE if either (a) any field of *r* is null or (b) *t* contains exactly one row, *r'* say, such that *r* = *r'* is TRUE; otherwise the result is FALSE.

■ *Case 5* (UNIQUE, PARTIAL): The result is TRUE if either (a) every field of *r* is null or (b) *t* contains exactly one row, *r'* say, such that each nonnull field in *r* is equal to its counterpart in *r'*; otherwise the result is FALSE.

■ *Case 6* (UNIQUE, FULL): The result is TRUE if either (a) every field of *r* is null or (b) every component of *r* is nonnull and *t* contains exactly one row, *r'* say, such that *r* = *r'* is TRUE; otherwise the result is FALSE.

I hope that's all perfectly clear! In all seriousness, though, I recommend as an exercise going back through the foregoing explanation to see what the effect would be if every field of *r* and every column of *t* had nulls not allowed.

Nulls and the MATCH specification together also have implications for the various options—CASCADE, etc.—that can be specified in the ON DELETE and ON UPDATE clauses, but I omit the details here.

Guaranteeing Predictable Behavior

As we saw in Chapter 2, certain combinations of

a. Referential structures (i.e., sets of [base] tables that are interrelated via referential constraints), along with

b. Specific foreign key rules, and

c. Specific data values in the database

can lead to conflict situations, and can cause unpredictable behavior, if not handled appropriately. Further details are beyond the scope of this chapter; suffice it to say that the standard identifies cases involving such potential unpredictability and requires the implementation to treat them as errors— meaning that in those cases the attempted update must be rejected at run time and an exception condition raised. Such exceptions can occur on DELETEs and key UPDATEs against certain referenced tables.

Note: A helpful analysis and explanation of this aspect of the standard can be found in Bruce M. Horowitz, "A Run-Time Execution Model for Referential Integrity Maintenance," in the Proceedings of the 8th International Data Engineering Conference (February 1992).

Chapter 6

Case Study:

Keys and Foreign Keys

in DB2 and SQL/DS

Between the idea
And the reality ...
Falls the shadow.

—T.S. Eliot:
The Hollow Men (1926)

This chapter is based on material from a couple of earlier books that I
wrote jointly with my friend Colin White—A Guide to DB2, 4th edition
(Addison-Wesley, 1993) and A Guide to SQL/DS (Addison-Wesley,
1988)—and I refer you to those books for more specifics. It's intended
to supplement, not replace, material on those products in earlier
chapters. Please note that (as with the discussion of the SQL standard
in the previous chapter) I've made no attempt to ensure the treatment
is 100% up to date and covers the most recent versions of the products
in question—the chapter is, again like the previous one, meant as a
case study, not a reference text.

I wrote the first version of this chapter in the late 1980s (like the previous
chapter, it began life as a brief appendix to my two-part paper "Referential
Integrity and Foreign Keys," which was discussed in Chapter 4). The key and
foreign support provided at that time by the IBM products DB2 and SQL/DS was

perhaps the most sophisticated then commercially available. I have no idea whether such is still the case—probably it isn't—but I think it's worth taking a look at those early implementations anyway (by way of another case study, I mean), and that's what this chapter is all about.

A few preliminary remarks:

■ The original versions of the DB2 and SQL/DS products—i.e., the versions I'm describing in this chapter—were intended at the time for two specific IBM environments: DB2 for the MVS environment, and SQL/DS for the VSE environment. The detailed picture has changed considerably since that time (see the annotation to references [2] and [3] in Chapter 4), but the changes are irrelevant as far as this chapter is concerned. For that reason I've made no attempt to reflect them in what follows, or even to keep up with them.

■ Please note that everything I said in Chapter 5 (in particular, everything I said in the section "An Important Clarification" and everything I said regarding SQL syntax) applies here also, unless explicitly contradicted. In other words, the present chapter isn't intended to stand alone—it assumes you've read the previous chapter first.

■ To simplify the presentation overall I'll deal with DB2 first, then summarize the SQL/DS differences in a section of their own.

TERMINOLOGY

Some of the terminology used by IBM in connection with keys and foreign keys seems to me a trifle unfortunate, to say the least. To be specific:

■ The IBM term for a referenced or target table is *parent* table—presumably a hangover from "the bad old days" of IMS.

■ Oddly enough, the IBM term for a referencing table isn't, as might have been expected, child table but *dependent* table.

■ The IBM term for a table that's not a dependent table *and also not a parent table* is *independent* table.

■ The IBM term for a dependent of a dependent table is *descendant* table.

Note, therefore, that, first, *dependent* doesn't mean *not independent*; second, a dependent isn't a descendant! There are rich possibilities for confusion here, it seems to me.

What's more, the IBM documentation—very perversely, to my mind— shows referential arrows *going the wrong way*: i.e., from the referenced ("parent") table to the referencing ("dependent") table, instead of the other way around. For example:

```
DEPT ──▶ EMP
```

instead of

```
EMP ──▶ DEPT
```

The convention I've been using in all previous chapters, the one illustrated in the second of these figures, accords better with intuition, surely. What's more, it's consistent with both relational and mathematical literature. (As I pointed out in Chapter 1, a referential arrow is basically just a functional dependency arrow in a different context.) I can't help feeling the IBM convention is likely to cause a great deal of unnecessary confusion, and I won't use it myself in what follows.

KEYS IN DB2

Let *T* be a DB2 base table. Then:

■ *T* can have any number of keys (possibly none at all), at most one of which can be designated as primary, i.e., defined by means of a PRIMARY KEY clause. Such a clause can appear on the pertinent CREATE TABLE statement or on some subsequent ALTER TABLE statement.
   Note: Key constraints can optionally be named, but I omit the specifics here. The same goes for foreign key constraints also (see the next section).

■ IBM doesn't seem to have a specific term for other ("alternate") keys, i.e., ones defined by means of UNIQUE clauses and thus not designated as primary. Note, however, that UNIQUE clauses are permitted only on CREATE TABLE, not on ALTER TABLE, and hence that all keys except possibly the primary key must be defined when the table is defined.[1]

- Every column involved in any key must be explicitly defined to be NOT NULL.

- Let *K* be a key for *T*; then a UNIQUE index must be explicitly defined on *K* in order to enforce uniqueness. That index must be on exactly the columns that make up *K*, no more and no less, in exactly the left to right order in which the columns of *K* are specified in the key definition for *K*. For example:

```
CREATE TABLE SP
      ( SNO ... NOT NULL ,
        PNO ... NOT NULL ,
        QTY ... ,
        PRIMARY KEY ( SNO , PNO ) ) ;
   ...
CREATE UNIQUE INDEX XSP ON SP ( SNO , PNO ) ;
```

Note: In practice I would certainly specify NOT NULL for column QTY also. I omit such a specification here purely for the sake of the example.

- Let *K* be a key for *T*; then *T* is considered to be "incomplete" until the corresponding index has been created, at which point it becomes "complete." (It'll become "incomplete" again if that index is subsequently dropped.)

- No access is allowed to a table while it's incomplete. *Note:* Prohibiting INSERTs and key UPDATEs on such a table is reasonable, of course, but I don't see why retrievals, DELETEs, or nonkey UPDATEs have to be prohibited. However, apparently they are.

---

[1] I can't help noting in passing how counterintuitive this is—the primary key is, well, primary, and you'd surely expect it to have to be defined when the table is defined (if you believe in primary keys in the first place, that is). By contrast, any other keys are secondary, in a way, and you might thus have thought it would be OK to add them later.

■ Suppose a primary key—call it *PK*—is to be "added" to table *T* via ALTER TABLE, thus:

```
ALTER TABLE T
      ADD PRIMARY KEY ( column name commalist ) ;
```

Then (a) *T* mustn't currently have a declared primary key; (b) the required UNIQUE index on *PK* must already exist; and (c) all existing access plans that refer to *T* will be invalidated.[2]

■ Let table *T* have primary key *PK*. Then *PK* can be dropped via ALTER TABLE, thus:

```
ALTER TABLE T
      DROP PRIMARY KEY ;
```

The index on *PK* won't be automatically dropped, but it'll lose its "primary" status. By contrast, any foreign key that previously referred to *PK* will automatically be dropped (the user performing the ALTER operation must hold the ALTER privilege on all of the tables to which those foreign keys belong).

■ Key constraint checking is always immediate, except that it's possible to load data via the LOAD utility with checking disabled (see the section "DB2 Utilities," later).

FOREIGN KEYS IN DB2

Foreign key definitions in DB2 can be specified on either CREATE TABLE or ALTER TABLE. Here's the syntax:

```
FOREIGN KEY ( column name commalist )
      REFERENCES base table name
              [ ON DELETE response }
```

---

[2] Loosely speaking, an *access plan* in DB2 is the compiled version of an application program (or, to be a little more precise, the compiled version of the database access portions of such a program). An invalidated access plan will automatically be replaced—i.e., an automatic recompilation will be done and a new access plan created—the next time the program is run.

The possible *responses* are as follows:

```
RESTRICT | CASCADE | SET NULL
```

If the ON DELETE clause is omitted, ON DELETE RESTRICT is assumed. Points arising:

- There's no ON UPDATE clause, but ON UPDATE RESTRICT is implicitly and effectively assumed. See the appendix to this chapter for further discussion of this point.

- The referenced key is required to be a primary key specifically.

- The referenced table must already exist and must be "complete" in the sense explained in the previous section.

- It follows from the previous point that in a referential cycle at least one of the foreign keys must be defined via ALTER TABLE.

- In particular, therefore, the foreign key for a self-referencing table must be defined via ALTER TABLE.

- The user defining a foreign key must hold the ALTER privilege on the referenced table.

- By contrast, a user who deletes a row from a referenced table that (thanks to the pertinent delete rule) causes an update to the referencing table requires no special privilege—not even the SELECT privilege!—on that referencing table.

- If the foreign key definition appears in an ALTER TABLE statement and the table being "altered" is nonempty, then that table—i.e., the referencing table—is placed in a "check pending" state.[3] All SQL operations on a table in a "check pending" state will be rejected until that state has been cleared (again see the section "DB2 Utilities," later).

---

[3] More precisely, it's not the table as such but the tablespace that contains it that's placed in that "check pending" state. See the section "DB2 Utilities," later.

- Oddly enough, dropping a referenced table has no effect on the referencing table. In particular, the delete rule and implicit update rule will *not* be invoked. (The foreign key will automatically be dropped, though, but— oddly enough again—the user doing the DROP doesn't need to have the ALTER privilege on that referencing table.)

- Foreign key constraint checking is always immediate, except as noted in the section "DB2 Utilities," later.

DB2 IMPLEMENTATION RESTRICTIONS

Referential integrity support in DB2 is subject to a number of implementation restrictions.[4] The restrictions in question all stem from one basic fact: namely, that DB2 applies key and foreign key integrity checking to each individual row *as it updates that row*, whereas—at least in some cases—it would be more correct not to do that checking until the end of the pertinent update statement. In other words, there's another logical difference involved here ... Let me illustrate:

- Suppose table *T* has just two rows, with primary key values 1 and 2, respectively.

- Consider the update request "Double every primary key value in *T*."

The correct result is that those rows should now have primary key values 2 and 4, respectively. However, DB2 will reject the request entirely, on the grounds—presumably—that if it were to update the row with primary key value 1 first (to yield 2) it would run into a primary key uniqueness violation.[5]

By way of another example, consider the update request "Add one to every primary key value in *T*." I can certainly imagine situations in which such a request might seem perfectly reasonable.

---

[4] At least, it did when it was first introduced; it's possible that some of these restrictions might have been relaxed by now. But even if they have, that's not the point. The intent of the chapter, rather, is (to say it again) merely to serve as a case study—to be specific, a case study of what key and foreign key support might look like in practice, and in fact did look like at one time in one particular case.

[5] Interestingly, the same problem exists in DB2 whenever a UNIQUE index is defined, regardless of whether or not the indexed columns constitute a declared key. However, the implementation restriction applies only to primary keys; in other words, the result in other cases really is unpredictable. Make of that what you will.

As the foregoing examples indicate, different row level implementations of a given set level update can yield different results. Thus, there could be situations—not just in DB2, but in fact in any system that implements set level updates in such a manner—where the result of such an update is unpredictable. DB2 in particular therefore imposes a number of operational restrictions in order to outlaw situations in which such unpredictability might otherwise occur. Here are the specifics:

1. Any UPDATE statement that updates a primary key must be "single row" (i.e., there must be at most one row *at run time* that satisfies the WHERE clause). Thus, for example, the following UPDATE is certainly legitimate, because supplier numbers are unique:

```
UPDATE S
SET    SNO = 'S10'
WHERE  SNO = 'S5' ;
```

   By contrast, the following is either legitimate or not, depending on the current state of the database:

```
UPDATE S
SET    SNO = 'S10'
WHERE  CITY = 'Athens' ;
```

2. In a self-referencing table:

   a. The delete rule must be CASCADE.

   b. DELETE CURRENT (i.e., DELETE via a cursor) isn't allowed.

   c. INSERT ... SELECT is allowed only if it inserts at most one row, i.e., only if the SELECT selects at most one row. (Note that "regular" INSERT, meaning an INSERT without that SELECT, inserts a single row by definition.)

The remaining restrictions, Nos. 3-5, all have to do with tables that are *delete connected* to one another. To elaborate:

■ First an intuitive explanation: Table T_n is delete connected to table T_1 if and only if a DELETE on T_1 can either *affect* or *be affected by* the current value of T_n.

■ More formally: Table T_n is delete connected to table T_1 if and only if (a) T_n references T_1 directly, or (b) T_n references some table T_{n-1} directly and there's a referential path from T_{n-1} to T_1 in which every delete rule is CASCADE:

$$T_n \xrightarrow{\;*\;} T_{n-1} \xrightarrow{\;C\;} T_{n-2} \xrightarrow{\;C\;} \cdots \xrightarrow{\;C\;} T_2 \xrightarrow{\;C\;} T_1$$

The "C"s in this diagram here denote a CASCADE delete rule; the asterisk stands for "any" (i.e., "don't care") delete rule. Observe that, depending on the current value of T_n, an attempt to delete rows from T_1 can:

a. Cause rows to be deleted from T_n, if the "*" rule is CASCADE;

b. Cause rows to be updated in T_n, if the "*" rule is SET NULL;

c. Fail, if the "*" rule is RESTRICT.

In other words, a DELETE on T_1 can indeed either "affect or be affected by" the current value of T_n.

Note that it follows from the foregoing definition that (a) every table is delete connected to every table it references directly, and hence that (b) every self-referencing table is delete connected to itself.

Now I can state the remaining restrictions:

3. If

a. The user issues a DELETE on table T_1, and

b. Table T_n is delete connected to table T_1, and

c. The DELETE involves a subquery,

then the FROM clause in that subquery mustn't refer to table T_n unless the last delete rule in the path—i.e., the one from T_n to T_{n-1}—is RESTRICT.

Example: Suppose the referential constraint from shipments (table SP) to suppliers (table S) has a delete rule of CASCADE. Then the following attempt to delete all suppliers who currently supply no parts will—unfortunately, and surely rather surprisingly—fail:

```
DELETE
FROM    S
WHERE   NOT EXISTS
        ( SELECT *
          FROM    SP
          WHERE   SP.SNO = S.SNO ) ;
```

Instead, the user must (e.g.) first compile a list of relevant supplier numbers, and then delete all suppliers whose number is given in that list as a separate operation.

4. (*Note: I discussed this one in some detail in the section "Implementation Issues" in Chapter 2, though I didn't use the term "delete connected" in that discussion.*) If table T_n is delete connected to table T_1 via two or more distinct referential paths, then every foreign key in table T_n that's involved in any of those paths must have the same delete rule, and that rule mustn't be SET NULL.

5. In a referential cycle of length greater than one, no table is allowed to be delete connected to itself.

Well, I suppose IBM is to be congratulated for at least grappling with these problems and coming up with some kind of solution to them. But it seems to me that some rather obvious questions arise:

■ How easy is it to remember all of these restrictions? *My answer:* Not very, I'd say.

■ How burdensome or difficult to apply are these restrictions likely to be in practice? *My answer:* I don't really know, but the example discussed above under the first of the restrictions above—"delete suppliers who supply no parts"—suggests that at least they're likely to be annoying.

■ Are the restrictions all in fact necessary? *My answer:* Don't know. Is there a proof?

■ Are the restrictions sufficient? *My answer:* Don't know. Again, is there a proof?

DB2 UTILITIES

The following existing DB2 utilities are affected by referential integrity: CHECK, COPY, LOAD, RECOVER, REORG, and REPAIR. There are also two new ones, QUIESCE and REPORT. This section briefly summarizes the situation.

First of all, as explained in the section "Some Operational Considerations" in Chapter 4, it's clear that point in time recovery—that is, *media* recovery— logically needs to operate in terms of "referential structures" (see Chapters 2 and 4 for an explanation of this term). However, media recovery in DB2 operates in terms of physical storage units called "tablespaces," not logical units such as tables or referential structures. DB2 therefore defines another construct, the *tablespace set*, which is the set of all of the tablespaces that, taken in combination, contain all of the tables in a given referential structure;[6] and it is the tablespace set, not the referential structure, that acts as the unit of integrity so far as DB2 media recovery is concerned.

Let *TS* be a tablespace. Then certain operations that affect *TS* will cause *TS* to be placed in the "check pending" state. "Check pending" means that *TS* contains, either actually or potentially, at least one value of at least one foreign key for which no matching value of the corresponding target key exists. The operations that set "check pending" are as follows:

■ Actual detection of such a "matching failure" via the CHECK utility (see below)

■ Definition of a new foreign key via ALTER TABLE for an existing nonempty table in *TS*

---

[6] Of course, "all of the tables" here really means *the physically stored versions of* those tables, and "tables" in turn really means *base* tables. Observe how easily, and how subtly, logical vs. physical confusions can creep into the picture!—into many pictures, in fact.

- Data load or recovery operations (via the LOAD or RECOVER utilities— see below), either on some referencing table in *TS* or on some target table that is referenced by some table in *TS*, if such operations might possibly violate some referential constraint

While *TS* is in the "check pending" state, data manipulation operations (SELECT, UPDATE, etc.) and COPY, REORG, and QUIESCE utility operations won't be accepted on *TS*. Data definition operations will be accepted, however. The "check pending" condition can be reset either by the CHECK utility or by the REPAIR utility (see below).

Next, the LOAD, RECOVER, CHECK, and REPAIR utilities have all been extended, as follows:

- LOAD on a table that contains a foreign key can be run with referential constraint checking enabled or disabled. If checking is enabled, input rows that violate the constraint won't be loaded (however, they can optionally be placed in a separate rejects file). If checking is disabled, a "check pending" condition will be set on the applicable tablespace.

- RECOVER can be used to recover an entire tablespace set as a unit. In general, RECOVER will set "check pending" on the applicable tablespace(s) unless (a) the entire tablespace set is recovered as a unit *and* (b) recovery is to a "point of consistency" (established via QUIESCE—see below).

- CHECK is extended to perform referential integrity checking. Would-be referencing rows that violate a referential constraint can optionally be copied to an exception table, and optionally deleted as well. If they're deleted, or if no such rows are found, any "check pending" condition will be reset.

- REPAIR is extended to allow the user to force a "check pending" condition to be reset.

Finally, two new utilities, QUIESCE and REPORT, are provided:

- QUIESCE is used to quiesce operations temporarily on a specified collection of tablespaces. The quiesced state corresponds to a single point in the log, so that the collection of tablespaces can subsequently be recovered as a unit. For example, QUIESCE can be useful in connection with dumping and subsequently restoring an entire disk volume as a unit. In particular, QUIESCE can be used to establish a point of consistency for a tablespace set, thus ensuring that subsequent recovery to that point will restore the data to a consistent state (see RECOVER above).

■ The REPORT utility can be used to determine the collection of tablespaces that constitute a tablespace set, and hence the tablespaces that need to be quiesced as a unit.

FURTHER DB2 CONSIDERATIONS

A few miscellaneous points:

■ All integrity checking is performed by DB2 itself, not by generated code in the access plans.

■ The action of adding a primary or foreign key to an existing table via ALTER TABLE can have the effect of invalidating existing access plans.[7] To be specific:

1. Adding a primary key to base table T will invalidate all plans that operate on T.

2. Adding a foreign key to base table T_2 that references base table T_1:

   a. If T_2 and T_1 are the same table, will invalidate all plans that operate on that table;

   b. If the delete rule in the new foreign key definition is CASCADE or SET NULL, will invalidate all plans that operate on any table to which T_2 is now delete connected (including in particular all plans that operate on T_1).

---

[7] I mentioned this point previously in connection with primary keys in particular, where I also explained what it means for a plan to be invalidated (see footnote 2).

The purpose of the foregoing invalidations is to allow DB2 to detect violations of certain of the implementation restrictions described earlier in this chapter—for example, the restriction that DELETE CURRENT isn't allowed on a self-referencing table. (As usual, invalidated plans will automatically be recreated the next time they're used. Though sometimes, of course, that recreation process will fail, and a source code change will be required.) Note that the foregoing could cause migration problems in some circumstances; that is, a plan that worked perfectly under DB2 Version 1 might fail to recompile properly under DB2 Version 2, when referential integrity support was first added to the product. Again, a source code change will be required in such a situation.

■ There are no new catalog tables; however, there are several new columns in existing tables, and several possible new entries in existing columns. For example, the SYSINDEXES catalog table has a new possible UNIQUERULE entry P, meaning primary index. (The other possible entries are U, meaning other unique index, and D—duplicates allowed—meaning nonunique index.) Further details are beyond the scope of this chapter.

SQL/DS DIFFERENCES

Note: The following is a far from exhaustive list of ways in which support for keys and foreign keys in SQL/DS differs from that of DB2. See the book A Guide to SQL/DS, by Colin White and myself (Addison-Wesley, 1988), for further details.

1. It's not necessary to create a UNIQUE index on the primary key—SQL/DS will create such an index automatically.

2. If table T_2 references table T_1 and the delete rule is CASCADE, then no table T_3 can reference table T_2 (i.e., T_2 can't be a target table). This is a major restriction! But it does have the effect of simplifying several aspects of the product; in particular, the DB2 concept of "delete connected" becomes totally irrelevant. The DB2 restrictions regarding delete connected tables therefore become irrelevant also, except that the following

two (simplified forms of two of DB2's "delete connected" restrictions) do still apply:

    a. If table T_2 references table T_1, then a DELETE on T_1 mustn't include a subquery in which T_2 is named in the FROM clause unless the delete rule from T_2 to T_1 is RESTRICT.

    b. If table T_2 has two or more foreign keys that reference the same table T_1, then the delete rules for those foreign keys must all be the same, and furthermore they mustn't be SET NULL.

3. Self-referencing tables aren't supported. The DB2 restrictions on self-referencing tables therefore don't apply.

4. To define a foreign key that references table T, the user needs the REFERENCES privilege on T. DB2 doesn't support the REFERENCES privilege but uses the existing ALTER privilege for the same purpose.

5. Individual primary and foreign key constraints can be dynamically deactivated, and subsequently reactivated, via ALTER TABLE. While a constraint is active, all checking is immediate. While a constraint is inactive, only the owner of the table (or the database administrator) can access the affected table(s). Reactivating an inactive constraint causes all applicable checks to be performed; if any of those checks fails, the reactivation fails also.

6. SQL/DS doesn't support the "check pending" condition. SQL/DS utilities aren't affected by referential integrity. (SQL/DS doesn't support point in time recovery.)

7. Integrity checking is implemented differently. The details are beyond the scope of this chapter, but one implication is there are many more situations in SQL/DS than there are in DB2 in which access plans (called access *modules* in SQL/DS) are invalidated.

Note: I have to say I think it's unfortunate that differences such as those described above exist. One obvious consequence is that programs that work on one product won't necessarily work on the other.

APPENDIX: WHY "UPDATE CASCADE" IS DESIRABLE

This appendix presents an example, based on the usual suppliers and parts database, to show why support for a CASCADE update rule is desirable. (As we've seen, neither DB2 nor SQL/DS supports such a rule. Of couse, I'm assuming for the sake of this appendix that we're operating in a DB2 or SQL/DS environment.)

Requirement: The supplier number for supplier Sx has changed to Sy, where Sx and Sy are given. Update the database accordingly.

Preliminary comments: Note first of all that a simple UPDATE statement along the following lines—

```
UPDATE  S
SET     SNO = Sy
WHERE   SNO = Sx ;
```

—won't work, because in general supplier Sx will have some matching shipments, and the implicit RESTRICT update rule will therefore come into play.

Second, note that the following sequence of operations will also not work:

```
UPDATE  SP
SET     SNO = Sy
WHERE   SNO = Sx ;

UPDATE  S
SET     SNO = Sy
WHERE   SNO = Sx ;
```

The attempt to UPDATE the shipment (SP) rows for supplier Sx will fail for at least two reasons:

- First, it would violate the foreign key constraint.

- Second, UPDATEs to a primary key column must be "single row"—i.e., there must be at most one row at run time that satisfies the WHERE clause. (Note that SP.SNO is a component of the primary key of SP, as well as being a foreign key.)

Interchanging the two UPDATEs won't make any difference, of course. Nor will embedding the two UPDATEs within a transaction work, because all key and foreign key checking is done immediately.

So we're going to have to write a program to handle the problem. An example of such a program (written in PL/I with embedded SQL) follows. *Note:* I assume for the sake of the example that any attempt to introduce a new shipment for some supplier (via an INSERT or UPDATE on table SP) will request at least a shared lock (S lock) on the row for that supplier in table S. Also, for clarity the code uses the "not equals" symbol "≠", even though it's not legal syntax in either SQL or PL/I.

```
UPDSNO: PROC OPTIONS (MAIN) ;
        /* change supplier no. Sx to Sy */

        DCL SX             CHAR(5) ;
        DCL SY             CHAR(5) ;
        DCL SNAME          CHAR(20) ;
        DCL STATUS         FIXED BINARY(15) ;
        DCL CITY           CHAR(15) ;
        DCL PNO            CHAR(6) ;
        DCL MORE_SHIPMENTS BIT(1) ;

        EXEC SQL INCLUDE SQLCA ; /* "SQL Communication Area" */

        EXEC SQL DECLARE Y CURSOR FOR
                    SELECT S.SNAME , S.STATUS , S.CITY
                    FROM   S
                    WHERE  S.SNO = :SX
                    FOR UPDATE OF SNAME ;

        EXEC SQL DECLARE Z CURSOR FOR
                    SELECT SP.PNO
                    FROM   SP
                    WHERE  SP.SNO = :SX ;

        EXEC SQL WHENEVER NOT FOUND CONTINUE ;
        EXEC SQL WHENEVER SQLERROR CONTINUE ;
        EXEC SQL WHENEVER SQLWARNING CONTINUE ;

        ON CONDITION ( DBEXCEPTION )
        BEGIN ;
           PUT SKIP LIST ( SQLCA ) ;
           EXEC SQL ROLLBACK WORK ;
           GO TO QUIT ;
        END ;
```

```
GET LIST ( SX , SY ) ;
EXEC SQL OPEN Y ;
IF SQLCODE ≠ 0
THEN SIGNAL CONDITION ( DBEXCEPTION ) ;

/* fetch column values for supplier Sx */
EXEC SQL FETCH Y INTO :SNAME , :STATUS , :CITY ;
IF SQLCODE ≠ 0
THEN SIGNAL CONDITION ( DBEXCEPTION ) ;

/* make sure supplier Sx stays locked exclusive (X locked), */
/* thus preventing concurrent creation of new shipments for */
/* supplier Sx and concurrent UPDATE/DELETE on supplier Sx  */
EXEC SQL UPDATE S
        SET    SNAME = :SNAME         /* effectively a no op */
        WHERE  CURRENT OF Y ;
IF SQLCODE ≠ 0
THEN SIGNAL CONDITION ( DBEXCEPTION ) ;

/* insert new supplier Sy row */
EXEC SQL INSERT
        INTO   S ( SNO , SNAME , STATUS , CITY )
        VALUES ( :SY , :SNAME , :STATUS , :CITY ) ;
IF SQLCODE ≠ 0
THEN SIGNAL CONDITION ( DBEXCEPTION ) ;

/* prepare to loop through shipments for Sx */
EXEC SQL OPEN Z ;
IF SQLCODE ≠ 0
THEN SIGNAL CONDITION ( DBEXCEPTION ) ;
MORE_SHIPMENTS = '1'B ;

/* loop through shipments for Sx */
DO WHILE ( MORE_SHIPMENTS ) ;
   EXEC SQL FETCH Z INTO :PNO ;
   SELECT ;                  /* PL/I SELECT, not SQL SELECT !!! */
      WHEN ( SQLCODE = 100 )
         MORE_SHIPMENTS = '0'B ;
      WHEN ( SQLCODE ≠ 100 & SQLCODE ≠ 0 )
         SIGNAL CONDITION ( DBEXCEPTION ) ;
      WHEN ( SQLCODE = 0 )
         DO ;
            /* update current shipment -- */
            /* but not via cursor Z  !!!  */
            EXEC SQL UPDATE SP
                    SET    SNO = :SY
                    WHERE  SNO = :SX
                    AND    PNO = :PNO ;
            IF SQLCODE ≠ 0
            THEN SIGNAL CONDITION ( DBEXCEPTION ) ;
         END ;
      END ;   /* PL/I SELECT */
END ;   /* DO WHILE */
```

```
   EXEC SQL CLOSE Z ;
   /* delete supplier Sx */
   EXEC SQL DELETE
           FROM    S
           WHERE   CURRENT OF Y ;
   IF SQLCODE ≠ 0
   THEN SIGNAL CONDITION ( DBEXCEPTION ) ;
   EXEC SQL CLOSE Y ;
   EXEC SQL COMMIT WORK ;
QUIT:
   RETURN ;
END ;   /* UPDSNO */
```

One final point: The original problem of changing supplier number Sx to Sy might be solved (albeit in a rather heavyhanded manner) in SQL/DS, though not in DB2, by making use of SQL/DS's facility for dynamically deactivating and reactivating constraints. Such a solution might look somewhat as follows. (Note that the operation of deactivating a particular primary key has the automatic effect of deactivating any foreign keys that refer to that primary key as well. It also has the effect of dropping the primary key index.)

```
   ALTER TABLE S DEACTIVATE PRIMARY KEY ;
   ALTER TABLE SP DEACTIVATE PRIMARY KEY ;

   UPDATE S
   SET    SNO = Sy
   WHERE  SNO = Sx ;

   UPDATE SP
   SET    SNO = Sy
   WHERE  SNO = Sx ;

   ALTER TABLE SP ACTIVATE PRIMARY KEY ;
   ALTER TABLE S ACTIVATE PRIMARY KEY ;

   COMMIT WORK ;
```

Note: Instead of deactivating (and subsequently reactivating) the primary key constraint for table S, we could alternatively have deactivated (and subsequently reactivated) the foreign key constraint from table SP to table S. This latter approach might be more efficient in practice.

Appendix A

Glossary of Terms

"When I *use a word," Humpty Dumpty said, in rather a scornful tone,*
"it means just what I choose it to mean—
neither more nor less."

—Lewis Carroll:
Through the Looking-Glass and What Alice Found There (1871)

In order to make it easy to check the meanings of terms used in various places throughout this book, this appendix repeats many of the definitions (sometimes in slightly revised form) from the body of the text. It also adds a few more. The definitions are based for the most part on ones in my book *The New Relational Database Dictionary* (O'Reilly, 2016).

alternate key Let relvar R have keys K_1, K_2, ..., K_n (and no others), and let some K_i ($1 \leq i \leq n$) be chosen as the primary key for R; then each K_j ($1 \leq j \leq n, j \neq i$) is an alternate key for R. The term isn't much used.

assertion In SQL, a constraint defined via CREATE ASSERTION, as opposed to a base table constraint.

assignment An operator that assigns a value (the source, denoted by an expression) to a variable (the target, denoted by a variable reference); also, the operation performed when that operator is invoked. The source and target must be of the same type, and the operation overall is required to abide by (a) *The Assignment Principle* (always), as well as (b) **The Golden Rule** (if applicable). Every update operator invocation is logically equivalent to some assignment, albeit possibly a multiple one.

Assignment Principle After assignment of value v to variable V, the comparison $v = V$ is required to evaluate to TRUE.

attribute A pair of names of the form <*A*,*T*>, where the first name *A* is the name of the attribute in question and the second name *T* is the name of the corresponding type. But it's common to ignore the type name *T* in informal contexts.

base relation The value of a given base relvar at a given time.

base relvar A relvar not defined in terms of others.

base table constraint Term used in the present book to mean what SQL calls just a table constraint—which is to say, a constraint formulated as part of CREATE TABLE or ALTER TABLE, not CREATE ASSERTION.

body A set of tuples all of the same type. The number of tuples in the set is the cardinality of the body in question. Every subset of a body is a body. In particular, the set of tuples appearing in some given relation—especially the relation that's the value of some given relvar at some given time—is a body, and so is any subset of such a set.

candidate key Let *K* be a subset of the heading of relvar *R*; then *K* is a candidate key (or just a key for short) for *R* if and only if both of the following properties hold:

  a. *Uniqueness:* No possible value for *R* contains two distinct tuples with the same value for *K*.

  b. *Irreducibility:* No proper subset of *K* has the uniqueness property.

cardinality The number of elements in a set.

coercion Implicit type conversion (usually best avoided, because it's error prone).

compensatory action An action performed automatically by the system in addition to some requested update, with the aim of avoiding some integrity violation that might otherwise occur. The requested update and the corresponding compensatory actions(s) should behave as a semantically atomic unit—that is, no integrity checking should be done until the update and compensatory actions have all been completed.

constraint A database constraint or a type constraint; usually understood to mean a database constraint specifically, unless the context demands otherwise.

database Strictly, a database value; more commonly used, in this book in particular, to refer to what would more accurately be called a database variable.

database constraint Let D be a database. Then C is a database constraint for D if and only if it's a named boolean expression, or something equivalent to such an expression, in which the only variables mentioned are relvars in D.

database value Either the actual (i.e., current) or some possible "state" for some database; in other words, a collection of relations, those relations being actual or possible values for the applicable relvars.

database variable Loosely, a container for relvars; more accurately, a variable whose value at any given time is a database value. Strictly speaking, there's a logical difference, analogous to that between relation values and relation variables, between database values and database variables; thus, what we usually call a database is really a variable, and updating that database has the effect of replacing one value of that variable by another, where the values in question are database values and the variable in question is a database variable. More precisely still, a database is really a tuple variable, with one attribute (relation valued) for each relvar in the database in question.

dbvar Database variable.

deferred checking Checking a constraint at some time (typically commit time) later than the time when an update is performed that might cause it to be violated. The relational model rejects such checking as logically flawed.

degree See heading.

delete connected A term used in DB2, defined as follows: Base table T_n is delete connected to base table T_1 if and only if (a) T_n references T_1 directly, or (b) T_n references some base table T_{n-1} directly and there's a referential path from T_{n-1} to T_1 in which every delete rule is CASCADE.

delete rule A foreign key rule that specifies the action to be taken by the system if some tuple t_2 exists that contains a foreign key value referencing some tuple t_1 and tuple t_1 is deleted.

derived relation A relation that results from evaluation of some relational expression; loosely, a relation defined in terms of others. *Note:* The value of a given derived relvar at a given time is certainly a derived relation—but so too is the current value of any relational expression *rx*, regardless of whether *rx* happens to be the defining expression for some derived relvar.

derived relvar A relvar defined in terms of others by means of some relational expression—for example (and especially), a virtual relvar or view.

domain Type. *Note:* The term *type* is preferred.

doubleton / doubleton set A set of cardinality two.

empty set The set of cardinality zero.

entity integrity The entity integrity rule states that no attribute that participates in the primary key of a base relation is allowed to accept nulls. *Note:* This rule is vacuous, in a sense, because it has to do with nulls; it's also suspect, inasmuch as it treats primary keys as special. I give the definition here for reference purposes only.

EQD Equality dependency.

equality dependency An expression of the form $rx = ry$, where *rx* and *ry* are relational expressions of the same type.

FD Functional dependency.

foreign key Let R_1 and R_2 be relvars, not necessarily distinct, and let K be a key for R_1. Let *FK* be a subset of the heading of R_2 such that there exists a possibly empty set of attribute renamings on R_1 that maps K into K', say, where K' and *FK* each contain exactly the same attributes (in other words, K' and *FK* are in fact one and the same). Let *FKC* be a constraint to the effect that, at all times, every tuple t_2 in R_2 has an *FK* value that's the K' value for some necessarily unique tuple t_1 in R_1 at the time in question. Then *FK* is a foreign key; the associated constraint *FKC* is a foreign key constraint (also known as a referential constraint); and R_2 and R_1 are the referencing relvar and the corresponding referenced relvar (or target relvar), respectively, for that constraint. Also, K—not K'—is the referenced key or target key. *Note:* The referencing, referenced, and target terminology carries over to tuples in the obvious way; that is, tuples t_2 and t_1 in the foregoing paragraph are a referencing tuple and the corresponding referenced or target tuple, respectively. Note too that R_1 and R_2 here aren't necessarily base relvars—they might be views, or even hypothetical views.

foreign key constraint See foreign key.

foreign key rule A rule specifying the action—the referential action—to be taken by the system to ensure that updates affecting the foreign key in question don't violate the associated foreign key constraint.

functional dependency Let H be a heading; then a functional dependency (FD) with respect to H is an expression of the form

$$X \longrightarrow Y$$

(where the determinant X and the dependant Y are both subsets of H). The phrase *with respect to H* can be omitted if H is understood.

FD holds The FD F holds in relvar R—equivalently, relvar R is subject to the FD F—if and only if every relation that can be assigned to relvar R satisfies F.

FD is satisfied Let X and Y be subsets of the heading of relation r; then the FD

$$X \longrightarrow Y$$

is satisfied by r if and only if, whenever two tuples of r agree on X, they also agree on Y.

Golden Rule No database is ever allowed to violate any applicable database constraint.

heading A set of attributes, in which by definition each attribute is a pair of the form $<A,T>$, where A is an attribute name and T is a type name (i.e., T is the name of the type of attribute A). Every subset of a heading is a heading. Within any given heading, (a) distinct attributes are allowed to have the same type name, but not the same attribute name; (b) the number of attributes is the degree (of the heading in question).

hold Constraint C holds for database D—equivalently, database D is subject to constraint C—if and only if every value d that can be assigned to D satisfies C. More specifically, constraint C holds for relvars $R_1, R_2, ..., R_n$—equivalently, relvars $R_1, R_2, ..., R_n$ are subject to constraint C—if and only if every set of relations $r_1, r_2, ..., r_n$ (in that order) that can be assigned to $R_1, R_2, ..., R_n$, respectively, is such that evaluating C with R_1 equal to r_1, R_2 equal to r_2, ..., and R_n equal to r_n yields TRUE. More specifically still, constraint C holds for relvar R—equivalently, relvar R is subject to constraint C—if and only if every relation r that can be assigned to R is such that evaluating C with R equal to r yields TRUE. Note, therefore, that to say that constraint C holds is to say C evaluates to TRUE at statement boundaries.

hypothetical view Let rx be a relational expression, and let there not be a view for which rx is the view defining expression. Then the hypothetical view corresponding to rx is the view that would have existed if a view with defining expression rx had in fact been defined after all.

identity projection The projection of a relation on all of its attributes. The identity projection of any given relation r is identically equal to r.

immediate checking Checking a constraint whenever an update is performed that might cause it to be violated. All constraint checking is immediate in the relational model.

inclusion dependency An expression of the form $rx \subseteq ry$, where rx and ry are relational expressions of the same type.

IND Inclusion dependency.

integrity constraint Constraint.

join Let relations r_1 and r_2 be joinable. Then the expression

```
r₁ JOIN r₂
```

denotes the join of r_1 and r_2, and it returns the relation with heading the set theory union of the headings of r_1 and r_2 and body the set of all tuples t such that t is the set theory union of a tuple from r_1 and a tuple from r_2.

joinable Relations r_1 and r_2 are joinable if and only if attributes with the same name are of the same type—equivalently, if and only if the set theory union of their headings is a legal heading.

key A candidate key (unless the context demands otherwise).

key constraint A constraint to the effect that a given subset of the heading of a given relvar is a key for that relvar.

literal Loosely, a self-defining symbol; a symbol that denotes a value that can be determined at compile time. More precisely, a literal is a symbol that denotes a value that's fixed and determined by the symbol in question (and the type of that value is therefore also fixed and determined by the symbol in question). Every value of every type, tuple and relation types included, is—in fact, must be—denotable by means of some literal.

multiple assignment An operation that allows several individual assignments all to be performed in parallel (in effect, simultaneously). In the important special case in which the target(s) for some or all of the individual assignments are database relvars, no database constraint checking is done until all of those individual assignments have been executed in their entirety. Note that multiple assignments, relational or otherwise, are involved implicitly in a variety of other operations—for example, updating some join or union view, or updating some relvar in such a way as to cause a cascade delete or other compensatory action to be performed.

Naming Principle Everything we need to talk about should have a name.

nonscalar Having user visible component parts. The most important nonscalar constructs in the relational model are tuples and (especially) relations themselves, where the "user visible component parts" are, of course, the pertinent attributes (and the pertinent tuples as well, in the case of a relation).

null A construct, used in SQL in particular, for representing the fact that some piece of information is unavailable for some reason. *Note:* Null isn't a value. Nor is it part of the relational model.

one to one relationship A correspondence between two sets *s1* and *s2* (not necessarily distinct) such that each element of *s1* corresponds to exactly one element of *s2* and each element of *s2* corresponds to exactly one element of *s1*.

primary key A key that has been singled out for special syntactic treatment. A given relvar can have any number n of keys ($n > 0$), but it can have at most one primary key. For a given relvar, however, whether some key is chosen as primary, and if so which one, are essentially psychological issues, beyond the purview of the relational model as such.

Principle of Cautious Design When we're faced with a design choice, say between option A and option B (where A is upward compatible with B), and the full implications of option B aren't yet known, then the recommendation is to go with option A.

Principle of Interchangeability There must be no arbitrary and unnecessary distinctions between base and virtual relvars; i.e., virtual relvars should "look and feel" just like base ones so far as users are concerned.

projection Let relation r have attributes $A_1, A_2, ..., A_n$ (and possibly others), of types $T_1, T_2, ..., T_n$, respectively. Then the expression

```
r { A₁, A₂, ..., Aₙ }
```

denotes the projection of r on those attributes, and it returns the relation with heading $\{<A_1,T_1>, <A_2,T_2>, ..., <A_n,T_n>\}$ and body consisting of all tuples t such that there exists a tuple in r that has the same value for attributes $A_1, A_2, ..., A_n$ as t does.

proper subset Set s_2 is a proper subset of set s_1 (written $s_2 \subset s_1$) if and only if it's a subset of s_1 and s_1 and s_2 are distinct.

proper superset Set s_1 is a proper superset of set s_2 (written $s_1 \supset s_2$) if and only if it's a superset of s_2 and s_1 and s_2 are distinct.

referenced key See foreign key.

referenced relvar See foreign key.

referenced tuple See foreign key.

referencing relvar See foreign key.

referencing tuple See foreign key.

referential action The action specification portion of a foreign key rule; also used to mean the corresponding action itself.

referential constraint See foreign key.

referential cycle A referential path from some relvar to itself:

referential path Let relvars R_n, R_{n-1}, ..., R_2, R_1 be such that R_n has a foreign key referencing R_{n-1}, R_{n-1} has a foreign key referencing R_{n-2}, ..., and R_2 has a foreign key referencing R_1. Then the chain of such references from R_n to R_1 represents a referential path from R_n to R_1 (and that path is of length $n-1$). Note that R_n, R_{n-1}, ..., R_2, R_1 here aren't necessarily base relvars—they might be views, or even hypothetical views.

referential integrity Loosely, the rule that no referencing tuple is allowed to exist if the corresponding referenced tuple doesn't exist. More precisely, let *FK* be some foreign key in some referencing relvar R_2; let K be the corresponding key in the corresponding referenced relvar R_1; and let K' be derived from K in the manner explained under **foreign key**. Then there must never be a time at which there exists an *FK* value in R_2 that isn't the K' value for some (necessarily unique) tuple in R_1.

relation Let H be a heading, let B be a body consisting of tuples with heading H, and let r be the pair $<H,B>$. Then r is a relation value (or just a relation for short), with heading H and body B, and with the same degree and attributes as H and with the same cardinality as B.

relation type   Let H be a heading; then RELATION H denotes the relation type with the same degree and attributes as H.

relation value   Relation.

relation variable   A variable whose type is some relation type; referred to as a relvar for short. Let relvar R be of type T; then R has the same heading (and therefore the same attributes and degree) as type T does. Let the value of R at some given time be r; then R has the same body and cardinality at that time as r does.

relational model   A theory of data; the formal theory, or foundation, on which relational databases in particular and relational technology in general are based. It consists of the following five components: (a) an open ended collection of types, including in particular the scalar type BOOLEAN; (b) a relation type generator and an intended interpretation for relations of types generated thereby; (c) facilities for defining relation variables of such generated relation types; (d) a relational assignment operator; and (e) an open ended collection of generic read-only operators (i.e., the operators of relational algebra or relational calculus or something logically equivalent) for deriving relations from relations. Note that the relational model is deliberately silent on everything to do with performance, including physical storage matters in particular.

relvar   Relation variable.

restriction   Let r be a relation and let bx be a restriction condition. Then the expression

```
r WHERE bx
```

denotes the restriction of r according to bx, and it returns the relation with heading the same as that of r (i.e., the result is of the same type as r) and with body consisting of just those tuples of r for which bx evaluates to TRUE.

restriction condition   Let r be a relation; then a restriction condition on r is a boolean expression in which all attribute references are references to attributes of r and there are no relvar references. Note, however, that WHERE clauses in real languages typically permit boolean expressions that are more general than just simple restriction conditions on the pertinent relation.

satisfy   Let C be a constraint that refers to relvars R_1, R_2, ..., R_n ($n \geq 0$) and no others. Then relations r_1, r_2, ..., r_n (in that order) satisfy C if and only if evaluating C with R_1 equal to r_1, R_2 equal to r_2, ..., and R_n equal to r_n yields TRUE. Otherwise relations r_1, r_2, ..., r_n (in that order) violate C.

scalar   (*Of a type, attribute, value, or variable*) Having no user visible component parts. The term is also often used as a noun, in which case it refers to a scalar value specifically. (*Of an operator*) Returning a scalar result.

self-referencing relvar   A relvar R with a foreign key that references some key of R itself (thereby giving rise to a referential cycle of length one).

set   A collection of objects, called elements or members, with the property that given an arbitrary object x, it can be determined whether or not x appears in the collection. Sets don't contain duplicate elements. Every subset or superset of a set is itself a set.

set difference   The difference between sets s_1 and s_2 in that order (written $s_1 - s_2$) is the set of all elements x such that x is contained in s_1 and not in s_2.

set intersection   The intersection of sets s_1 and s_2 (written $s_1 \cap s_2$) is the set of all elements x such that x is contained in both s_1 and s_2.

set union   The union of sets s_1 and s_2 (written $s_1 \cup s_2$) is the set of all elements x such that x is contained in at least one of s_1 and s_2.

singleton / singleton set   A set of cardinality one.

sixth normal form   Relvar R is in sixth normal form, 6NF, if and only if it can't be nonloss decomposed at all, other than trivially (i.e., into the corresponding identity projection). Equivalently, relvar R is in 6NF if and only if it's in 5NF, is of degree n, and has no key of degree less than $n-1$. *Note:* A relvar in 6NF is sometimes said to be irreducible.

subject to See hold.

subset Set s_2 is a subset of set s_1 (written $s_2 \subseteq s_1$) if and only if every element of s_2 is also an element of s_1—in which case s_1 is said to include s_2 (equivalently, s_2 is included in s_1). Every set is a subset of itself.

subset constraint Inclusion dependency. The term is slightly deprecated.

superset Set s_1 is a superset of set s_2 (written $s_1 \supseteq s_2$) if and only if every element of s_2 is also an element of s_1. Every set is a superset of itself.

target key Referenced key.

target relvar Referenced relvar.

target tuple Referenced tuple.

tuple Let H be a heading, and let t be a set of pairs of the form $<<A,T>,v>$, called components, obtained from H by attaching to each attribute $<A,T>$ in H some value v of type T, called the attribute value in t for attribute A. Then t is a tuple value (or just a tuple for short) with heading H and the same degree and attributes as H. Every subset of a tuple is a tuple.

tuple type Let H be a heading; then TUPLE H denotes the tuple type with the same degree and attributes as H.

tuple value Tuple.

tuple variable A variable whose type is some tuple type; referred to as a tuplevar for short. Let tuple variable V be of type T; then V has the same heading (and therefore attributes and degree) as type T does.

tuplevar Tuple variable.

type A named—and in practice finite—set of values; not to be confused with the internal or physical representation of the values in question, which is an implementation issue. Every value, every variable, every attribute, every read-only operator, every parameter, and every expression is of some type. Types can be either scalar or nonscalar (in particular, they can be tuple or relation types); as a consequence, attributes of relations in particular can also be either scalar or nonscalar. Types can also be either system defined or user defined. They can also be generated or "constructed" (see **type generator**).

type constraint A definition of the set of values that make up a given type.

type generator An operator that's invoked at compile time instead of run time and returns a type instead of a value; also known as a type constructor.

update rule A foreign key rule that specifies the action to be taken by the system if some tuple t_2 exists that contains a foreign key value referencing some tuple t_1 and the corresponding target key in tuple t_1 is updated.

value An "individual constant" (for example, the individual constant three, denoted by the integer literal 3). Values can be of arbitrary complexity; in particular, they can be either scalar or nonscalar (for example, a value might be an array). Values have no location in time or space; however, they can be represented in memory by means of some encoding, and those representations (or encodings, or occurrences) do have location in time and space—indeed, distinct occurrences of the same value can appear at any number of distinct locations in time and space, meaning, loosely, that the very same value can occur as the value of any number of distinct variables, at the same time or at different times. Note that, by definition, a value can't be updated, because if it could, then after such an update it would no longer be that value. Note too that every value is of some type—in fact, of exactly one type (and types are thus disjoint), except possibly if type inheritance is supported.

variable A holder for a representation of a value. Unlike values, variables (a) do have location in time and space and (b) can be updated (that is, the current value of the variable can be replaced by another value). Indeed, to be a variable is to be updatable, and to be updatable is to be a variable; equivalently, to be a variable is to be assignable to, and to be assignable to is to be a variable. Every variable is declared to be of some type.

view A virtual relvar; a relvar whose value at any given time is the result of evaluating a certain relational expression (the view defining expression, specified when the view itself is defined) at the time in question.

violate See satisfy.

virtual relvar View.

Index

For alphabetization purposes, (a) differences in fonts and case are ignored;
(b) quotation marks are ignored; (c) other punctuation symbols—hyphens, underscores,
parentheses, etc.—are treated as blanks; (d) numerals precede letters; (e) blanks
precede everything else.

www.ingramcontent.com/pod-product-compliance
Lightning Source LLC
Chambersburg PA
CBHW080630060326
40690CB00021B/4871

* 9 7 8 1 6 3 4 6 2 4 0 5 3 *